Kamenets-Podolsk and its surroundings (Kamyanets Podilskyy, Ukraine)

Translation of
Kamenets-Podolsk u-sevivata

Original Book Edited by:
A. Rosen, Assoc. of Former Residents of Kamenets-Podolsk
and Its Surroundings in Israel

Originally published in Tel Aviv, 1965

JewishGen
מרכז עולמי לגנאלוגיה יהודית
The Global Home for Jewish Genealogy

A Publication of JewishGen
Edmond J. Safra Plaza, 36 Battery Place, New York, NY 10280
646.494.2972 | info@JewishGen.org | www.jewishgen.org

MUSEUM OF
JEWISH HERITAGE
A LIVING MEMORIAL
TO THE HOLOCAUST

Kamenets-Podolsk and its surroundings (Kamyanets Podilskyy, Ukraine)
Translation of *Kamenets-Podolsk u-sevivata*

Library of Congress Control Number (LCCN): 2024949118

ISBN: 978-1-962054-10-2 (hard cover: 282 pages, alk. paper)

About JewishGen.org

JewishGen, is a Genealogical Research Division of the Museum of Jewish Heritage - A Living Memorial to the Holocaust, serves as the global home for Jewish genealogy.

Featuring unparalleled access to 30+ million records, it offers unique search tools, along with opportunities for researchers to connect with others who share similar interests. Award winning resources such as the Family Finder, Discussion Groups, and ViewMate, are relied upon by thousands each day.

In addition, JewishGen's extensive informational, educational and historical offerings, such as the Jewish Communities Database, Yizkor Book translations, InfoFiles, Family Tree of the Jewish People, and KehilaLinks, provide critical insights, first-hand accounts, and context about Jewish communal and familial life throughout the world.

Offered as a free resource, JewishGen.org has facilitated thousands of family connections and success stories, and is currently engaged in an intensive expansion effort that will bring many more records, tools, and resources to its collections.

Please visit https://www.jewishgen.org/ to learn more.

Vice President for JewishGen: Avraham Groll

About the JewishGen Yizkor Book Project

Yizkor Books (Memorial Books) were traditionally written to memorialize the names of departed family and martyrs during holiday services in the synagogue (a practice that still exists in many synagogues today).

Over the centuries, as a result of countless persecutions and horrific atrocities committed against the Jews, Yizkor Books (Sefer Zikaron in Hebrew) were expanded to include more historical information, such as biographical sketches of famous personalities and descriptions of daily town life.

Following the Holocaust, the idea of remembrance and learning took on an urgent and crucial importance. Survivors of the Holocaust sought out other surviving residents of their former towns to memorialize and document the names and way of life of those who were ruthlessly murdered by the Nazis. These remembrances were documented in Yizkor Books, hundreds of which were published in the first decades after the Holocaust.

Most of these books were published privately, or through *Landsmanshaftn* (social organizations comprised of members originating from the same European town or region) that still existed, and were often distributed free of charge. The languages used to document these crucial histories and links to our past were mostly Yiddish and Hebrew. JewishGen has undertaken the sacred responsibility of translating these books into English so that the culture and way of life of these communities will be preserved and transmitted to future generations.

In 1986, a group of farsighted JewishGenners started a project to pool their efforts together in groups based upon their ancestors' towns and donate funds to translate the Yizkor books of their ancestral towns into English. As the translated material became available, it was made accessible for free at https://www.JewishGen.org/Yizkor . Hardcover copies can be purchased by visiting https://www.jewishgen.org/Yizkor/ybip.html (see below).

It is our hope that the translation of these books into English (and other languages) will assist the countless Jewish family researchers who are so desperately seeking to forge a connection with their heritage.

Director of JewishGen Yizkor Book Project: Lance Ackerfeld

About JewishGen Press

JewishGen Press (formerly the Yizkor Books-in-Print Project) is the publishing division of JewishGen.org, and provides a venue for the publication of non-fiction books pertaining to Jewish genealogy, history, culture, and heritage.

In addition to the Yizkor Book category, publications in the Other Non-Fiction category include Shoah memoirs and research, genealogical research, collections of genealogical and historical materials, biographies, diaries and letters, studies of Jewish experience and cultural life in the past, academic theses, and other books of interest to the Jewish community.

Please visit https://www.jewishgen.org/Yizkor/ybip.html to learn more.

Director of JewishGen Press: Joel Alpert
Managing Editor - Jessica Feinstein
Publications Manager - Susan Rosin

Notes to the Reader

The images in the original book were reproduced from photographs from the time of the first edition. These reproductions were already of poor quality, being pre-war and at least 30 or more years old. As a result, the images in the book are the best achievable.
A reader can view the original scans of the book on the websites listed below.

The original book can be seen online at the Yiddish Book Center website:

https://www.yiddishbookcenter.org/collections/yizkor-books/yzk-nybc314200/rosen-avraham-bernshtain-kaminits-podolsk-u-sevivatah-sefer-zikaron-li-kehilot-yisrael

OR

at the New York Public Library Digital Collections website:

https://digitalcollections.nypl.org/items/fdab7750-5eff-0133-a2f8-00505686d14e

To obtain a list of Shoah victims from **Kamenets-Podolsk (Kamyanets Podilskyy, Ukraine),** the reader should access the Yad Vashem web site listed below; one can also search for specific family names using family name option. These lists are continually updated by Yad Vashem, so it is worthwhile to periodically search them.

There is more valuable information (including the Pages of Testimony, etc.) available on this website: https://yvng.yadvashem.org/

A list of all books available from JewishGen Press along with prices is available at:
https://www.jewishgen.org/Yizkor/ybip.html

For additional information, please visit: https://kehilalinks.jewishgen.org/Kamyanets-Podilskyy/

Cover Photo Credits

Cover Design by: Irv Osterer

Front Cover:

Image from Postcard c.1910 - Kamenets Podolsk. "East side. Synagogue and Turkish Tower". Publisher: Magazin Wargaftinga.

Back Cover:

Top Left:
 Yankel Fillerman, 1910 carte de visite photo provided by Moshe Braitman
https://jewua.org/kamenets_podolski/

Top Right:
The"Haganah" in 1909 [Page 41]

Middle:
Contemporary view of The Great Synagogue and Hochar Tower
https://jewua.org/kamenets_podolski/#jp-carousel-2914

Bottom:
Zionist Youth Organization "Ha-Techiya" in 1919 [Page 48]

Geopolitical Information

**MAP OF UKRAINE
AUGUST 2022**

//// Russian annexed or separatist area

Map of Ukraine showing the location of **Kamianets-Podilskyi**

Kamianets-Podilskyi

Kamyanets Podilskyy, Ukraine is located at 48°40' N 26°34' E and 215 miles SW of Kyyiv

	Town	District	Province	Country
Before WWI (c. 1900):	Kamenets Podolskiy	Kamenets Podolskiy	Podolia	Russian Empire
Between the wars (c. 1930):	Kamenets Podolskiy	Kamenets-Podolski	Ukraine SSR	Soviet Union
After WWII (c. 1950):	Kamenets Podolskiy			Soviet Union
Today (c. 2000):	Kamianets-Podilskyi			Ukraine

Alternate Names for the Town:

Kam″yanets'-Podil's'kyy [Ukr], Kamenets Podolskiy [Rus], Komenetz [Yid], Kamieniec Podolski [Pol], Cameniţa [Rom], Camenecia [Lat], Kumenetz-Podolsk, Kamenets Podolsk, Kamenets Podolski, Komenitz Podolsk, Kamenets Podilski, Kamenez Podolsk

Nearby Jewish Communities:

Zhvanets 9 miles SSW
Shatava 10 miles NE
Ataky 10 miles SSW
Orynyn 10 miles NW
Kytaihorod 11 miles E
Makiv 11 miles NE
Okopy 12 miles SW
Khotyn 13 miles SSW
Balin 15 miles NNE
Studenitsa 17 miles ESE
Zarechanka 18 miles NNW
Melnytsya-Podilska 19 miles W
Smotrych 20 miles N
Dunayivtsi 20 miles NE
Velikiy Zhvanchik 20 miles ENE
Verkhneye Krivche 21 miles W

Skala-Podilska 21 miles NW
Klishkivtsi 21 miles SW
Ustya 22 miles W
Sokilets 24 miles ENE
Zbryzh 24 miles NW
Rzhavyntsi 24 miles WSW
Chemerivtsi 25 miles NNW
Borshchiv 25 miles WNW
Tsyhany 25 miles WNW
Stara Ushytsya 27 miles ESE
Oliyevo-Koralivka 27 miles W
Myn'kivtsi 27 miles ENE
Losyach 28 miles NW
Vikno 28 miles WSW
Lanivtsi 29 miles WNW
Lipcani, Moldova 30 miles SSE
Kupyn 30 miles N

Jewish Population in 1900:   16,211

Dedication

To the people of Kamenets-Podolsk— those who perished in darkness and those who carried the light forward.

Your stories echo through time, your memories endure in the stones of the fortress, in the whispers of the Smotrych River, in the hearts of those who remember.

For those who were lost, and those who survived to rebuild, to remember, to live, to tell.

May your legacy be a blessing.

Stefani Elkort Twyford

Houston, TX

December 2024

Table of Contents

TOC translated by Sara Mages

Kamenets-Podolsk and its surroundings (Kamyanets Podilskyy, Ukraine)

48°40' / 26°34'

Translation of
Kamenets-Podolsk u-sevivata

Editors: A. Rosen, Assoc. of Former Residents of Kamenets-Podolsk
and Its Surroundings in Israel

Published in Tel Aviv, 1965

Acknowledgments

Project Coordinator

Stefani Elkort Twyford

**Our sincere appreciation to Yad Vashem
for the submission of the necrology for placement on the JewishGen web site.**

This is a translation of: *Kamenets-Podolsk u-sevivata* (Kamenets-Podolsk and its surroundings),
Editors: A. Rosen et.al., Tel Aviv, Assoc. of Former Residents of Kamenets-Podolsk
and Its Surroundings in Israel, 1965 (H, 263 pages).

JewishGen, Inc. makes no representations regarding the accuracy of the translation. The reader may wish to refer to the original material for verification. JewishGen is not responsible for inaccuracies or omissions in the original work and cannot rewrite or edit the text to correct inaccuracies and/or omissions. Our mission is to produce a translation of the original work and we cannot verify the accuracy of statements or alter facts cited.

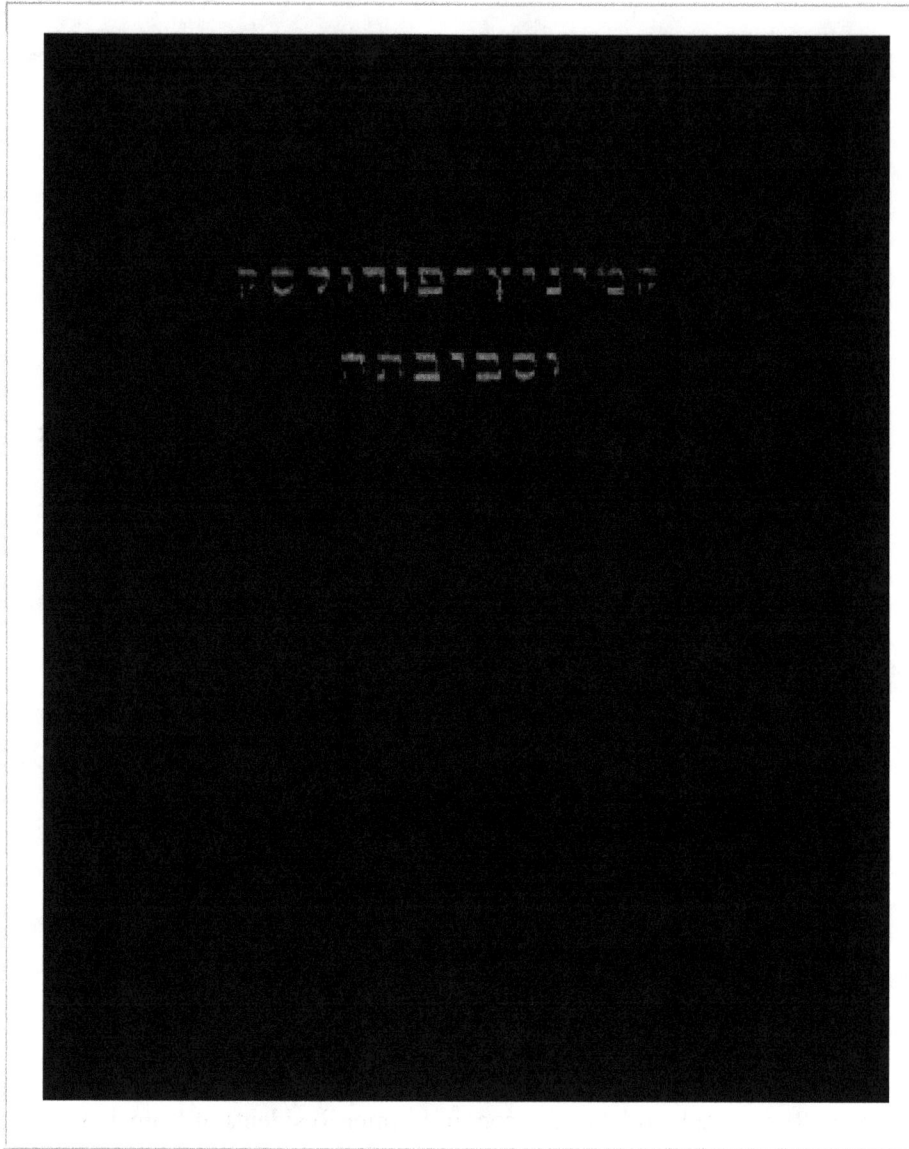

קמיניץ-פודולסק

וסביבתה

[Page 9]

Foreword

Translated by Monica Devens

At the end of the Second World War, when the shocking news about the destruction of the Jewish communities in Europe - and among them the Jewish communities in Kamyanets Podilskyy and its surroundings - reached Israel, some of the expatriates of these places came up with the idea of a book in memory of the aforementioned communities.

In order to achieve this goal, in 1946 the organization of expatriates of Kamyanets Podilskyy and its surroundings was founded. However, due to the deaths of the two main initiators - Y. Goldman and B'Z Shteklis - and for reasons brought about by the times, the organization's operations ceased. Over time, there were several more attempts to publish the book of remembrance, but the indifference and passivity of the people from these aforementioned places delayed the start of the activity. Only in the summer of 1961 were the organization's activities renewed at the initiative of some of the expats of Kamyanets Podilskyy and its surroundings, led by the late Matityahu Segal. At the general assembly of the members of the organization, a council and an editorial committee of three members were elected.

The committee that was chosen by the council established a memorial plaque in the Chamber of the Holocaust at Mount Zion in Jerusalem, where the names of the communities in Kamyanets Podilskyy and its surroundings that were exterminated by the Nazis, were perpetuated. The committee also organized a fundraiser in order to publish the book through contributions and subscriptions.

Thanks to the efforts, and the material and spiritual support, of many of the members of the organization in Israel and of the expatriates of the aforementioned communities in the United States, Canada, Colombia and other countries, we have brought this project to completion.

Due to the non-responsiveness of many of the expatriates of the aforementioned communities, both regarding the creation of literary material and regarding the provision of the necessary means, the preparation of the book continued for almost three years.

[Page 10]

We are grateful to those who participated in the book with the fruit of their pen and those who took an active part in preparing it by organizing and rounding up the necessary financial means. We are also grateful to the directors and employees of "Israel" publishing, who invested a lot of work and effort in the printing of the book, to the owners of "Ha-Tsinkographia Ha-Yisraelit," which prepared the engravings for the book, as well as to the members of the editorial team, who did not spare their time and energy in preparing the book without receiving a reward, and with their great dedication carried out the important task. All will be blessed.

Organization of Expatriates of Kamyanets Podilskyy and the Surrounding Area

The Committee:

Bar-Levi, Y. A.
Michaeli, Uri
Rechter, N.D.
Sharig, Hayyim
Sharir, Yaakov
Shilmover, Ben-Zion, Engineer

The Council:

Avnei-Kamenetzky, A.
Bahat-Buchhalter, Y.
Bar Levi-Weissman, Y. A.
Ben Avraham-Feldblit, Y.
Bernstein, Y.
Fuchs, D.
Golan-Yigolnitzer, R.
Goldschmidt, S.
Kaplan, S.
Landon, S.
Lerner, Z.
Leskov, Ts.
Michaeli-Pressman, A.
Pollack, Y.
Rechter, N.D.
Rosen-Rosenzweig, A.
Schor-Schwartz, G. (deceased)
Schrier, Y.
Segal, M. (deceased)
Sharig-Schreiberman, H.
Sharir, Y.
Shilmover, B.
Wasserman, A. (deceased)
Yaakovi-Kizhner, A.
Yigolnitzer, D.

[Page 11]

*

Translated by Monica Devens

While recognizing the sacred national duty imposed on our contemporaries to establish a memorial for the Jewish communities of the European diaspora that were destroyed by the Nazi oppressor during the Second World War, we, too, have come to fulfill with this book the duty towards the cities of our origin, Kamyanets Podilskyy and its surroundings, which, too, were laid waste and erased off the face of the earth during the Holocaust.

Russian Jewry, including that of Podolia, occupied an important and valuable place in shaping the image of our people over the last centuries and contributed a lot to its national revival and the establishment of its homeland in the land of our ancestors. As an integral part of the entire nation, the communities of Kamyanets Podilskyy and its surrounding cities also participated in these actions, and many of their members even became famous among the various national movements that arose for us over the generations. In faithfully coming to this blessed collaboration, future generations will find this book of remembrance, which we present to them as a precious bequest from their ancestors in the diaspora.

The plan of the book was based mainly on a description of the life of the Jewish community, its history and way of life, its institutions and people, as well as its history during the Holocaust. Following the number of cities included in it, it is divided into ten sections, city by city and its section with, at their introductions, a concise overview of the city according to the data from before the Second World War. Except for assessments of personalities, the articles and notes on the aforementioned topics were written by local people who lived and worked in them in the diaspora, and their words serve as unshakable testimony to the recent past, which has passed and is no more, and an unfailing source for historians of the future.

We are very sorry that, due to a lack of material, we were unable to include in this book also the remaining cities and towns in the vicinity of Kamyanets Podilskyy. All our efforts to obtain the necessary material from the expatriates of these places were in vain. Let us hope that they will finally wake up and fill the gap by publishing another volume.

Finally, we thank all those who helped with our enterprise, whether with material or spirit, and thereby made possible the perpetuation of the memory of the holy communities of our cities of origin. May the blessing come upon everyone.

Tel Aviv, Nisan Tash"kah [5725=1964-65]

[Page 12][Blank][Page13]

Podolia

by A. R.

Translated by Monica Devens

A

The region of Podolia covers 36,910 square versts in northwest European Russia. It borders Galicia and is separated from it by the Zbruch River. Its territory is a flat plain that flows towards the southwest and is dissected by the rivers Dniester (415 versts; bordering Bessarabia), with its tributaries: Zbruch, Smotrych, Ushitza, Liadva, Murafa, and others, and Bug (508 versts), with its tributaries: Buzuk, Ikva, Rob, Seniboda, Sinyota, and others.

Podolia soil is black and very fertile. In some places in the south, it contains lime. Its quarried substances: building stones, lithography stones, gypsum, and phosphates.

The climate is warm (the average annual temperature in the urban region of Kamyanets Podilskyy +8.6°).

Number of inhabitants[1]: 3,544,000, of which 247 thousand live in cities. The densest settlement (96 inhabitants per square verst) of the rest of the regions of European Russia except for the Polish regions. 81% of the population are Ukrainians, the rest are Jews (12%), Russians, Poles, Moldavians, and others. There are 17 cities and 120 towns in the region.

The branches of agriculture: all kinds of grains, potatoes, beets, flax, tobacco and cotton plantations, fruits and vegetables, and cattle breeding. 293 factories for sugar, flour, schnapps, and textiles.

Trade: wheat, oats, flour, sugar, skins, and schnapps. In 1905, exports (wheat, eggs) reached 3037 rubles and imports (wooden materials) reached 899 rubles.

Transportation: train (1213 versts) and cargo ships across the Dniester. 2168 schools, of which 9 are high schools with 166 thousand students.

The county is divided into 12 districts, the city of the region Kamyanets Podilskyy.

[Page 14]

B

The beginning of the settlement of Podolia is very ancient. According to the Father of History, Herodotus the Greek, different peoples lived in Podolia for five hundred years before the Christian era. After Hadrian, Emperor of Rome, conquered the lands of Germany and Romania, this region, too, came under his rule. For about five hundred years after that, various wild peoples ruled until, at the beginning of the sixth century A.D., the Slavic tribes expelled them and replaced them.

From the fourteenth century until the second partition of Poland between Russia and Prussia in 1793, Lithuania, Poland, Russia, and Turkey ruled by turns. In 1793, this region, together with several other districts, passed from the country of Poland to the full possession of Russia.

C

The origin of the first Jewish settlers is disputed. Some historians believe that they came to Podolia from the countries of Russia and Poland, to which they immigrated from Western Europe, while others see them as deportees from Spain, who came via these countries. There is also an opinion that says that the Jews came to Podolia from the land of the Khazars and the Crimean Peninsula or from the principality of Kiev, from which they were expelled during the reign of Vladimir Monomakh in 1120.

There is also no uniform and agreed-upon opinion regarding the time of the Jews' settlement in Podolia. In any case it is clear that, already by the end of the twelfth century, there was a Jewish settlement there, which engaged in trade, leasing, and crafts, and was very successful. During the Thirty Years' War (1618-1648), many of the Jews of Ashkenaz were added to them, among them families known there for Torah and wisdom.

During the entire time that Podolia was under the rule of the princes of Lithuania and Poland, the Jewish residents enjoyed certain rights and their economic and civil status far exceeded that of their brothers in the other provinces.

The study of the Torah was also widespread among the people who produced from their midst famous rabbis and scholars. The rabbis of the cities of Nemyriv, Tulchin, Beer, and Medzhybizh became famous.

However, this situation changed for the worse in 1648 with the outbreak of the uprising of the Cossacks living in Ukraine against their Polish enslavers, who severely struck not only at their civil and political rights, but also at their religion and traditions. In particular, the rebellion worsened under the leadership of Bohdan Khmelnytsky who poured out his wrath on the Jewish residents, too, who were in trade and leasing relationships

[Page 15]

with the owners of the Polish estates. In a flash, the Cossack regiments attacked the Jewish communities in Podolia and, like beasts of prey, oppressed, slaughtered, and murdered mercilessly, whether man, woman, child or elderly. Whole communities were destroyed and of all the Jewish population in Podolia, only a tenth remained. Many were forced to convert or were captured and ransomed by their brothers in the diaspora.

These horrible conditions of constricted life and calamities, along with fear of death by the sword of an enemy, prepared the ground among the masses for mysterious delusions and belief in supernatural miracles. And these days were the days of Shabbetai Zvi, when the belief in his Messianism flooded almost all of the diaspora, including Podolia. This great Messianic movement hit in waves (especially in the years 1676-1700) and breathed a spirit of hope into the hearts of the oppressed masses. However, the bitter disappointment that followed this movement did not spare Podolia either and shook the lives of its Jewish residents quite a bit.

In particular, the evil increased with the arrival (in 1787) of the successors of Shabbetai Zvi's Messianic movement, Jacob Frank and his group. As a result of their identifying themselves to the bishop of Kamyanets Podilskyy, he arranged a public religious debate between them and the rabbis who excommunicated them, which ended with the imposition of a heavy fine on the Jews and the confiscation of the books of the Talmud from the entire district and their public burning in the city market (in the year 5518=1757).

Thus, as a healing drug for the broken spirit of the people, discouraged from the suffering of their many hardships, Hasidism arose in the mid-eighteenth century, whose creator and founder was Rabbi Israel Ba'al-Shem-Tov (The Besht), born in the Podolia town of Okopy. This doctrine, which grew and was nurtured in the land of Podolia mainly among the simple people, expanded and deepened over a short period of time until it became a complete philosophy of life encompassing all avenues of the Jewish people, and despite the disputes and divisions between the various Hasidic sects and despite the opposition from the rabbis and Torah scholars, it paved a path to the diaspora of Israel as a popular movement with many virtues and content.

The "Enlightenment," founded by the Jews of Western Europe ("the Berlin Enlightenment") in the eighteenth century, also took root in Podolia. It destroyed the "Chinese wall" that surrounded the closed Jewish street, closed to outside influence, and introduced into it the spirit of the new times. Among the writers of the Jewish Enlightenment in Russia were also some who came from Podolia, such as: Yitzhak Satanov, writer and thinker; Menachem Mendel Lefin, writer and translator; Ben-Ami (Mordechai Rabinowitz), writer in Russian, and more.

[Page 16]

In the wake of the Enlightenment, the Zionist movement, too, visited Podolia Jewry in the mid-nineteenth century and found a loyal foothold among all its social sections. Zionist organizations of varying streams arose and began to prepare the generation for redemption. The new Hebrew school, which gave to its students a national Zionist education, replaced the old "Cheder," which was only sufficient for religious studies, and trained them for a new life in the Land of the Fathers. And indeed, many of them even immigrated to Israel and contributed their part in building it.

Podolia Jewry also took part in the new Hebrew literature that arose with the Zionist movement and produced writers, poets, and thinkers, such as: M. Y. Berdyczewski, Prof. Yehezkel Kaufmann, Eliezer Steinman, Prof. Zvi Scharfstein, S. L. Blank, Avraham Rosen, Mordechai Michaeli, M. Poznansky, David Fogel, Yitzhak Shinhar, S. Shafan, B. Karu, A. Ashman, and more.

Thus, in the healthy body of former Russian Jewry, that of Podolia was a living and active part which contributed quite a bit of its life to the soul of the entire nation. However, with the Nazi severing of our people in the diaspora, it, too, was almost completely destroyed from the face of the earth. And it's a shame, a great shame for a large and important Jewish community that was and is no more.

Original Footnote:

1. With the intention of the numbers being about the stable condition of the region, which was progressively weakened after the First World War, they are brought here from the period that came before it.

[Page 17]

Kamyanets Podilskyy

Translated by Monica Devens

More or less agreed upon information about Kamyanets Podilskyy comes from the beginning of the 14th century during the time of the Lithuanian ruler, Gediminas. From the 14th century to the end of the 18th century, rule of the city passed from the Lithuanians to the Poles, from them to the Turks and finally, with the partition of Poland, it was annexed to Russia in 1793.

The first news about the Jews in Kamyanets Podilskyy comes from the year 1447. With the city's annexation to Russia, Tsar Pavel issued a special decree permitting the Jews to remain and live in Kamyanets Podilskyy, a right that was denied them by the previous government. As a result of this, the Jewish community in Kamyanets Podilskyy and the district grew and expanded, and the Jewish population once again had a significant position in the economic life of the place.

Even as the Jews were an important cause for the development of the economic life of the city, haters of Israel could not be reconciled to this fact, that the Jews enjoyed equal rights and the right to live in the city. In 1832, the mayor requested from the central authorities that they forbid the Jews from living in Kamyanets Podilskyy. However, the Council of Ministers did not accept the proposal and decided to leave the right for Jews to live in the city, and also to purchase non-mobile property and to repair their old houses. New houses and stores were permitted to be built only in the new sections of the city. The Jews were forced, therefore, to live in the Russian and Polish "Folwarks" and to build their houses there. In 1843, the government forbade accepting immovable property from the Jews as collateral.

In 1793, there were 40,134 inhabitants of the city, of whom 32% were Ukrainian, 16% Polish. At the end of the First World page 19]War, it was estimated that there were 60,000 inhabitants, half of them Jews.

[Page 18][Blank][Page 19]

Kamyanets Podilskiyy

by Y. A. Bar Levi (Weisman)

Translated by Monica Devens

A. The City and its Economy

The Structure of the City and its Location

The city, whose historical background the reader will find below, lies sixteen versts from the great Dniester river that connects Podolia with Bessarabia. With the end of the First World War in 1917, Bessarabia passed to Romania and this river was a natural border between two foreign and mutually hostile countries. Also the city was close to the border between Russia and Eastern Galicia.

The city itself was built on a high cliff, one of the offshoots of the Carpathians, and around it the river Smotrych sends its quiet waters to the Dniester, which surrounds the city on three sides and so it looks like a peninsula. On the other side of the city, the topographic structure consists of ups and downs, except for its central part where rocks that extend over large spaces rise up higher and higher out of the fertile, black soil. The suburbs are built on these rocks: "Novi-Plan" (the new city), "Polski Folvarek" (the Polish suburb), "Ruski Folvarek" (the Russian suburb), "Podzamcze," Zinkovitz, and the Karvasari.

Transportation between the city and these suburbs was carried out over three bridges: the new bridge (built in the seventies of the 19th century), which connected the city with the Novi-Plan, the second

From views of the city: "The New Bridge"

[Page 20]

bridge, which led from the city to "Polski Folvarek," and the third bridge, "the Turki" (built by the Turks in the last quarter of the 17th century), which connected the city with "Podzamcze."

The "Podzamcze" suburb is apparently named after the fortress built by the Turks at the end of the bridge (in Russian and Polish - "Zamuk"). Apart from these bridge roads, side roads and paths led from the city to the suburbs.

The Smotrych flowed under the third bridge, in a noisy and roaring waterfall, on the one side to Zinkovitz and on the other to "Ruski Folvarek." On the bank of the river across from Zinkovitz stretched the Karvasari suburb, which, in the days of the rule of the Poles, being a town in itself, served as the first ghetto in Kamyanets. The Jews who were not from the area were forced into this ghetto at nightfall and had to stay there until the next day.

According to the records of 1847 (the "Revizia"), the community of Karvasar numbered 752 souls and, according to the census of 1897, 720 souls out of the general population of 1264 souls. When Kamyanets

Podilskyy was declared the regional and district city, it expanded its borders and also "swallowed" this small town, which became a suburb of the city.

From views of the city: "The Turkish Bridge"

Usually the streets of the city went uphill and downhill, and only the main streets extended over a flat surface, with a square plaza in the center. On the four sides of the plaza stood large two- and three-story buildings, of which the upper stories were for residences and the lower ones for business and commerce. In the middle of the plaza, there were again tall buildings and among them the municipal police building. Above the police building rose a high square tower with a railing at the top, which served as a look-out in all directions. In this tower, the municipal clock was also installed.

[Page 21]

On either side of the central block of houses that were in the middle of the square, two groves ("Skverim") were planted, which served as a resting place for passers-by, for children's games, as well as a meeting place for various brokers and craftsmen. Besides the mentioned groves, there were also two large city gardens ("Boulevarim") "Old" and "New." The first one was inside the city and extended on the slopes of the mountain next to the Smotrych River, from the Governor's Square to the "Podzamcze." This garden was the older of the two gardens. The second, "New" garden was larger in dimensions than its predecessor and spread over a huge and wide area on the land of the "Novi-Plan" between the new bridge and the "Polski Folvarek" on the left - a walk of about a kilometer. Standing on the slope in this garden in the evening, you could see the city in all its beauty, as it beckons you with its lights from the residents' houses and the street lamps. This sight was very charming and it seemed to you as if God had scattered the star system not only in the sky, but also on earth. The beauty of the city left a deep and unforgettable impression even in the hearts of people who were not local who happened to visit. Among these I will mention two writers and thinkers, Chaim Greenberg and Shmaryahu Gorelik, may their memory be blessed, who expressed to me their admiration for the landscape images and delightful corners they found in Kamyanets Podilskyy.

Special mention should be made of "the path" ("Dorozhka") within the "New" city garden that stretched over the top of the rock from the right side of the bridge to the "Ruski Folvarek." This "trail" attracted the hearts and affection of most of the city's residents, especially the young ones, who used to hang out there in groups until late at night. Quite a few novels were planned there, and quite a few love relationships came as a result of meetings on "the path."

From views of the city: "The Turkish Fortress"

[Page 22]

The Population

In the last quarter of the nineteenth century the city was counted among the twelve districts of the Podolia region. According to its geographical situation, the city and its district lay close to the border of eastern Galicia. Its closest neighbors were - the new Ushitza district on the east side, and Proskorov= Khmelnytskyi on the northwest side.

As a result of the "movement of peoples" (Germans, Poles, Lithuanians, Tatars, Turks, Ukrainians, etc.) from Western to Eastern Europe, and the frequent wars between them, layers of different peoples were formed in Podolia, who settled on its land as farmers in villages, and as residents, artisans, and merchants - in cities and towns. The proportion between the nationalities was different in each place. The population in Podolia, including in the western districts close to Galicia (Ushitza, Yampil, Mohyliv-Podilskyy, Proskorov= Khmelnytskyi, Kamyanets Podilskyy), was mixed with Poles, Ukrainians, Jews, Germans,

Armenians, and others. In the cities and towns, the Jews were the majority. In the villages - the Ukrainians, and in the manor houses - the Poles (the "Paritzim"). In the religious sense, the population was also divided according to this composition: Jews, Pravoslavs (Orthodox), Catholics, and Lutherans. The Germans made up a small part of the general population and were scattered throughout the whole district. Only in the town of Dunayivtsi was a significant part of them concentrated.

In Kamyanets Podilskyy itself, the population consisted of Jews, Ukrainians, Poles, and Germans. The Jews made up fifty percent of the total population. During the days of Khmelnytsky's attacks on Kamyanets, over ten thousand Jewish families were concentrated there. This number was accidental and ephemeral because, at that time, many Jews from other settlements were concentrated in the city, having fled to Kamyanets because it was a fortified city. With the cessation of fighting and skirmishes, many of them returned to their places and the Jewish population in Kamyanets continued to decrease.

We only find accurate numbers about the general and Jewish population in Kamyanets Podilskyy starting in the 19th century. According to the census ("Revizia") of 1847, there were 4,629 Jews in the city; in 1893, their number reaches 13,866 out of 36,951 in the general population (Pravoslavs - 18,211, Catholics - 4,150, others - 494). According to the census of 1897, there were in Kamyanets - 16,211 Jews, who constituted, at that time, forty percent of all residents. In the twenty years after this census, the Jewish population in the city grew and, according to the estimate, the number of residents reached 60,000 by the end of World War I, of whom half were Jews. The growth of the Jewish population came partly from natural increase and partly from the arrival of thousands of refugees from the towns near the border of Galicia who were expelled in 1915-1916 by the persecutor of the Jews, the commander-in-chief of the army, Nikolai Nikolayevich. The revolutions of February and October 1917, the change of regimes and governments, the rule of all kinds of local and foreign groups (Ukrainians, Bolsheviks, Poles, Czechs, etc.) resulted in the Jewish population looking for ways to escape from the oppression and hardship, some by internal migration around Russia or Ukraine and some by emigration, legal and illegal, abroad (the Land of Israel, the United States and Canada, South America, etc.). As a result, the number of Jews in Kamyanets also decreased and, according to the 1927 census, we find in Kamyanets in 1923 only 33,172 residents,

[Page 23]

of whom 50 percent are Jews. According to the 1951 census, there were in Kamyanets in 1926 only 31,000 residents (Jews and Ukrainians). For some reason, the author of the list does not mention the Poles.

A final, unofficial, and imprecise census, a blood census, was conducted by the Hitler murderers (may their names be obliterated) at the beginning of the month of Elul 5701 (end of August 1941), with their extermination in Kamyanets Podilskyy of about ten thousand Jews from the people of the area and the nearby towns and another six thousand Jews who were brought from Western and Eastern Europe (Hungary, Belgium, Holland, and Romania). God will avenge their blood.

Employment

Until 1915, there was no railroad in Kamyanets that would connect the city with the rest of Russia near and far, with the all-Russian industrial centers or with the cultural centers of the

From views of the city: "The Polish Suburb"

large and vast empire. The only means that served the city's transportation purposes with the wider world were very primitive and, in order to get from Kamyanets to any nearby train station, the city's residents had to move themselves in wagons in the summer and in sleds in the winter.

It goes without saying that the absence of the railroad that would connect Kamyanets with the rest of the country was the fault of the city. Its merchants, who were going to Warsaw or to Moscow, to Riga or to Odesa, to Nizhny-Novgorod or to Kyiv - for fairs and contracts - deliberated a lot over the question of transportation since transportation by horses was very expensive. Two offices took care of bringing goods and cargo: one was the "All-Russian Transportation and Insurance Company" ("Vserossiyskaya transportnaya i strakhovaya obtshistav"), under the management of H. Shabati, a native of Berdychiv, and the other, "The Southwest Transportation Office" ("Yugo-Zapadnoe transportnoe kontura"), under the management of Abraham Branzon and Menachem-Moshe Lichtman. These two offices kept large warehouses where the goods brought from far away were stored until the merchants - their owners - could take them out after paying the transportation, insurance, storage, and guarding fees, etc.

[Page 24]

These transport companies would help the merchants by providing loans against the stored goods and thereby enable them to last through the "dead" seasons. The merchants who could not bring their goods from far away were helped by the annual fair that was held in the town of Yarmolyntsi, sixty versts from Kamyanets, in the months of June-August, which attracted many vendors, factory owners or their agents from all over Russia. Here they bought and sold the agricultural produce of Podolia and the industrial products of the industrial centers in Russia and Poland.

Industry

There was no developed industry in our city. The main reason was again the lack of a railroad and the location of the city geographically at the edge of the region and also at the southwest edge of Russia. There was only light industry, aimed mainly at the local market. There existed: a beer factory of the Kleiderman family, tobacco factories, cigarette pouch factories, two mineral water factories, two cotton wool factories, a large flour mill, and a few other smaller enterprises. In Kamyanets, the mechanical factory of Kramm (German) which dealt in mechanical casting and welding was considered a heavy industry.

Maccabi-ha-Esh's observation tower (the "Kolancha")

[Page 25]

The Governmental and Public Institutions

The city served as an administrative center of the region and the district, and the government institutions were concentrated there: the district court, the local courts, the state treasury, the Office of the Inspector of Taxes, the Regional Administration and the Office of the Minister of the Region, the governmental and public banks, as well as educational institutions (four gymnasiums, a technical high school, a Russian religious seminary) and culture (theatre, etc.) and medical institutions. Two army battalions were also camped in the city with their commanders and officers.

Trade and crafts

As in all the cities of the "Pale of Settlement," trade and crafts in Kamyanets Podilskyy, too, were mainly in the hands of the Jews. We find statistical information about trade and crafts in the city only beginning in 1847 (according to the Revizia). Among the Jewish population at that time, there were 370 merchants, who were, apparently, of the wholesaler type. In addition to them, there were also retail merchants. In agricultural products - 759 self-employed (2,278 family members); in clothing - 270 self-employed (740 family members); in brokerage - 119 (370 family members); in just trade without a special type - 123 (392 family members), and in total 1,750 self-employed (6,300 family members) were engaged in trade. In crafts, the Jews took the first place: in tailoring - 713 self-employed (1,562 family members); in processing food products - 115 self-employed (397 family members); in metal (sheeting, framing, etc.) - 108 self-employed (227 family members). There are no numbers from that period about other types of craftsmen (carpenters, engravers, painters, watchmakers, goldsmiths, hatters, cobblers, etc.). And it can be assumed that there were close to five hundred self-employed like this (about 2,000 family members).

The Various Professions

According to the same count from 1947, there were engaged in clerical work and non-professional jobs 679 (men - 131, women - 548); in the professions - 190 (253 family members); those with fixed income 304 (612 family members).

All the professionals mentioned worked for the local population as well as for the surrounding area. The clerks, the teachers, the clergy, the police, the gendarmerie and the army, as well as the farmers and the owners of the estates, formed a group of customers from whom the Jews of Kamyanets made a good living. Also, the Jews of the towns that belonged to the district of Kamyanets or Ushitza would come frequently to Kamyanets to settle their affairs here, either in commercial matters or in financial matters in banks, or in matters concerning the various government offices. All this necessitated the existence of hotels and guesthouses, most of which were owned by the Jews.

The Banks

The three major banks played a large part in the city's economic development: the State Bank, Union Bank, and the "Russian Bank for Commerce and Industry." The Jewish merchants were also represented in the councils of these banks. These representatives were not elected, but rather were added or sometimes invited by

[Page 26]

the bank managers. From them, the managers obtained their information about the economic situation in the city and about the economic situation of those who applied to them for credit. For the most part, the big merchants or the owners of the estates and the various institutions were helped by these banks, but not the shopkeeper or the small craftsman, or the clerk, the teacher, etc. These circles, therefore, turned to private lenders who were engaged in providing loans at high interest rates and the borrowers never managed to get rid of their debts … In the broad community, the recognition grew that new ways to sources of cheap credit must be sought and that it is necessary to add penny to penny in order to save. That's when the two mutual credit institutions were founded, which played a large part in the development of the city's economic life.

The Cooperative Banks

The first association that was founded under the name of "The Mutual Credit Cooperative Association" mostly included among its members the estate owners, the upper office workers, and the big merchants, Jews and Christians. And even though this association did not close its doors to "Amcha" (=average people) of all nationalities - because according to the regulations, it was impossible to behave in a discriminatory fashion - nevertheless, the financial politics of the management was to restrict the advancement of Jewish "Amcha" in granting credit, even though there were also Jewish representatives among the members of the council. This desire to seclude themselves among privileged circles only was even more felt in the selection of the necessary clerks. In the staff of clerks of this financial institution, which was larger than a "minyan" (= 10), there was not a single Jew, despite the considerable number of Jewish members of the association. This came about as a result of the anti-Semitic attitude of the chief accountant, Biletsky (a Pole), who was supported by the Christian members of the management. Only after the death of the aforementioned anti-Semite Biletsky, and especially with the outbreak of the First World War, when some of the Christian clerks were drafted into the army, did the opportunity for Jews to join the group of clerks also come.

When the broad circles of the residents came to know that the aforementioned cooperative society did not stand at the service of "Amcha," they rose up and founded the second mutual credit society, which opened its doors to the shopkeeper, the craftsman, the low-level clerk, from the city and the surrounding area. The members of management and the council as well as the staff of clerks were all Jewish. The association absorbed a large number of members from all Jewish and Christian circles. In general, it should be noted that the relations between the nationalities in the city in daily contact were among the improved ones and this was also reflected in the composition of the institutions as mentioned above.

The Insurance Company

Private insurance companies operated in our city, whose centers were in St. Petersburg and Moscow, and they had agencies in Kamyanets, whose managers were only Jews. But there were many who could not meet the payment conditions of private companies and it was necessary to take care of the sustenance of families of this type in the event of a disaster. For this purpose, the "Society for Mutual Aid in Case of Death" was founded in 1912. Even this company served as an example of good relations between all parts of the population, and Jews and Christians were elected to its management as well as to the audit committee.

[Page 27]

B. Spiritual and Social Life

Authors

As mentioned above, the population in Kamyanets was mixed with different nationalities, but at all times, the Jews were 40-50 per cent of the residents. Until the second half of the 19th century, the spoken language of the Jewish community was only Yiddish, however, the "Revizia" (=census) of 1847 already knows to point out that, within the Jewish population of 16,112 people, only ninety-nine did not speak Yiddish - at the end of the century, the number of Jews who also knew other languages kept increasing. According to the statistics from that time, 24 per cent of the Jews of Kamyanets knew Russian and there were another about 14 percent who knew other languages.

In the 60s and 70s of the preceding century, Shalom Yaakov Abramovich (Mendele Mocher Sforim) and A.D. Gottlober lived and worked in Kamyanets. In 1857, the man who was later known as Baron David Ginzburg was born there. Professor Fischl Schneerson z"l and Menachem Poznansky z"l were also born in Kamyanets.

From the later generation, we should mention the teacher and writer Shlomo Shafan z"l (born in Yarmolyntsi), who received his general education in our city, and even studied at the university that was founded there during the days of Ukrainian rule, and the teacher and writer Aharon Ashman and teacher and poet Avraham Rosen were distinguished for long lives.

Hassidism and Frankism

With its positioning on the border of Galicia and Wallachia Moldavia, the city was open to attacks and wars from its near and far neighbors, and even to spiritual influences. On the other hand, the 17th and 18th centuries were the most difficult for the Jews of Podolia in general and the Jews of Kamyanets in particular. The devastation of the years of 1647 and 1648 at the hands of Khmelnytsky's troops; the wars between the Poles and the Turks, as a result of which the city was conquered by the Turks and was under their rule in the years 1672-1699, put great fear into the Jews and greatly weakened their economic situation. With this, the circle of economic relations expanded and the Jews of Podolia reached Kushta and Smyrna in trade relations. Some of them even sent their sons there to study with the Sephardic rabbis. Among them were those who were influenced by the pseudo-Messianists (the Shabbtais) and the teachings of the Frankists. In particular, the members of the Frankist sect also found a foothold in the towns near the border: Lyantskorun=Zarechanka, Sataniv, and others. It goes without saying that the rabbis and all the ultra-Orthodox could not sit quietly when they saw that the new teachings, which contained kernels of Christianity, captivated the souls of the weak in spirit, and they began to persecute the members of the sect. The latter sought protection from the Polish authorities and the Catholic clergy until finally the rabbis had to submit to the demand of Bishop Dembowski and stand in a public debate with the Frankists. With the results of the same debate, about 1000 books of the Talmud were burned.

Around the same time, the Hasidic movement arose, whose founder and originator was Rabbi Israel Ba'al-Shem-Tov z"l. This movement, whose cradle was almost at the gates of our city (The Besht was born in the town of Okopy,

[Page 28]

close to Kamyanets), had many supporters and fans. And when, as is known, after the departure of the Besht and his first disciples, the "rabbis' courts" on both sides of the border multiplied. There were also some among the Jews of our city who would travel to their rabbis who were across the border and there were rabbis who came from time to time to their followers in Kamyanets.

The majority of the Jewish population in the city was made up of "Mitnagdim," or more precisely, of those who were indifferent to Hasidism and behaved in their religious lives according to the accepted tradition. The style of prayer was the Sephardic style and, as Professor Balaban explains in his book "The History of the Frankish Movement" ("Dvir Press", Tel Aviv, 1933), it was influenced by the Jews of Spain who immigrated to Eastern European countries and came into contact with Judaism in Poland, Austria, and Hungary.

The Cathedral

In the New Time

With the annexation of Podolia by the Russian Empire at the end of the 18th century, the spiritual life of the Jewish settlement also changed. Even under the new conditions, the Jews were limited in their rights, such as the prohibition of settling in the villages, the purchase of land, "numerus clausus" in the high schools and colleges, and the prohibition of permanent settlement in cities outside of the "Pale of Settlement," etc., etc. Even so, new winds were blowing and the ideas of the new time also influenced Russian Jewry. The Jews of Kamyanets Podilskyy, as in the rest of the cities of the country, were no longer satisfied with providing their sons with a traditional education in the "cheder" and the yeshiva, and they began to send their sons away

[Page 29]

to the general schools, elementary, high, and universities. After the boys came the turn of the girls.

As a result of this, the number of people who knew Russian and other languages kept increasing among the Jewish residents. The encounter with the culture and literature of the Russian people and other peoples of Western Europe came about. The influence of various social movements also penetrated the peoples and Israel. The daily life of the Jews of Kamyanets took on a new shape and a different tone, especially among the young generation, and the deviation from a traditional way of life began. Despite this, there were no breaches in the wall of traditional Judaism in our city (desecration of Shabbat and the like) until the days of the Revolution of 1917.

The founders of the Zionist youth organization "Kadima"

"Hibbat Zion" and political Zionism

The national revival movement in its first manifestation - the "Hovevei Zion" movement - and later on the Zionist movement had considerable influence in our city.

The "Hovevei Zion" was headed by the lawyer David Schleifer z"l, who was in his time one of the founders of the BILU Association in Kharkiv, but for various reasons did not immigrate to Eretz Israel with his BILU associates and worked as a prosecutor in our city.

"Hovevei Zion" in Kamyanets were not satisfied with just collecting membership fees or donations from the "bowls," but were alert to the general questions of the movement and participated in the general meetings and conferences of the "Odesa Committee."

With the appearance of the book, "The State of the Jews" by Dr. Binyamin Ze'ev Herzl, and the gathering of the first Zionist Congress in Basel, many of the "Hovevei Zion" joined the Zionist movement, as is known, including many of the "Hovevei Zion" in Kamyanets. From them, David Schleifer founded the first "chug" of the organization, the Zionist Federation, in Kamyanets Podilskyy.

In this way of "chugim," more male members joined the movement, as well as female members ("B'not Zion") from among

[Page 30]

the middle class, educated and young, and in the years 1904-1905, the Zionist Federation had six chugim in our city. The writer of these columns was then tasked by the general municipal committee, which consisted of representatives of all the chugim, to organize an additional chug in the Polish suburb, mainly from among the local youth.

The "third chug" was the most outstanding, since most of its members were educated people who knew Hebrew and were supporters of Hebrew literature, young people aged 20-25, members of more or less economically established families. They excelled in activity and daring activism.

The influence of David Schleifer, who was the chief spokesman of the Zionist Federation and even of the Jewish public in the city, was evident on all "chugim," except for the members of the diplomaed intelligentsia who saw their world in the pursuit of profits from their professions and of their private pleasures and hardly took part in public work. These (except for a few of them) were imbued with the spirit of assimilation and looked at Schleifer, who, despite his occupation and troubles as a lawyer specializing in civil law and famous throughout the region, devoted himself to Zionist work and other public affairs as abnormal. In his work for the Zionist ideal, David Schleifer was helped by a loyal and dedicated Zionist like Mr. Israel Goldman z"l who served for many years as the secretary of the Zionist Federation in our city.

As we know, all the Zionist work in the first years of the movement's existence was conducted by the institution "Ha-Morashim." The Zionist Federation in Kamyanets Podilskyy, along with all the other Federations in the Podolia region and in the region of Bessarabia, including the Khotyn district, were in the circle of activity of the Morasha, the member of the Executive Committee Dr. Yaakov Bernstein-Cohen z"l, who lived in Chisinau. However, apparently, it was impossible to be satisfied with the management of the Zionist work from the center in Chisinau and, therefore, Kamyanets Podilskyy was chosen as the appropriate place for this and it was there that the first regional conference was held in 1901. Of the leaders of the Zionists, Dr. S. Bendersky, Dr. Y. Bernstein-Cohen, Menachem Sheinkin, and others participated. Of the 24 conference delegates, Kamyanets was represented by 8 delegates and at their head, the lawyer D. Schleifer and Mark Nudelman.

Kamyanets Podilskyy also sent its delegates to other Zionist congresses and conferences. At the Second Conference of Russian Zionists in Minsk in 1901, D. Schleifer participated as a delegate from Kamyanets. At the Third Conference in Helsinki (1906), Israel Drachler, who also participated as a delegate from our city in the Fourth Conference in The Hague (1907) as well as in the Eighth Zionist Congress there that same year, represented Kamyanets. At the Ninth Zionist Congress in Hamburg (1909), Kamyanets was represented by Israel Drachler and Israel Goldman.

The first 20th of Tammuz

I was then a boy of fifteen and, until this day, that bitter and hasty day when the news of Dr. Herzl's passing came is retained in my memory. And the Jewish city of Kamyanets, with all its chugim and classes, religious and secular, Zionists and non-Zionists, was in heavy mourning. On that day, a mourning meeting was called at the time for the prayers of Mincha and Ma'ariv in the tailors' synagogue, the largest and most magnificent in the city. The news

[Page 31]

Regional Zionist Conference

[Page 32]

of the death of Dr. Herzl and of the meeting quickly spread to all corners of the city and even reached the nearby towns, and long before the appointed time crowds began to flock to Purlasky Street where the synagogue was. Many people came to the meeting, not only from the Zionists, but just Jews "all year round," sympathizers of Zionism and even those who opposed it; many came from the intelligentsia who until now had mocked the "dreams" of the Zionists, people from the local government also came. I don't remember if the Zionist Federation announced the cancellation of work and the closing of shops, but during those hours of the meeting, the streets of the city were deserted because all the workshops and shops were closed as a sign of mourning. The great hall of the synagogue was too narrow to accommodate the entire crowd and many stood outside.

During the Days of the Uganda Debate and the First Coup in Russia

The great debate in the Zionist movement on the question of Uganda - the Land of Israel found its expression even in Kamyanets Podilskyy. However, the number of those inclined to the territorialist idea was very small in Kamyanets and most of the members of the Zionist movement in our city remained loyal to the Land of Israel and supported "Tsiyonei Tsiyon."

The Zionist movement had not managed to heal its wounds after the Uganda debate when the days of the first coup in Russia came in October 1905. Czar Nikolai II announced the granting of a constitution that would allow the people to take part in the management of the affairs of the state through its emissaries to the first Russian parliament - the "Duma." The Jewish population pinned a lot of hopes on the new system that came to the country and, along with the rest of the inhabitants, rejoiced in the coup and looked forward to good days. However, this joy did not last long. Almost the day after the constitution was given, riots and pogroms took place organized by the "Black Hundred" under the auspices of the police and the Jews were chosen as the "scapegoat." For 2-3 days, pogroms were held in dozens of cities and towns, Jewish property was looted, and quite a few victims even fell. In Kamyanets Podilskyy, rioters who were recruited from among the Gentiles of the suburbs of the city went wild and to them were added a number of "Katsafs," who were brought especially from the center of Russia. Admittedly, the pogrom in Kamyanets manifested itself only in the breaking of windows of a number of Jewish houses and the looting of several sales stalls in the market and there were no victims, although the Jews locked themselves in their houses until the anger passed.

The Political Birzha

The socialist parties that had been working clandestinely until now came to light and began to conduct broad written and mainly oral propaganda among all segments of the population, including the youth and the working classes. In order not to have to rent special halls for meetings, a meeting place was arranged for them in the streets in the evening hours after the male and female workers had finished their work. The propagandists of the parties would "catch" the workers on their way home from work and hold informative talks with them about the essence of their program and their ideals and about the democratic rights declared for them in the constitution. The meeting place was known as the "Birzha" (stock exchange).

The parties that operated in the "Birzha" were: the Social Democratic Party, the Socialist Revolutionaries, the Anarchists, and "Po'alei Tsiyon." Each party had its "Birzha" on one of the four broad sidewalks of the central square in the city.

[Page 33]

The First Seeds of "Tse'irei Tsiyon"

In those days, young people from the ranks of the workers and the students who sought in Zionism not only the fulfillment of the aspiration for a Jewish state like all the states, but also aspired to a state of social justice, began to gather and organize. At that same time, an emissary from Odesa arrived in our city, a skinny guy, with black hair and deep piercing eyes, wearing a black "Rovshka" and sash, about 18-19 years old, who made a great impression on everyone who met him. This young man was Chaim Greenberg z"l.

Chaim Greenberg came then to lecture on matters of Hebrew culture and literature, however he did not wash his hands from the political questions either and he spoke respectfully in a lively and comprehensive debate with the opponents of Zionism. The power of his warning and persuasive speech (he spoke in Russian), his noble appearance, and the ways of pure conceptual debate captured the hearts of all his listeners, especially the youth. In this visit, Chaim Greenberg sowed the first seeds of the "Tse'irei Tsiyon" movement in our city.

The Student Organization "Kadima" in 1918

C. Between the Two Revolutions 1905-1917

"The Work of the Present"

After the Russian Zionist Conference in November 1906 in Helsinki (Finland), during which the "Helsinki Program" in the matter of "The Work of the Present" was accepted and in which Israel Drachler participated as a delegate on behalf of the Zionists of Kamyanets Podilskyy, Zionist activity increased in our city, too. The People's Bank was founded and special attention was paid to strengthening the girls' school of Mrs. S. L. Blobstein, and the "Jewish Club" was also established, whose role was to bring the assimilated intelligentsia closer to the national movement and the national cause. Various cultural activities were carried out in this club and there was also a library there of 3000

[Page 34]

volumes in Russian, Yiddish, and Hebrew. The Zionist Federation also gave its opinion on the matter of the "Talmud Torah" in Polski Folvarek, which, until the years 1905-1906, was in very poor condition. A new curriculum was implemented, which also included learning the Russian language and arithmetic as well as craft lessons. Poor students also received clothing and shoes. The Zionists also took care to improving the institution of "hospitality" and to expand it.

Thus the Zionist activity in our city flowed in two channels: the usual Zionist work for the education of the masses for Zionist national consciousness and the collection of funds for the institutions and funds of the movement, and the care of the local public institutions.

At the Helsinki conference, a central committee was elected, whose seat was in Vilnius. However, Kamyanets in particular, and Podolia in general, had an organizational and spiritual connection to the Odesa center headed by M. M. Ussishkin. In 1907, the well-known Zionist writer and publicist A. M . Borochov (bless him) was sent to Kamyanets from Odesa in order to organize here, at a regional conference of Podolia Zionists, an active center for the entire region. At this conference, the following were elected to the regional council: David Schleifer, Israel Goldman and Israel Drachler from Kamyanets Podilskyy, Menashe Altman from Balta, Shalom Altman from Zhvanets, Zvi Isserzon from Vinnytsya, and Yosef Blank from Dunayivtsi.

The committee went to work body and soul and vitality was introduced in all the local cells of the Zionist Federation in Podolia. The connections with the two centers - Vilnius and Odesa - worked miracles and helped a lot to put the work and the propaganda on a high level, and Kamyanets was both the plaintiff and the defendant for all kinds of actions, including cultural actions. And indeed, the year 1908 was rich in cultural events in Kamyanets. In the summer of that year, the famous writers Shimen Frug and Leib Yaffe visited our city and, with their participation, two literary banquets were held in the municipal theater, which attracted many Zionists and just Jews from the country towns as well. On behalf of the central committee in Vilnius, its member Dr. Daniel Pasmanik visited Kamyanets. At the end of the summer of that year, the writer Shmaryahu Gorelik, member

A group of Zionists from Kamyanets and the surrounding area
who were imprisoned at the Zionist Conference in Mohyliv-Podilskyy in 1920

[Page 35]

of the "Das Yiddische Falk" council in Vilnius came to our city. The members of the "Bund" and "Po'alei Tsiyon" also regarded his visit positively, as a writer who writes Yiddish and as a lecturer on literary matters and not as a Zionist speaker.

All these actions of the guests were arranged with a license from the local authority (the police). In order to disguise the purpose of these "guests'" coming, "neutral" topics were chosen for their lectures. At the same time, there were secret meetings and gatherings of the Zionists of Kamyanets and the surrounding area, in which we discussed organizational questions and practical day-to-day matters.

And here one bright day, on the intermediate days of the holiday of Pesach (April 1909), the gendarmerie appeared - apparently, according to the information of someone among the "Haters of Zion" - at the apartment of the Secretary of the Regional Committee, Israel Goldman z"l, conducted a long and thorough search, and confiscated all the material related to the Regional Zionist Committee's activities. This time they were satisfied with only this. A few days later I. Goldman was invited to the gendarmerie office and was required to translate into Russian all the material taken from him during the search. The translation of the material was finished about a year later and, contrary to the opinion of the gendarmerie, that the matter should be dismissed, the investigator of the district court saw fit to file a complaint against the Committee. And indeed the trial took place in the district court in Kamyanets Podilskyy in the summer of 1911 and, thanks to the defense of the local lawyer D. Schleifer, all the members of the committee were found innocent.

In connection with the "War of Languages" that was going on at that time in the Jewish street between Hebrew and Yiddish, Zev Jabotinsky, whose reputation as a brilliant orator and a gifted publicist preceded him, was invited to give a lecture in our city. His lecture on "Jewish Language and Culture," which was held in the municipal theater hall, attracted a huge audience and many of those who came remained outside. At the end of the first lecture, the representatives of the "Bund" and of "Po'alei Tsiyon" and the rest of the left-wing parties were invited to come up on stage to argue with the lecturer, but the great victory of the lecturer on the Hebrew matter discouraged them and none of them dared to ask permission to speak, and they did not appear any longer for Jabotinsky's second lecture on the same subject. In a proclamation issued jointly by these parties, they accused the Zionists of deliberately inviting the regular police and the secret police to ensnare the representatives of the "proletariat" when they took the stage to argue with Jabotinsky, but the words of the conspiracy did not elicit any response and the victory of the Zionists and the "Hebrews" was complete.

Among the other activities, it is worth noting the two Purim receptions, which were held as part of "Eretz Israel Week." Thanks to these receptions, which were very successful, the light of Zionism was raised in the city.

The Beginning of the First World War

Since our city was very close to the Austria-Hungary border, it was the first to experience the taste of war and its horrors. And indeed on August 5, 1914, the city received authoritative information that the Austrian army had crossed the border, was already on Russian territory, and was approaching Kamyanets. And this was immediately felt: the enemy, who was already within firing range of field artillery, began to bombard the city thinking that a Russian army was in the city. The bombings continued with slight breaks. On that day, the Austrian soldiers entered, including a Hungarian regiment, and passed through the main streets of the city together.

[Page 36]

For the hostilities of the retreating Russian army, a penalty of 300,000 rubles was imposed on the city in money or its equivalent, as well as the provision of certain amounts of food and various supplies to the army. The army demanded that this be provided by 9 o'clock in the morning the next day, otherwise it would continue its operations against the city. The Polish mayor and two of the city's Jews were arrested as hostages against the fulfillment of the demand.

All night the residents were worried that the necessary amount would not be collected and the next morning, when they saw that the hostages had not yet been released, many began to leave the city.

A few days later, the city's conquerors left and the Cossacks entered. It was on Shabbat and when the Jews came out of the synagogues, the Cossacks greeted them with curses and whipping and, after venting their anger on the heads of the Jews, they continued on their way towards the border to Galicia. Life in the city returned to its normal course and the refugees began to return.

"New Faces"

During the war years, the residents of the towns near the border and the front suffered in particular, and many of them left the place they had resided for generations and moved to other settlements. Thus was created a very considerable flow of refugees who demanded the help of the central Jewish institutions in the capital city: "YKUF," "OZE-YIVO," "ORT," and more. The administrations of these institutions had the hand of the left-wing parties, the anti-Zionists, at the top and most of the people who were sent to the refugee centers were "theirs." Mr. Eliyahu Gumener, a lawyer from Vilnius and a socialist Zionist, was also sent to our city as an agent.

A person with energy, organizational skills, and a dynamic speaker, but at the same time a clear "Zion Hater" and even more a hater of Zionists in all their shades. He appeared in Kamyanets in 1915 in the midst of the war and his "authority" also reached other cities and towns in the districts of Kamyanets and Ushitza. And since he had the "century" in his hand, he tried to have the "opinion" as well. As a party member, he aspired to increase and glorify the forces of the left in our city in order to create for himself an influential public home front. Indeed, all the anti-Zionist forces in the city were concentrated around him: "Po'alei Tsiyon," the "Bund", and the "Folks-Party," which usually did not have a large number of friends or sympathizers in their ranks, but all of them were imbued with the spirit of militant "Yiddishism." In this anti-Zionist assemblage, the lawyer Yaakov Krayz, who created for himself the popular spirit of a public businessman close to the "Folks-Party," and Israel Drachler (brother of Sarah Drachler, who was killed in the defense of Tel Hai), who previously represented the Zionist Federation in riots and congresses, also stood out. By profession, he was a Hebrew teacher, but at the same time he created for himself the theory of Yiddishism and became close to the "Po'alei Tsiyon" and became their spokesman. As a serious public figure, with a quiet temperament and pleasant manners with people, he was accepted by all the chugim, including his former friends in the Zionist movement. Of the few "Bund" people, S. Bograd and Feibush Morgenstern, and of the socialist Zionists - Moshe Sister (now Dr. Sister, researcher and teacher of Tanach at the Kibbutzim College in Israel), who was strongly opposed to the movement and the Zionist Federation in his public appearances on the party stages, along with E. Gumener, his friend, stood out.

New and fresh forces appeared in the Zionist camp as well. With the expulsion of the Jews of Zhvanets on the Austrian border, by the decree of the commander-in-chief of the Russian army Nikolai Nikolayevich, most of the deportees came

[Page 37]

to nearby Kamyanets. The people of Zhvanets quickly integrated into the economic, social, and cultural life of their new place of residence and introduced new blood into the life of the Jewish community. The younger generation especially excelled among them, who had grown up and were educated in an atmosphere of Hebraism and Zionism in their place of origin and continued their activity in this area here, too. The driving and encouraging force of all this cultural activity was one of the young people of Zhvanets, Yehoshua Salzman (Malchi) or, as they called him at the time - Schika Salzman, who was a student at the "Herzliya" Gymnasium in Tel Aviv and returned home for his annual vacation and because of the war could not return to the Land of Israel. This Salzman excelled in his warm temperament and in the polemical talent of a popular orator who stood out the most over the years after the Revolution of 1917 in his debates on public platforms against the anti-Zionist parties. He was also the originator of the idea of "Ha-Mitnadvim ba-Am" (an organization of "He-Halutz") and the organizer of the youth chug,

First group of members from Kamyanets in Kiryat Anavim

which was centered around him in "Beit Ha'Am" (Community Center), his handiwork. From here also came the young forces who adhered to the idea of pioneering and were among the core members who immigrated to the Land of Israel in 1920 and founded, together with pioneers from the city of Pryluky, the "Kiryat Anavim" collective farm in the vicinity of Jerusalem.

However, it was not only the younger generation of Zhvanets refugees who were involved in the life of the Jewish population in Kamyanets. The elderly among them, led by veteran businessman Shalom Altman z"l, also took an active part in the life of our community.

In those years, Meir (Muni) Zak, who was later the general manager of the main office of the Keren Kayemet Le-Israel in Jerusalem, under the name of Meir Ha-Ezrachi, became famous. He stood out as a talented Zionist orator and was one of the few who remained within the framework of the Association of General Zionists throughout his life.

In those days, young forces who belonged to the "Tse'irei Tsiyon" also appeared in the public arena and they were: Zalman Pretkin (born in Pryluk), known in Israel as Zalman Porat, director of the supervisory alliance of the agricultural cooperative and active in the Aliyah Bet mission; the teacher the writer Aharon Ashman (born in Balin); Mendel Goldstein, who graduated from the Faculty of Law and excelled in the power of his speech and pen; Israel Bashirovker

[Page 38]

(born in Lyantskorun=Zarechanka), a Hebrew teacher, known in Israel as Y. Bar-Shira, a lawyer and law lecturer at the Tel Aviv branch of the Hebrew University in Jerusalem; Yaakov Sharir, director of the "Zion" Insurance Company in Israel and head of the Association of Insurance Companies in Israel; Y. A. Weisman (now Bar Levi), the only Yiddishist in the Zionist camp and in the "Tse'irei Tsiyon" Party in Kamyanets; Etti-Hadassah Lerner (born in Zhvanets), kindergarten teacher, having a gentle soul and advanced intelligence.

A non-Zionist religious party, "Ahdut Israel," which united and consolidated the religious circles in the city from the worshippers of the synagogues and the Beit Midrash led by R. Leib Kley-Darman, owner of a beer factory, also appeared then for the first time.

Education and Culture

In the last years of the war (1915-1917), the struggle between the Zionists and their opponents intensified and this time not only for the sake of abstract ideological values, but also over matters of money received from the central aid institutions. These funds were intended not only for physical needs, but also for things in the spirit: maintaining kindergartens, schools, and various cultural activities.

In the years 1900-1902, two "reformed rooms" were founded in our city. Only one of them lasted 3-4 years. Better than that was the fate of the school for girls named after S. L . Blobstein, the daughter of the "Ha-Rav Mita'am," which was founded in 1902 and existed until approximately 1916.

At the end of the First World War, two Hebrew schools were founded in our city under the auspices of the local "Ha-Tarbut" called Tushiya and Moledet. In the field of Hebrew education, the following teachers worked at the time: Aharon Ashman, Avraham Rosenzweig (Rosen), Israel Bashirovker (Bar-Shira), Haim Schreiberman (Sharig) and others. Two Hebrew kindergartens were also founded, under the management of kindergarten teachers Etti-Hadassah Lerner and Batsheva Hat.

"Beit Ha'Am" and "Kadima"

The last three years before the February coup were marked by lively activity among all the chugim of the Jewish population in the city, and especially in the area of culture among the youth. Each chug worked according to its ability and according to its achievements. In addition to the two mentioned Hebrew schools, which were nurtured with love and devotion by their teachers and administrators, the left-wing chugim also founded their own schools in Yiddish. Even the older generation and the maturing generation among the youth broke their own paths and created two important institutions for themselves: "Beit Ha'Am" and "Kadima."

"Beit Ha'Am" opened in one of the houses on Dolgaya Street and the evening classes for boys and girls aged 15-18 were held there, on Hebrew, Hebrew literature and history, as well as lectures and debates on the questions of the time and on the future of the Jewish people.

The Jewish youth who were students, the students of the Russian gymnasiums, found their place in the "Kadima" organization.

[Page 39]

The Histadrut was founded on April 28, 1916. Here, too, the orientation was nationalist-Zionist, and although most of the speeches and lectures were conducted in Russian, the Hebrew language was also studied in this chug. With the February coup of 1917, "Kadima" appeared as a defined Zionist group and participated in all the Zionist activities in the city.

"Kadima" Student Organization

One of the initiators and organizers of the "Kadima" chug was the young Israel Brandman, a violinist and music prodigy, a student of the conservatory in Petrograd, who came from a family of musicians. His older brother Yaakov, a cellist, and his sister Ada (then Bromberg), a pianist, were also active in this chug. In March 1917, the choir and orchestra named "Kadima" were founded. This institution in its new incarnation became a dear project not only of its founder Israel Brandman, but also of the wider Jewish public in the city. In the tumultuous years of 1918-1920, "Kadima" appeared on the concert stages of all the regimes of those days (Bolsheviks, Ukrainians, Poles), a special concert was even given in honor of the delegation of the Joint arranged by Professor Friedlander, Max Fein, and others on June 27, 1920.

In November 1920, with the resumption of Bolshevik rule in the city, the activities of "Kadima" ceased as most of its members left Kamyanets and immigrated to the Land of Israel. In Israel, "Kadima" gave two more concerts: one with the participation of the choir of Gedud Ha-Avoda in Petah Tikva and one in Jaffa. Some of the members of "Kadima" who remained in Kamyanets organized themselves as a professional musical group and performed in a concert in early 1921. After a Yevsektsiya man reported them to the Bolshevik government as a "counter-revolutionary" Zionist organization, the group ceased to exist.

[Page 40]

D. In the Confusion of the Time

Regime changes and riots

In the first years after the February 1917 revolution in Russia, there were regime changes frequently. According to the book by E. Gumener, "A Kapitel Ukraine" ("Ukraine Chapter"), the regime changed sixteen times in Proskorov= Khmelnytskyi during the first two years of the revolution. The same was also the case in Kamyanets. Of course, the entire civilian population suffered from this, especially the Jewish communities. The rule of various militias under the leadership of all kinds of adventurers, men of hand and fist, to whom human life was worthless, instilled in the Jewish population a constant fear of riots. And indeed it was not a vain fear. A wave of riots passed over the Jews of Ukraine and, in our surroundings, it befell the cities and towns: Orynyn, Dunayivtsi, Velikiy Zhvanchik, Vurbovtsi, Murovani Kurylivtsi, Yarmolyntsi, Solovkovyts, Kytaihorod, Kopaihorod, Shatava, and other settlements. This wave did not skip over our city, Kamyanets Podilskyy, either and reached it on the eve of Shavuot (June, 1919). The pogrom lasted for 3 days during which the Heidemaks of Petliura ran amok in the city and were helped by the local people, who took advantage of the window of opportunity to steal Jewish property from apartments, shops, and warehouses. About 72 Jews were killed in these riots.

These lives of fear and riots had a considerable effect on worsening the economic and cultural situation of the Jewish residents. Due to the changes of regimes, the value of the currency decreased and the crowds thinned out, the roads were disrupted, and trade and crafts dwindled. Nevertheless, these were years of lively political and public activity on the part of all parties and all circles.

For its part, the Ukrainian government recognized the right of the Jewish population to organize its communal life

The leadership of the Jewish community

[Page 41]

on a democratic basis. In Kamyanets, the community committee and its council were elected in democratic elections according to the spirit of the times and the laws of the state, which managed all the affairs of the Jewish public in the city. The community committee also served as an address for help in times of need for all public businessmen in the nearby towns.

The "Haganah" in 1909

"Self-Defense" and the Chomsky Trial

After the pogrom in Kishinev=Chisinau in the spring of 1903, a number of young Zionists, educated and "house owners," organized themselves and began collecting funds to buy small arms (pistols), learned the "craft" as "amateurs," and went out to fulfill the obligation of "self-defense." The "mild" pogrom in Kamyanets in October 1905, the day after the first revolution, reminded the Jewish youth in the city that they should not remain complacent and quiet. And then the reduced circle of the young Zionists began to broaden the framework and to bring the common working people, porters, butchers, and blacksmiths closer for defense matters. In the meantime, years passed and there was no need for "self-defense." Those who were at the head of the organization grew up in the meantime and dispersed to different places and the city was left without "defense."

However, the unstable security situation that arose due to the frequent changes of government in the years 1918-1919 required the creation of some kind of framework of security and defense and the residents, principally the Jews, organized a night watch in every house. At a later time, a sort of "Civil Guard" was organized under the authority of the municipality. The men of the guard also received a limited number of rifles from the city militia, although not all of them were trained and knowledgeable in the rules of the rifle and its use.

And here, on one of the days at the end of May 1919, the chairman of the Bolshevik "Revkom" informed the Jewish Civil Guard that gangs of Heidemaks had entered the town of Orynyn, near Kamyanets,

[Page 42]

and were organizing a pogrom there, and suggested that the Jewish population take care of the defense of the Jews of Orynyn, and the safety of the Jews of Kamyanets as well, and to mobilize the Jewish youth for this purpose. From the Jews of Orynyn, too, came a cry and a demand to come to their aid. Immediately, the call went out among the Jewish youth in the city, regardless of party or ideological outlook, to volunteer and to come to the aid of the Jews of Orynyn. The number of young people who volunteered reached eighty-ninety and they were joined by several tens of soldiers from the "Red Army" and two officers at their head and, along with them, one cannon.

The company barely managed to move about 8 versts away from Kamyanets and suddenly it was subjected to heavy fire from cannons and machine guns. The volunteers were ordered to lie down on the ground and a fierce battle ensued between the young Jews who were not used to weapons and war, and the Ukrainian army, experienced in battles and murders, who also had more men. But in this critical and desperate situation, the Jewish volunteers concentrated their forces and switched from defense to counterattack, and overcame the Heidemaks. The results of the battle were: 60 Heidemaks were killed, excluding the number of wounded taken by the retreating Ukrainian army, and on the side of the Jews, two fell, one of them Avraham Korman z"l (a member of "Tse'irei Tsiyon"), and three were wounded.

When the victorious volunteers returned to Kamyanets, it became clear that the Bolsheviks' intention in sending the Jewish youths to Orynyn was to use them as "cannon fodder" in order to gain time for the evacuation of the city. And indeed it did not take many hours and the city was emptied of its Bolshevik rulers, who fled eastward.

It was clear to the Jews that, if the city was captured again by the Ukrainian army, they would not be silent about the defeat that the Jewish youths had caused the Heidemaks and they would want to take revenge on the Jewish population. And in fact the Heidemaks arranged the pogrom in Kamyanets, which we mentioned above, at the beginning of June 1919.

Many of the Jews fled the city to other settlements. Among them was Alexander (Shura) Chomsky, the deputy commander of the "Civil Guard," who participated in the "Orynyn campaign" as the commander of the volunteers, but about two weeks later returned to Kamyanets and was arrested by the secret police of Petliura. He was charged with being the leader of armed Jewish forces in the "Red Army" who fought in the Orynyn front against the Ukrainian army and the matter was handed over to a military court.

The trial was conducted behind closed doors. The defense was headed by the defendant's brother-in-law, M. Alter, an excellent and very talented lawyer. As defense witnesses there appeared at the trial the best businessmen of the city - Jews, Ukrainians, and Poles. But all the testimonies in Chomsky's favor were of no use and he was sentenced to die for his "crime." However, for some reason, the verdict was not carried out immediately, as is customary in such cases, but was delayed for a long time. In the meantime, the defense tried with the Petliura government to pardon the accused or to cancel the verdict and to investigate the matter anew. And although the government circles recognized Chomsky's righteousness, they encountered resistance from the army, which sought revenge.

In the end, the government had the upper hand and Alexander Chomsky was released from prison. The whole city, and the Jews in particular, breathed a sigh of relief.

[Page 43]

The Help of the Jews of America

The echoes of the terrible pogroms reached abroad, even though the suffering Ukrainian Jewry was cut off from the wider world. The communities that suffered from the pogroms could only expect a small amount of help from the local aid organizations who were also cut off from their centers in Petrograd and

Kyiv. Indeed, a small amount of help did come from the Jewish Ministry in the Ukrainian government, but this government itself wandered from place to place and the connection to it was extremely loose.

The community committee in Kamyanets Podilskiyy, which was the largest community in the area, served as an address to which the people of the small towns in the nearby districts turned for help and the community responded to them to the best of its ability. However, the financial means of the community were very limited and it maintained its institutions with great difficulty and met the needs of the local population.

And then at the same time the first emissaries of the "Joint" arrived in Bessarabia, which was then under the rule of Romania, and Mr. Zelig Shuchtman (now Z. Eligon) came to Kamyanets from Kishinev=Chisinau to establish a public committee that would deal with proffering help under the auspices of the American "Joint." Since the committee was composed mostly of the parties: "Ahdut," the general Zionists, and "Tse'irei Tsiyon," the left-wing parties that remained in the minority established a parallel separate committee. In January 1920, the first delegate of the "Joint," Mr. Becker, came from Bucharest and brought with him a large amount of money for help, but he stipulated that the two committees must unite and, accordingly, a new committee was assembled on an equal basis.

The large financial means of the "Joint" allowed the committee to conduct its work for the benefit of the needy in all the surrounding communities that had suffered from the pogroms, providing them with material and spiritual help.

In February 1920, during the rule of the Poles in Kamyanets, the "Joint" envoy came from Warsaw. After the Poles left and the Ukrainians entered again, the "Joint" envoys arrived in Kamyanets: Max Fein and Judge Fisher from Chicago, followed by Professor D. Friedlander, Moshe Katz, and Dr. Lev.

During one of the delegation's trips across the Jewish settlements, Professor Friedlander stopped with his friends in the town of Yarmolyntsi and on the 19th of Tammuz Tara"f (July 5, 1920), he and Dr. Cantor were shot there by "Red Army" patrols, who mistook them for Polish military personnel.

When word of the disaster became known in Warsaw and in America, help from American Jewry stopped. The central committee in Kamyanets nevertheless continued its work for some time. However, when the Bolsheviks returned to the city in November 1920, they confiscated all the funds found in the hands of the central committee and distributed the goods in the committee's warehouses among the "Red Army" soldiers and even among the farmers in the surrounding area. The committee dissolved and its work was banned.

Lights Out of the Darkness

In those three years after the second Russian revolution (1917-1920), years of confusion and despair, years of hardship and constant fear for the future, our city also knew good days and one of those was "San Remo" Day.

[Page 44]

On April 24, 1920, the San Remo Peace Conference confirmed the rights of the Jewish people to the Land of Israel and the Balfour Declaration was included as a clause in the peace treaty between the Great Powers and Turkey. When the news was received in Kamyanets, about two weeks later, it was decided to celebrate the event in a big public way and on May 12 the celebrations were held with great pomp and a great procession went through the main streets

A celebration in honor of the acceptance of the
Balfour Declaration by the San Remo Peace Conference in 1920

of the city. The city was decorated with flags, flowers, carpets, and pictures of the leaders of world Zionism: Dr. Herzl, Nahum Sokolov, Dr. Weizmann, and others. Delegations from the nearby communities as well as Jewish soldiers from the Polish army who were stationed there participated in the procession.

Towards evening, a large public meeting gathered in "Shevchenko Beit Ha'Am" (Shevchenko Community Center). The hall was decorated with blue and white flags and on the stage sat distinguished guests invited to this meeting, among them: Minister of the State Prof. Ogienko, Substitute Head of the Ministers; the Jewish Minister P. Krasny; the Mayor and his Deputy; a representative of the "Zemstvo"; professors from the university; the editors of the daily newspapers and representatives of Western European governments.

Indeed, the festive mood of "San Remo" Day did not last long. In September of that year, the Ukrainians returned to Kamyanets and in November, the Bolsheviks captured the city for the third and last time.

"He-Halutz"

The "He-Halutz" movement that encompassed many of the youth circles in the communities of Israel in Russia also attracted the hearts of the youth in our city. Among the members of "He-Halutz" was the local organization "Ha-Mitnadvim ba-Am," whose members came from the ranks of the General Zionists and "Tse'irei Tsiyon."

In order to acquire practical knowledge in agriculture, some of these young people left their parents' homes and went to work as laborers for the Jewish farmers in the agricultural colonies in the Kherson region. Others also came to Odesa and learned the theory of agriculture from the renowned agronomist, A. Sussman, in practice.

[No page number]

"Podolskiyy Kray" (Podolia geographic region), a daily paper in Russian, which appeared in Kamyanets Podilskiyy.
The May 12, 1920 issue was dedicated to the celebration of the acceptance of the Balfour Declaration at San Remo.
(See the contents of the issue on the opposite side of the page.)

[No page number]

Podolskiyy Kray

A daily newspaper for political, social and literary matters

Sunday, May 16, 1920   **No. 529**

Churchill on the government in Israel

London, May 6. Churchill responded to the question in Parliament concerning the future of the government in Israel that, following the decision for a solution of the question of Israel at San Remo, the military government will be converted to a civilian government.

The first steps towards peace between the Jews and the Arabs

Krakow, May 6. The Pantara Agency announces from San Remo that, after the decision was taken on the question of Israel, a banquet was held of all the representatives of the Zionists and the Arabs, during which the two sides announced in their speeches their readiness for joint work in the Near East ("the call").

The celebration following the recognition of the rights of the Jewish people to the Land of Israel

Already on the evening before the day of celebration, the city was decorated with the national flags and with pictures of the Zionist leaders. In one of the houses on Rehov Ha-Do'ar, a picture from the lives of the Jewish farmers in the fields of the Land of Israel was displayed and the entire city was lit up with a strong light as if it were daytime. On the morning of May 12, various organizations began to gather in Governor's Square: Jewish soldiers from the Polish Army, Jewish "Scouts," "Maccabi," a group of Jewish horsemen, bicycle riders, and also delegations from the surrounding towns.

All the demonstrators arranged themselves in a circle around the stage upon which sat members of the community committee, the rabbis, the Ukrainian Republic Minister for Jewish Affairs P. Krasny, the Regiment Head from the Ukrainian Officers School, the Professor from the Ukrainian university in Kamyanets Podilskiyy, and others, Mr. Ashman, head of the community committee, opened the celebration and after him, Mr. M. Goldstein, a member of the community committee, and representatives of the various authorities and institutions spoke. After the speeches, the entire community went out in a procession throughout the streets of the city, while the playing of gramophones was heard through the open windows, accompanying the demonstrators with marches.

At 5 p.m., a festive meeting of the community committee was held at the Shevchenko Beit Ha'Am, dedicated to marking the important event.

After each speech, the musical organization, "Kadima," played the national anthem, "Ha-Tikva."

We will remember them ...

On the day of our national holiday, when above the heads of the celebrating masses the great news was carried, when from the depths of the shocked heart a stormy wave of happiness and joy burst out - we will remember them, the first ones, the good ones, and the chosen ones ... on the day of our great joy, when our thoughts rise up to the heavens in a celebratory flight to meet the nearness of our desire to be realized, to meet the miraculous fairy tale and wonderful dream about to become reality - we will remember them, the proud and heroic and fearless originators of our movement ...

M. Goldstein

[Page 45]

Pioneers from other cities also worked in this place, among them from the city of Pryluky, some of whom joined the Kamyanets pioneers when they immigrated to Israel and together with them established the Kiryat Anavim collective farm near Jerusalem.

Some of the pioneers of our city who did not go for training in Kherson and Odesa received a piece of land free of charge from local resident Pinchas Oksman and established a farm there. The local community and the adherents of "He-Halutz" from among the Zionists supported with their money the budget necessary for the farm equipment and for the members' sustenance until the new harvest, and living together qualified them as members of the Kiryat Anavim collective farm.

A group of pioneers from the Kamyanets district on their way to Israel

In the Path of Anguish

The Poles ruled Kamyanets until September 1920 and in their place came the Ukrainians led by Petliura. This rule lasted less than three months this time and, in November, the city was conquered by the Bolsheviks who remain there to this day. Even before the arrival of the Bolsheviks, a notice was published in the city under the auspices of the city commandant of the Ukrainian army, according to which all holders of a passport stating that they were born in Bessarabia or were former residents might return to it and take their property with them. The returnees would arrive in the town of Zhvanets, where they were received by a Romanian army officer and transported by way of the Dniester River to the town of Khotyn. Quite a few took advantage of the legal possibility to cross the border into Bessarabia. But there were also many who "stole" the border to there by way of the same Dniester River, abandoning themselves and their property to the hands of border smuggling "goyim" and not a few were taken down to the bottom of the river by these "saviors."

Another stream of those fleeing the rule of Petliura, and then from the Bolshevist rule, followed a different path through Galicia. They also had to "steal" the border in the dark of night. These two countries, Bessarabia and Galicia, served many of the refugees as intermediate stations only, while for others they became like a second homeland in their view that they had already reached a state of tranquility. Until the war came, followed by the Holocaust, and the cruel hand of Israel's bitter enemy, Hitler (may his name be obliterated), caught up with them, too.

[Page 46]

However, not all the Jews of Kamyanets could, or did not want to, "steal" the borders and flee from the city. Many remained in place under the Bolshevik rule and adapted to its regime. Some of them moved to other cities in Russia, where no one knew them nor did they know about their "bourgeois" or "petty-bourgeois" past.

Annihilation and Destruction

Thus gradually the city emptied of its Jewish inhabitants and when Hitler's goons arrived in 1941, they found ten thousand souls in total, a third of the Jewish population in 1920. The Jews of Kamyanets and the surrounding area were imprisoned by the Nazis in a ghetto with about six thousand more Jews who were brought by the murderers from Czechoslovakia, Hungary, Romania, Belgium, and the Netherlands, and were destroyed in the suburb of Podzamcze on the 3rd, 4th, and 5th days of Elul Tash"a (August 27, 28, 29, 1941) (may God avenge their blood).

This is how the Kamyanets Podilskiyy community lived and died. The city was ruined and destroyed. Partly by the actions of the last war, and mainly by the local non-Jewish residents who looted all the Jewish property left behind after the destruction.

Are there still Jews in Kamyanets? - It is impossible to answer that with certainty. The Soviet authorities do not allow foreigners to visit the city and only a few succeed once in a while to get in there. In any case, some estimate the number of Jews currently in the city at fifty families (?). These are mostly elderly people who are no longer able to work and live only on the pension they receive from the government.

4-5 years ago, one of its native sons visited the city and found it in great ruins, and in the summer of 1963, one of the city's native daughters (now in Colombia) visited Kamyanets and searched for her parents' house, but all her efforts were in vain. The street where the house stood, as well as the large synagogues and the several Beit Midrash of the city, were completely destroyed and of all that was in it, only one ruin remained: the ruins of the building of the tailors' synagogue and two Beit Midrash of the cobblers and of the "Kov'ei Itim" - a memory of eternal sorrow for future generations.

From views of the city: The Military Hospital

[Page 47]

The Hebrew Revival Movement in Kamyanets Podilskiyy

by Avraham Rosen

Translated by Monica Devens

The years 1917-1921 were years of prosperity and flourishing for the Zionist movement and for the revival of Hebrew culture in Kamyanets Podilskiyy. Until that period, there was almost no record of this city in these territories in the Eparchy and the large-scale activity and achievements in the field of national revitalization on the part of the cities and the nearby towns to a certain extent overshadowed it. As a regional city, various government institutions with their clerks and administrators were mainly concentrated in it, and many of its Jewish residents earned a living as lawyers, mediators, lobbyists, hotel owners, and more. The trade and crafts in the city did not exceed the normal limits of every town, and Jewish industry was almost completely absent. One thing set it apart for the better from the rest of the surrounding cities: it had several government high schools, which, despite the entry difficulties faced by Jews, also attracted many from the nearby towns. On the other hand, Hebrew education was neglected and retarded to a considerable extent and, apart from the "Cheders" and "Yeshivas" of the old-fashioned type, there was not a single modern institution, such as the "Updated Cheders" or the Hebrew schools, which had been established and operated for years now in several nearby cities, such as Zhvanets, Dunayivtsi, Kupyn and more.

With the outbreak of the 1917 revolution, a new wind blew through the Jewish settlement in Kamyanets Podilskiyy. Thanks to the nationalist awakening that began throbbing in the hearts of all the peoples of the country in those days, and especially thanks to the young Jewish students, who thronged then from all of the surroundings to the educational institutions in the city, after they opened

The "Moledet" School Committee
*With the permission of "Yad va-Shem," the memorial authority of the Holocaust and heroism.

[Page 48]

their gates wide for them as well - the Zionist movement began to leave its mark there as well. Zionist groups from various ideologies were founded, among them "Tse'irei Tsiyon," "Po'alei Tsiyon," "He-Halutz," "Tarbut," and more, and also Hebrew schools and kindergartens, evening Hebrew classes, a library, a choir, a community center, and more were established. The young revival movement made waves in the frozen public life, and many of the old and half-dead community institutions were revived and renewed. Thus, for example, the Hebrew Community Committee was established, which was composed by means of elections of all the Jewish parties in the city, and the institutions managed by it or under its supervision were henceforth placed on democratic foundations.

The Zionist Youth Organization "Ha-Techiya" in 1920

At the head of the cultural activity one must note the founding of the two Hebrew schools in the city: the "Tushiya" school on behalf of the local "Tarbut," headed by the Zionist businessman Shalom Altman (died in Kiryat Anavim near Jerusalem) and the "Moledet" school in the new quarter of the city (Novi-Plan), founded and managed by a group of local youth. The Tushiya school had 4 classes with about 140 male and female students. The curriculum included: Tanakh, Aggadah, Hebrew and its grammar, the history of the people of Israel, and also Russian and general studies in that language. The Hebrew studies were conducted in the Sephardic accent, according to the method then accepted in all "Tarbut" schools: Hebrew in Hebrew, and in one of the classes, an experiment was tried to study math in Hebrew. Sometimes celebrations and shows for children were organized by the students in one of the public halls, and this made a lot of publicity for the revival of the Hebrew language. The school in the new quarter had 3 classes with about 80 male and female students. Its curriculum was that of "Tushiya," and there, too, they taught Hebrew in Hebrew and with a Sephardic accent. The budget of both schools came mainly from the tuition fees that they received from their students, but the municipality also supported them with certain amounts. With the establishment of the first Soviet government in the city, in the spring of 1920, the Yevsektsiya took over the

[Page 49]

The music organization "Kadima" in 1919

[Page 50]

"Tushiya" school, fired the Hebrew teacher, and replaced him with a Yiddish teacher. However, 3 months later, after the Soviet government was expelled from the city by the Ukrainian army, the teacher returned to his position and the school - to its Hebrew program. It is worth mentioning that the students opposed the Yiddish program and many of them preferred to leave the school during those three months than to submit to the decree of the Yevsektsiya.

A second important place in the Hebrew revival movement in Kamyanets Podilskiyy was occupied by "Beit Ha'Am" [Community Center] and the evening classes in Hebrew given there. "Beit Ha'Am," which contained 3 spacious rooms and a large hall in one of the streets populated entirely by Jews, served as a center for all the Zionist youth in the city. It was where the assemblies and the meetings, the celebrations and the lectures, were held and where the various actions on the part of the youth groups were organized to spread the Zionist idea among the masses. Indeed, the highlight of all these activities were the evening Hebrew classes that took place there throughout that period. In this institution, teenagers between the ages of 15-16 from different social levels and positions studied, among them also apprentices and high school students. The curriculum was: Tanakh, Hebrew, Hebrew literature, and the history of the people of Israel. Usually there were 2-3 classes in the institution with 50-60 students. Tuition was minimal and those without means were freed from it. Some of the graduates joined the local "He-Halutz" as members, "Ha-Mitnadvim ba-Am," headed by Yehoshua Salzman (Malchi, a member of the Kiryat Anavim group), who later immigrated to Israel. "Beit Ha'am" was for a short time the creative home of the revival of the Hebrew language in the city, and within its walls could be heard the sound of the lively and fluent Hebrew speech. Every evening it served as a meeting place for youth activists and in its rooms, bustling with the joy of young life, a new Hebrew generation full of strength and courage was forged for a great future of building a nation and a country.

Next to "Beit Ha'am," there was also a literature club called "Bamatenu," whose members included the teachers of the institution and its employees, and among the other activities of the club (lectures, banquets, etc.) it is worth noting the publication of a literary collection, which, due to lack of means, was printed in a limited number of copies by spirograph. The collection included articles on various questions and problems (among them an article on self-defense), poems and stories, critiques and articles from the provincial towns. Among the participants were the writers S. Shafan (deceased) (then a high school student), A. Ashman and the writer of these columns (two of the institution's last teachers at the time).

Alongside "Beit Ha'am" a troupe of theater lovers was also established, which over time was an institution of

The administration of "Kadima"

[Page 51]

its own. The purpose of the band was to present on the Jewish stage, which at the time was mainly a place to present uninspiring and tasteless plays, the modern literary play in Yiddish and Hebrew. The plays took place in the halls of the municipal theater and were very successful. Plays by Asch, Hirschbein, Dymov, Chirikov and more were performed. The band's program also included performances in the provincial towns, but due to the difficulties of transportation and the road disruptions that arose on the occasion of the frequent changes of regime, this section of activity was fulfilled only once in one of the nearby towns (Lyantskorun=Zarechanka).

As an institution in itself, there was also "Kadima," the mem's and women's choir, founded and managed by the brothers Yaakov and Israel Brandman (the latter currently conducts the Ha-Poalim Choir in Tel Aviv), who received their musical education in Petrograd and later dedicated themselves to the development of Jewish music in their city. Apart from the concerts it held itself and the partial performances at all the Zionist celebrations and parties, "Kadima" held a "Kabbalat Shabbat" reception every Friday evening in its clubhouse with a program of Jewish folk music. During the days of the first Soviet regime in the city, the entire choir was recruited to sing at the Bolshevik propaganda meetings and this recruitment freed the members of the choir from forced labor, which was imposed on the residents then.

In 1920, "Ha-Moreh," a professional association of Hebrew teachers in the city, was also founded. The association was considered a branch of the national union of Hebrew teachers in Russia and a section of the Ukrainian teachers' union in Podolia. At the beginning of its operations, the association mainly aimed to benefit the material situation of the teacher, especially those engaged in private teaching, and for this purpose it opened a cooperative store for its members. The economic situation of the city was very difficult at that time, food supplies were very limited and often at exorbitant prices, and only cooperative institutions received supplies from the central authorities for their members and at discounted prices. The "Ha-Moreh" cooperative, therefore, saved some teacher families from real hunger.

This is how the remarkable and constant activity of the Hebrew revival in Kamyanets Podilskyy branched off in several different directions, which in total constituted a quite important and noticeable achievement in the field of Hebrew education and culture. The sleepy regional city, lagging behind in the Zionist movement's campaign, infected its daughters and sisters in Podolia and at certain points even surpassed them. And all this without instructions and guidance from the outside, without "Shlichim" and leaders from high central places, but rather with the independent forces of the local youth.

Indeed, when the Soviet stranglehold was lifted on the Zionist race within the borders of its country, the soft and refreshing branch of revival was cut off in this city as well, and the institutions of Hebrew culture, which were nurtured by its devoted and loyal sons-builders, were closed and eliminated one by one. A few years after the period in question, 1917-1921, the holy fire of the revival of the Hebrew language and culture still flickered here and there, boys and girls still worked hard to study Hebrew in small groups and in private rooms, but in the end, the whispering ember in the pile of fertility was completely extinguished.

[Page 52]

The Girls' School Named After Blovstein

by Sarah Reznik-Gluzman

Translated by Monica Devens

It has been about fifty years since I finished the Blovstein girls' elementary school in Kamyanets Podilskyy, and I would like to mention in connection with this jubilee some details about the aforementioned school that was unlike the others in our area and where I spent six years of my childhood. It seems to me that these were years of light, joy, and much happiness for all my friends with whom I sat on the study bench, especially for me, being fatherless. In this school, I found a lot of understanding and consideration on the part of my teachers and educators, or rather on the part of my female teachers, who made up the majority of the teaching staff. And when I now bring up my memories of those days, I am filled with feelings of gratitude and appreciation for them, who knew how to set before us as a goal in life not only the acquisition of the knowledge taught in every school, but also showed us a path to lofty ideals.

When I was 7 years old, I was accepted as a student in the preparatory level A. My sister, who is two years older than me, already studied there in the first grade. The curriculum of the school was for six years. The institution could serve as an example and model for excellent education in the academic and social sense, imparting general human values and the values of Judaism and Zionism.

The school was attended by girls from all social levels among the Jewish population in our city. Tuition was graduated: the rich and the wealthy paid three rubles a month, the middle class two rubles, and those of little means one ruble. It is worth noting that never was a student sent home for not paying tuition on time. The dress of the students was uniform. A gray dress and a blue apron, and during celebrations and vacation days - a white apron. The purpose of these modest uniforms, in their singular form, was to make the poor and the rich equal, so as not to cause jealousy between the daughters of the rich and the daughters of the poor.

At school we studied Hebrew according to the Hebrew in Hebrew method, the chronicles of Israel, the main prayers,

The Blovstein School for Girls

[Page 53]

Russian and its literature, German, general geography, arithmetic, and handicrafts (sewing and embroidery).

And may our teacher for Hebrew and the chronicles of Israel, Rabbi Pinchas Hasid (z"l), a man in his middle years, a man of spirit and an enthusiastic Zionist, be fondly remembered. When he was lecturing with great enthusiasm about the Land of Israel, his eyes would overflow with tears and he was very emotional and excited. It goes without saying that we were greatly influenced by his lessons, which instilled in us a love and a yearning for the land of our ancestors.

The teacher of mathematics and the German language was Sophia Levovna Blovstein, the daughter of the founder of the school, Rabbi Leib Blovstein. She was also the director of the institution. This Sophia Levovna was an ideal personality and a gentle soul. The language of instruction was Russian, as required by the authorities. The teacher was called, as was customary in Russian at that time, by the girl's name and her father's name such as: Sophia Levovna, Anna Isakovna, etc. The students were called by their family names only. In addition to the aforementioned directorate, there was a supervisory committee for the institution who mainly took care of its material condition. The members of the committee were: the lawyer D. S. Schleifer (Chairman), Ms. Schleifer, Ms. Wahrhaftig, and Ms. Goldentrester. In addition to its concern for the existence of the school, the committee also gave its opinion on its general direction.

The government inspector in charge of elementary schools would often visit the school. The visits of this gentile inspector would always strike fear into both the teaching staff and the female students because we would study neither according to the official program of our superiors nor according to the textbooks recommended in the official program. Our teachers tried to expand our knowledge and to impart it according to more sophisticated textbooks, even if not recognized by the authority. We had, therefore, to be on guard and during the aforementioned inspector's visits to take the official textbooks he wanted out of the drawers of our school desks.

Despite the great efforts of the students at this school of ours, not everyone completed their studies there.

The "Kadima" Committee

[Page 54]

In 1908, two of our great national poets, Shimen Frug and Leib Yaffe, visited our city. The purpose of their coming to Kamyanets Podilskyy was to arouse the nationalist feeling and to strengthen Zionist awareness among the Jews of our city and the surrounding area. On the occasion of this event, the local Zionist Organization organized a mixed choir of boys, "Talmud Torah" students, and girls, students of our school.

The choir was conducted by Mr. Menashe Brandman, the regular conductor of the choir and the orchestra of the opera in the municipal theater. The theater excelled in its beautiful interior arrangement, which created an intimate atmosphere for its visitors. The reception at which the two aforementioned guest poets appeared took place in this theater. The guests read from their works and the choir sang from their songs and from the songs of Zion from the days of the first and second Aliyah.

From What Was[a]

by Y. Bernstein

Translated by Monica Devens

"Kamyanets Podilskyy, a magnificent community, a large and important city in Israel, its people God-fearing and thoughtful of His name, pursuers of charity, philanthropic, influential people and officers, charitable and important, benevolent, giving to the poor, they do God's charity" - such is the description of the character of this holy community sixty-eighty years ago in the words of my grandfather, R. Gedalyahu the Ritual Slaughterer, z"l, in the introduction to his book "A Committee of Sages" (Warsaw 1899), and it was like that even in the period after that.

A magnificent community, in which the life of Torah and Hasidism and the traditional Jewish way of life of holy communities in Israel since time immemorial abounded. A large and important city in Israel.

Rabbis

There is little historical material about the life of the community in the distant past. From the period of two hundred years ago, the matter of the debate with the Frankists that took place in Kamyanets in 1757 by their count before Bishop Dembowski and a burning of the books of the Talmud after it on November 13, 1757 is known. Of the rabbis participating in the debate, the name of the rabbi from Kamyanets is not mentioned (although in Eisenstein's "Otsar Yisrael" R. Yosef from Kamyanets is mentioned, but this is probably a mistake and should be understood as from Kremenets). About seventy years later, R. Yitzchak Meisels, the father of the Rav R. Dov Ber Meisels who was famous as a supporter of the Polish uprising, was a rabbi in Krakow and finally in Warsaw.

Among the rabbis who headed the community from about seventy-ninety years ago, I remember the names of the Rav R. Zalman Lerner z"l, who was called by the people of our city by the name R. Zalminyu, and they used to mention him

[Page 55]

with awe and admiration as one who would be called holy; and the Rav R. Dov-Brish Eliash z"l (the grandfather of Dr. Mordechai Eliash z"l, the first Israeli ambassador in London, and his brother (may he live long!), Mr. Alexander Eliash, one of the dignitaries of Jerusalem), who was known as a prodigy and exceptional in Torah. In the book of my grandfather z"l mentioned above, an agreement from him was printed from the 19th day of Menachem-Av the year of /tamlo"kh betsyo"n/[b] (Tarna"d=1893-94) was printed and this is his title at the top of the agreement "the famous and genius Rabbi for praise and glory, sharp and knowledgeable, who smells and judges and arrives at practical Halachic rulings, living up to his principles, may his name be honored, the rabbi, Dov Ber (may his light shine), presiding judge of here Kamyanets Podilskyy."

For a while the famous tzaddik and genius, the Rav R. Avraham David Wahrman zatsa"l, author of "Da'at Kedoshim" and "Birkat David," who was known as the rabbi of Buchach in Galicia, a student of R. Levi Yitzchak of Berdychiv and R. Moshe Leib of Sasiv of blessed memory, sat on the chair of the rabbinate in Kamyanets. It is true that he did not continue in this rabbinic office and returned to Buchach. And as I heard from my father z"l, the reason for his preferring Buchach - was the abundance of men and women scholars there, with which Kamyanets could not compete. But there were excellent scholars in Kamyanets who were well-versed in all aspects of Torah, whether from among "holy vessels" or from among those for whom Torah was not their expertise; some of them "wealthy and charitable" and some poor and destitute -

their common ground that Torah and its study was their spiritual life all the days of their lives. There were even "Jews all year round" who set times for Torah study in a group and in public, some for the Gemara, the Mishnayot, or for "Ein Ya'akov," and some for the Parasha of the Week or for studying the "Or Hayyim" on the Torah. And there were those who kept "the law of Israel" daily, and the words of the Torah and the sayings of the Sages were spoken fluently by them.

From about sixty years ago until the year 1920, the Rav R. Israel Gutman z"l, a descendant of the Besht and of R. Pinchas of Korets z"l, sat on the rabbinical chair in Kamyanets Podilskyy. He was one of the followers of Husyatyn and he himself was "half a rabbi" in his manners and behavior. He had refined intellectual facial features, clever and shrewd and involved with mankind. He went to the United States and died there.

Kept in my memory is the name of someone special in our city, whom everyone called R. Hershli Hasid and he was like his name, righteous and a Hasid in all his ways and in all his actions. And I heard from my father z"l that, in addition to his Hasidism and his righteousness, R. Hershli was a great scholar and had a wonderful knowledge of the Bavli and the Yerushalmi, the books of the Sifra and the Tosefta, and the first and last adjudicators. And his wisdom was great and his deeds were great.

Among the great scholars in our city was my grandfather, R. Gedalyahu z"l mentioned above. He was the grandson of the famous saintly Rav, R. Gedaliah of Linits zatsa"l, author of "Tesu'ot Hen" about the Torah and one of the students of the Besht and of the Maggid of Mezhyrichi zatsa"l and, as my grandfather z"l writes about him, he was "the 52nd generation of scholars and heavenly saints, from whom the teaching did not stop generation after generation." My grandfather published his book, "Va'ad Hachamim," at the end of his life when he was blind, in which there is "Kuntres Derekh Tshuva" about an exchange of questions and answers with the geniuses of his generation.

Members of his family continued after him in the work of the ritual slaughterer in Kamyanets: my father, my teacher z"l R. Yehoshua

[Page 56]

Eliyahu - he was also known as great in the Torah and Hasidism and had high charitable values - the husband of R. Gedaliah's granddaughter, Rivka, she was my mother (may she rest in peace); so after R. Gedaliah, his son-in-law, R. Avraham Rechter z"l, continued, the husband of his daughter, Miriam - from his second wife - who perished brutally by the hands of the Nazi oppressors in Kamyanets and with her daughter, Haya (Haika), and her husband and their sons - may God avenge their blood.

Synagogues and the Various Beit Midrash, Rite and Way of Life

The life of the community was imprinted with the stamp of Torah and tradition, and public life was centered in synagogues and the various Beit Midrash. But there was one street that was unique in that it was named after the synagogues that were located there, the "Shul Gasse." On this street was the Great Synagogue, the main synagogue in the city. This is where the Eruv wire hung and this is where the rabbi used to give his sermon on Shabbat HaGadol and Shabbat Shuvah. Near it, on the downhill slope of the street, to the left of the Turkish minaret, was the Smotrych Beit Midrash. To the right of the Turkish minaret stood, one behind the other on a slope: the Tailors' Synagogue, the most magnificent of the synagogues in the city, which excelled especially in the beauty of its Ark; below it - the Cobblers' Synagogue; and below it - the "Kov'ei Itim la-Torah" Beit Midrash.

There was a large concentration of Beit Midrash buildings and enclaves on Dolgaya Street (Yatke Gasse) - the street of the butcher shops that was near Shul Gasse. Here were: the Sadigura enclave; the enclave of R. Gedaliah Heller (Zinkaver

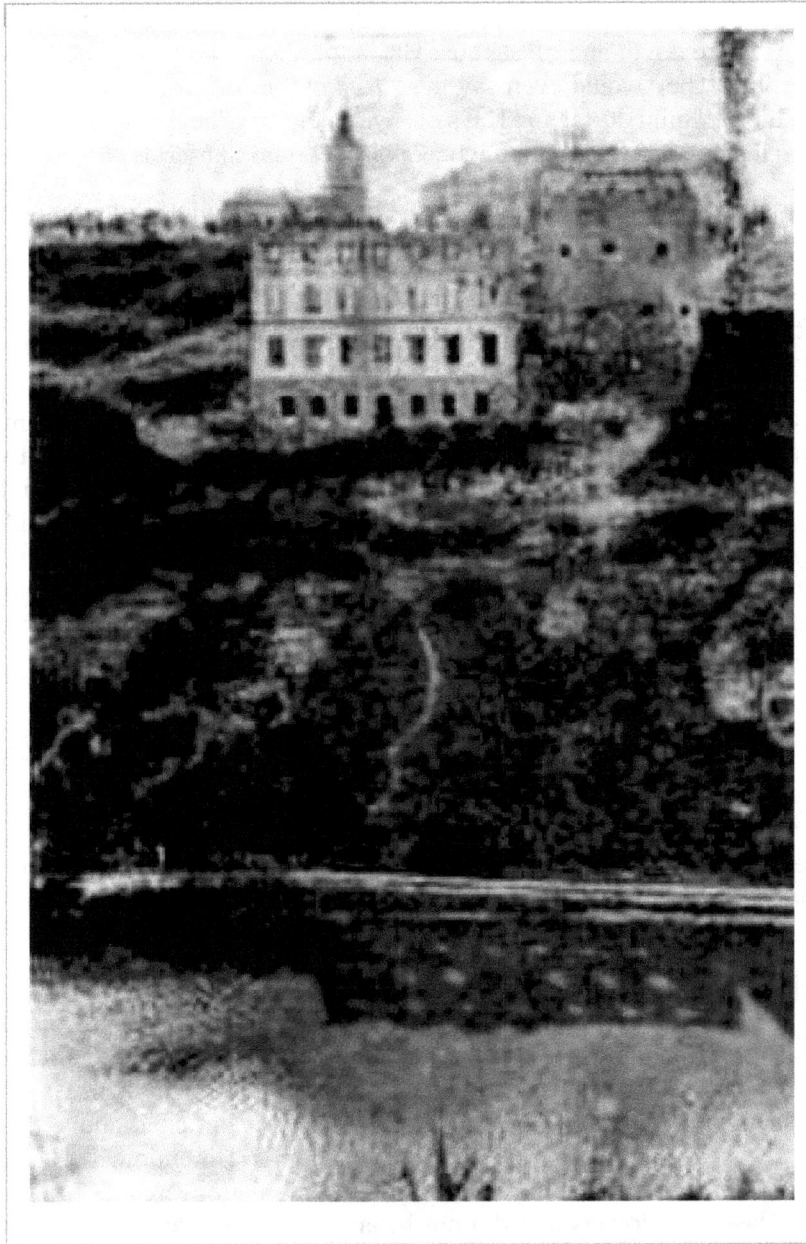

A destroyed synagogue from the time of the Holocaust

[Page 57]

enclave) the enclave of R. Yitzchak the Blacksmith; the enclave of R. Moshe Yonah Rubinstein (Boyaner enclave); the Stambolski Synagogue; the Beit Midrash of the Rabbi R. Naftali Rabinovitch (R. Naftalzis Shulechel); the Axelrod Synagogue; "Nos'ei ha-Mitah"; the Ashkenazi Synagogue; the Blacksmiths' Synagogue; on the other side of this street were: the Husyatyn Hasidim Synagogue; the Chortkiv Hasidim; the Weislovich Synagogue; and the Mermelstein Synagogue; to the list of synagogues that were in the city center should be added the Rabinowitz Synagogue and the Sheindelis Synagogue.

Apart from this, there were large and small synagogues in the other parts of the city: in "Plan Hadash"; (the new city) in the Polish suburb, in Karvasari, in Zinkovitz, and in Podzamcze and others.

The prayer rite in all the churches was the Hasidic Sephardic form, except for the Ashkenazi Synagogue. On the Shabbats of Arba Parshiyot and of Shabbat HaGadol, they used to say the "Yotsrot" and they also said "Krovetz for Purim." They would even say the "Yotsrot" during the prayers of the three pilgrimage festivals and most of the piyyutim during the Days of Awe (including the piyyutim that are in the "Kedusha" and also the piyyutim that are between Malkhuyot, Zikhronot, and Shofarot).

On the three pilgrimage festivals they would "say" the three Megillot of the Song of Songs, Ruth, and Kohelet, not from the parchment and without a blessing.

They would "say" the Haftarah on Shabbats and holidays, the whole congregation together with the Maftir and the Maftir would say only the blessings in chanting.

In the last years before the First World War, the traditional way of life was already loosening up and there were many breaches in the wall of religious life in the city. The "Cheders" became far fewer and the young men of the enclaves almost disappeared (apart from the Yeshiva students about whom more will be said further on). Many of the wealthy and affluent sent their sons and daughters to public schools, and the sons who strayed from traditional Jewish life would be brought to prayer on the holidays, and especially during the Days of Awe. And there were the young men with the shiny buttons looking in the prayer book like a rooster at "human beings" and all the words of the prayer like a sealed book in front of them. However, the life of the community as a whole was imprinted with the stamp of tradition, which was reflected in the essence of life in all its corners.

Saints and Hasidim

Kamyanets was mostly a city of Hasidim. I don't recall the names of any significant "Mitnagdim" except for the name of one "Litvak" from among the wealthy of the city, R. Shaul Pines (may he rest in peace). The rest were more non-Hasidim than "Mitnagdim" and the Hasidim called them "Ba'alei Batim" (bourgeoisie).

In general, the Hasidim were divided into two camps: the Hasidim of the House of Ruzhin - in Boyan, Sadigura, Chortkiv, and Husyatyn - and the Hasidim of Zinkov, Medzhybizh and Kopychyntsi. The Hasidic leaders of the House of Ruzhin had their courts across the border in Austrian Galicia and their followers would travel to them. Whereas the Hasidic leaders of Zinkov and Medzhybizh would come to visit their followers. In Kamyanets itself, there was R. Naftaltsi whom we mentioned above, but he had almost no followers from the townspeople. Apart from the rabbis whom we mentioned, Hasidic leader from the Chornobyl dynasties would come to the city. From time to time there were also "grandsons" who did not have an audience of Hasidic followers and did not behave as Hasidic leaders, but Hasidim helped them thanks to their ancestors.

[Page 58]

The Rebbes would set up "Shulchanot" in one of the synagogues on Friday nights or at the third meal and, in addition to their followers, rabbis and ritual slaughterers and other important people from the city would come.

On weekdays, many people, men and women, came to the Rebbe's lodgings to be counted and to be personally blessed by submitting notes and "ransoms." In particular, a crowd gathered at the doors of the Rebbe of Kopychyntsi in Galicia, the Grand Rebbe Heschel zatsa"l - the son-in-law of the Hasidic leader of Husyatyn - who was famous as a "miracle worker." The Rebbe of I?cani, R. Menachem-Nachum Friedman, the son-in-law of the Hasidic leader of Chortkiv zatsa"l, also visited Kamyanets, received with great respect by all the followers of the House of Ruzhin and the important members of the community.

A special event was the visit of the Hasidic leader of Sadigura, R. Avraham Yaakov Friedman zatsa"l, to Zhvanets near Kamyanets in the year 1912. Since the imprisonment of the one from Ruzhin and his escape to Sadigura, his descendants were not allowed to come to Russia and the visit to Zhvanets was a new development and was limited to this town only. Because of this, many of the Hasidim in Kamyanets went to Zhvanets, some for Shabbat and some on weekdays. This Hasidic leader from Sadigura immigrated to Israel during the occupation of Vienna by the Nazis, settled in Tel Aviv, and died here some years ago.

Of the Hasidic leaders from the House of Beit Zinkov, the brothers R. Pinchasele and R. Moishele zatsa"l used to visit Kamyanets. The Hasidic leader, R. Israelnyu of Medzhybizh, the son-in-law of the Rav R. Avrohom Yaakov of Sadigura zatsa"l, also visited our city.

Of the Hasidic way of life in our city, I especially remember the style and practices of the Boyan Hasidim and similarly the Hasidim of the other Ruzhin houses. These, as mentioned, would travel to the Rebbe and this trip involved quite a few difficulties. It was not easy to get a passport to go abroad and they would try to get a "tsetil" - a temporary license - which allowed leaving Russia and returning, and entering Austria. And in those days, there were ultra-Orthodox Jews who were strict with themselves to not be photographed, although according to the law there is no prohibition except for an obvious human form. But when the thing was needed for a trip to the Rebbe, they had to give up the strictness.

At that time there was still no rail transport in Kamyanets and they had be carried by cart to Larga and from there to continue by train, but of course it wasn't "express." At last, after tiring wanderings, they reached the desired district - and it was all worth it.

They would travel at regular times, mostly on holidays. On the return, the Hasidim would bring with them, apart from the teaching that they had heard from the Rebbe, also new tunes composed by the court cantor, R. Pinchas (Pinye) Spector (may he rest in peace), one of the students of the famous Nissi Belzer. He was a gifted composer and his works gained a reputation in the Hasidic world. In particular, his "Yedid Nefesh" was published and disseminated. The tunes were of two types: compositions for Shabbat songs, prayers, piyyutim; and "Freilichs" for singing and dancing. His works were sung in chorus during the "Shulchan" and then afterwards, the "Freilich" tunes, as mentioned. And the tunes were "tradeable" and spread among all the Hasidic circles, and it was part of the forms of sacred worship that led to the hours of exaltation and elevation of the soul.

They would sit together even on weekdays, especially on the days of a public celebration of a saintly rabbi. They would sit with a glass of schnapps and have "Eier Kichlich" for dessert, toasting "Le-Chaim" and talking about the saintly ones and their words. On Shabbat, after the prayer, they would go to the "Kiddush" in one of the group's houses and while enjoying the physical delights of Shabbat, they would sing the songs of Pinye and others.

[Page 59]

Pleasantness and festivity were part of the group's parties on the long winter Friday nights. Pure white snow, and intense and pinching cold from the outside, and the radiant whiteness of Shabbat, and a hearty warmth, mixed and pleasant inside, in the room and in the soul. Sitting together sweetens the secret of conversation about righteous people, their ways and their sayings. Shabbat songs, "Kol Mekadesh," tunes of devotion and longing, an atmosphere of sanctity and spiritual elevation, hours of satisfaction "like the world to come."

Among the followers of Boyan, I especially remember R. Alter Rubinstein z"l. One of the well-known rich people in the city, the son-in-law of R. Gur-Aryeh Hornstein z"l from Radomyshl, a famous and known Hasidic family with Torah and greatness in one place. A type of "silk and velvet." Smart and shrewd. Pleasant ways and pleasant speech. As is the way of the Hasidim, he would wear a silk kapoteh and a velvet cap on Shabbat and holidays. And so, elegant in his Hasidic clothing, he would carry with him on Sukkot the etrog and the lulav from his home in the new city to the Boyan enclave on Poshtova Street. Wealthy and generous, abounding in charity and kindness, and his home was wide open. And the Hasidim who came to his house would multiply happiness and celebrations of the memory of a saintly rabbi, especially on Simchat Torah and Purim. It goes without saying that these "guest visits" "turned the house upside down" with its luxurious rooms and furniture, expensive curtains and tapestries - but what does it have to do with? ... Usually, in those hours of high spirits, all the partitions were removed and the wealthy were not distinguished from the poor. Each man with his arm on his friend's shoulder fit together in the dance and, in the enthusiasm of the dance, you even saw one of the Hasidim, R. Shalom Nissenholtz (may he rest in peace), embracing R. Alter Rubinstein and lovingly calling out, "Hoy Altronyu…"

R. Shalom Nissenholtz (may he rest in peace) was unique. They said about him that in the winter days, he went on foot to Sadigura. Then he continued to travel to Boyan and his righteous faith was unmatched. At bad times, when he was "drunk," he would sing Cossack songs in their language. Once when he was tipsy and they saw him walking home in the wrong direction, they asked him: Where are you going, R. Shalom? - "Priyamo du Boyano" (straight to Boyan). was his answer.

And here's a typical saying of his:

- When the righteous Messiah comes soon in our day, we will go out to face him with song and tunes, with a drum and dance, celebrating and rejoicing in the redemption of Israel and - we will continue to travel to our holy rabbi (may he live a good long life) …

Similarly, I heard from Mr. Yosef Cohen about another of the same group: at one of the parties during the difficult years of the First World War, the Boyan Hasidim sat and discussed the issue of redemption and the expectation of the coming of the Messiah who would redeem Israel from the terrible troubles. One of the participants answered, he was R. Avraham the Scribe z"l, and said in these words: I - I don't know. I do not know Messiah. But I know the Rebbe and I want to see him… so much!

The "Tiferet Israel" Yeshiva

The young man of the enclaves almost disappeared before the First World War, as mentioned above, and the students of the "Cheders" dwindled. At the same time, a Yeshiva began to be founded in Proskorov (= Khmelnytskyi) under the leadership of the Rav R. Shmuel Zosia Bloch z"l from the country of Lithuania - and it didn't take hold there, but its seeds continued to grow in Kamyanets. The ultra-Orthodox of the city woke up to strengthen the Torah and its study and in the year 1907-1908

[Page 60]

the "Tiferet Yeshiva" was founded. The founders and heads of it were the brothers, R. Shmuel and R. Avraham Breitman z"l (later the last rabbi of Kamyanets) and the head of the Yeshiva was the Rav R. Shmuel Zosia Bloch, mentioned above. The two Breitman brothers, Chortkiv Hasidim, were wealthy and privileged and impressive looking. R. Shmuel had a firm and energetic character and conducted his presidency in the management of the yeshiva with strength and vigor - and with success. Not many of the townspeople sent their sons to the Yeshiva, but not many days had passed and its name became famous and students flocked to it from cities and towns near and far.

After the Rav R. Shmuel Zosia Bloch was elected rabbi of Orynyn near Kamyanets, my teacher and rabbi, the Rav R. Yechiel Michal Tribuch Margalit z"l, who after his immigration to Israel served as the rabbi in Neve Sha'anan and a member of the rabbinate of Haifa, was invited to serve as head of the Yeshiva.

The program included: beginning Gemara, study of Gemara and Tosafot and commentators in detail, and finally also adjudicators, without the purpose of getting a teaching permit for the students.

R. Moshe Hirsch Baynvelman z"l, who endeared himself to the students with the purity of his heart and his cleanliness, inside as out, and his dedication of heart and soul to his educational role, taught Gemara for Beginners.

The class of advanced students, who reached Gemara and Tosafot and even to self-study, heard the lesson of the supervisor, R. David Stern z"l, who was brought to the Yeshiva from Poland. He was an energetic and affectionate man. At the same time, strict and pleasant. He used a firm hand to discipline the students, and on the other hand, he was nice and would indulge in a cordial and pleasant conversation. He would even spice up his conversation with parables and pictures that draw the heart.

The Yeshiva supervisor,
R. David Stern

The mature students heard lessons and innovations of Torah from the head of the Yeshiva and learned Gemara, rabbinic rulings, and responsa in theory and in practice. The head of the Yeshiva, the Rav Margalit, published his innovations at the Yeshiva in his book "Me'irat Einayim."

Although they were not intended for instruction nor for the work of the ritual slaughterer, indeed while they were studying the tractate Hulin, the students went to the municipal slaughterhouse to familiarize themselves tangibly with the laws of slaughter and non-kosher food, the lung examination, and other details regarding the internal organs. Those who studied "Yoreh De'ah" with "Pri Megadim" deepened their studies in Tur and in Beit Yosef, "Drisha u-Ferisha," and even in the Acharonim.

A special one in the group of graduates was

[Page 61]

R. Shlomo Feingold z"l, who was called "Shlomo Ga'on" because of his sharpness and his depth, his clear logic and common sense.

The place of study for all the members of the Yeshiva was in the "Kov'ei Itim La-Torah" Beit Midrash. They studied persistently and diligently until late at night. And there were those who managed to get up and study early in the morning until prayer time. And on the weekly Friday nights, there was a "Mishmar" to study until the morning light. When it was a Mishmar night at "Kov'ei Itim," they would go in at the end to drink a glass of hot milk for the price of half a kopeck from the wife of R. Raphael the Scribe in the courtyard at the corner of Shul Gasse and Yatke Gasse streets; and on Mishmar nights in the Boyan enclave, the wife of the furrier, R. Nachum Helak (may he rest in peace), one of the residents of the same courtyard, would prepare kahwa for the members of the Yeshiva. She would even serve them a delicious "malai," but it was taken out of the oven.

Some of the members of the Yeshiva outside the city ate "days" with hosts; and there were some whose parents took care of the needs of their lodgings.

At fixed times and vacations, they would hold parties for the students. For the Tu BiShvat party, some of the dignitaries of the city were invited, the "fifteen fruits" were distributed, and speeches and sermons were given on matters of the day. In particular, the joy increased at the Purim parties at R. Shmuel Breitman's house.

The Yeshiva was called "Tiferet Yisrael," named after the saint R. Yisrael Merizhin zatsa"l, and was a Hasidic yeshiva in essence and point of view. The members of the Yeshiva also organized an association called "Oreach Le-Tzadik," which pooled financial means to travel to the rabbis. And when the Rebbe of Sadigura happened to be in Zhvanets, as mentioned above, many of the Yeshiva's students went to be there.

Generally, the Yeshiva continued to progress and develop and there was every chance for a good future. The First World War came and shook it to the core. The students scattered and dwindled and the Yeshiva barely continued its existence until it was finally closed.

Religious Pioneers

There was no religious Zionist organization in Kamyanets and there was even opposition to Zionism in the Hasidic community. But Zion and Jerusalem lived in everyone's heart. And the yearning for redemption from time immemorial did its part. Even in the years before the First World War, the buds of religious Zionism sprouted among the young members of the Yeshiva. And with the great Zionist awakening at the beginning of the revolution in Russia, these buds grew and sprouted, even bore fruit.

There was then a time of unrest and a great awakening in the Jewish public all over Russia, which also did not skip over our city. Even the religious young people in Kamyanets came in contact with the religious organizations that were formed in the big central cities at the time: "Netzah Yisrael" in Petrograd, "Masoret ve-Herut" in Moscow, and "Ahdut Yisrael" in Kyiv. The last was the closest and was headed by the Rav R. Shlomo Aharonson z"l, the Rav R. Levi Grossman z"l, (may he live long!) the Rav R. Shlomo Yosef Zevin, the Rav Yaakov Berman, and more. Rabbi Berman's name was famous in Ukraine at that time, not only as a speaker and a religious leader, but as one of the excellent and successful orators in the debates between all the Zionist streams and the "Bund." He was invited to visit Kamyanets at that time and the tickets for his lecture were already sold, but due to the road disruptions in those days, the visit did not

[Page 62]

take place. In the meantime, a civil war became stronger and the confusion and commotion increased all over the country. A regime goes, a regime government comes, and the first to suffer disaster in all this anarchy were the Jews in all their settlements.

With this, the Zionist activity continued and in many places "He-Halutz" associations were organized, including in Kamyanets. A training farm was established where the "He-Halutz" members trained themselves for agriculture. Even the writer of this list was for some time among those being trained at this farm, but the problem of kosher food prevented continuing. Then consideration was given to the foundation of a special group of religious pioneers. Despite the difficulties of connections with outside the country, we exchanged letters with the "Mizrachi" Center in Poland headed by the Rav Yitzhak Nissenboim z"l in Warsaw, but without practical results.

In the meantime, in the summer of 1918, Professor Israel Friedlander z"l visited our city having been sent by the "Joint" in the United States. The writer of these columns met with the guest at the house of the Kleiderman family who hosted him in connection with the group of religious pioneers and, at the end of the conversation, Prof. Friedlander took with him a letter from the "He-Halutz Ha-Mizrachi" in Kamyanets to deliver to the "Ha-Mizrachi" federation in America. After that same day, Professor Friedlander was murdered by Ukrainian murderers on his tour of Yarmolyntsi in the surrounding area - may God avenge his blood.

Some time later, some young men from the aforementioned group crossed the border into eastern Galicia and their goal - to immigrate to Israel. Here they were in contact with the "Mizrachi" centers in Poland and Galicia in their efforts to reach the desired district. In the meantime, disturbances broke out in Jaffa - in the year 1920 - and immigration to Israel stopped until it resumed in the winter of 1921. Finally, after a year of hardships and wanderings, they reached Tel Aviv on January 31, 1921.

General events

This was on the "honeymoon" of the revolution in the summer of 1917, on the day of Lag Ba-Omer 1917. At that time, the Russian army was facing a general offensive at the front and the main headquarters under the command of General Brusilov was then located in Kamyanets. On that same splendid day of spring, a Zionist procession, also splendid, went out through the main streets of the city. The girls of Israel marched in white clothes, the school students marched with the radiance of youth on their faces and songs of Zion in their mouths, thousands marched, carrying Zionist banners and above them fluttering blue and white Zionist flags. Among the Gentiles who witnessed the procession were those who said to each other: "Kanitz Sveta!" "Židy edut du Palestini"… (The end of the world! The Jews are going to Palestine).

When the procession passed by the Chief of Staff's residence, General Brusilov came out to greet it. A military band played "Ha-Tikva" and the head of the army of Great Russia stood still and saluted in honor of the Zionist national anthem and flag…

Everyone who remembered the time of Tsar Nikolai and the expulsion of the Jews by Chief of Staff Nikolai Nikolayevich - which was almost over, stood open-mouthed and dumbfounded at this miracle. We were like dreamers: the beginning of "the end of days" … "and a wolf lives with a lamb"…

* * *

The honeymoons did not last and very quickly the dreams and aspirations, human and Jewish, evaporated.

[Page 63]

The October Revolution came and with it the civil war. Chaos in all the cities of the country and the communities of Israel were drenched in a flood of blood. Not even Kamyanets was spared the evil and during Shavuot 1918, Petliura's people ravaged the Jews of the place and about eighty people of Israel were murdered there in a day. Riots in and around Kamyanets and in all the cities of Ukraine. Petliura's people from here, the Denikin camps from here, and the rest of the rebellious gangs took out their anger at the Jews. Sword and killing and loss.

The wolves did not change their nature.

* * *

And once again the sun shone and from San Remo came a bright and refreshing message: the British mandate over the Land of Israel for the fulfillment of the Balfour Declaration was approved, for the establishment of the Jewish National Home in the Land of Israel. The Poles then ruled the city and there was a period of relative peace. Upon hearing the good news, the Rav R. Israel Gutman z"l then commanded people to gather in the synagogues and the various Beit Midrash, to light candles, as on the days of public celebrations in memory of saintly rabbis, and to recite "Hallel" without a blessing.

And still in front of my eyes is the image of my teacher and rabbi, the Hasid R. Moshe Hirsch z"l, as he stands with awe and mercy and trembling with holiness, and lights the candles for the time of saying "Hallel" in the Husyatyn enclave, and his face glows with the glow of a sense of redemption...

* * *

And once again, a regime goes and a regime comes - and the people of Petliura return to the city, and in the midst of Yom Kippur in the year 1919, the entire community of Israel, men and women and children, from the synagogues and the various Beit Midrash led by the Rav Gutman and the Torah scroll with him, came out to Governor's Square (Guvernatorskaya Ploshad) - to welcome Petliura's troops in their entry from Podzamcze; and the women of Israel spread flowers on the path of the murderers...

Indeed, this time the wolves did not devour... and the crowd quietly returned to the end of the fast day. But the whole depth of the abyss of humiliation and the horrors of destruction of diaspora life horrified the hearts in preparation for the horrors to come - and a short time later they did indeed come...

Original footnotes:

1. Most of the things on this list are specific to the fields of Torah life and Hasidism in Kamyanets Podilskyy, as they are preserved in my memory and according to rumor.

2. After R. Zalman, R. Isaiah Dayan z"l held the high office, who was not given the title of rabbi, as was the custom in much of the Diaspora, that the successor of a great and holy rabbi was not called by the same title - the comment of Mr. Yosef Cohen of Kfar Hasidim.

[Page 63]

Religious Life in Our City under Soviet Rule

by Rabbi Ben-Tzion Fendler

Translated by Rabbi Dov Peretz Elkins

The first World War and the Revolution that followed changed the lifestyle in Russia completely, as is well known. The changes in the country caused major shocks in the realm of Judaism.

In our area [Kamenets-Podolsk], as in all places where the Bolsheviks ruled, they prohibited study of Torah and all Hebrew study in general; they prohibited Shabbat observance, kashrut, and every matter connected remotely with tradition. In daily life there was not a sign of Yiddishkeit. Overtly this was apparent, but covertly the situation was totally different. Throngs of Jews were faithful to all the sacred practice of Judaism, and clandestinely they observed the mitzvot of the Torah with deep commitment. In Kamenets there were people of many different backgrounds, among whom were artisans and unskilled workers, who during many years

[Page 64]

under Soviet rule, never tasted meat, since they did not want to be defiled with forbidden foods, and were scrupulous about the observance of the other mitzvot in all their details.

Synagogues all remained open until 5696 (1936), and many of them made hummed with the sound of prayers. The "Yevsektzia" [the Jewish section of the Communist Party] in Kamenets was moderate in its actions, and did not pursue religious Jews with rage as it did in other locations. The head of the "Yevsektzia" in Kamenets was a passionate Communist, but with regard to the religious he was a bit subdued. His view was that living conditions in the area were sufficient to terminate all the outmoded customs, and there was no need for special activities to accomplish this. Thanks to this viewpoint synagogues in the city were not destroyed until the summer of 5696 (1936). In that year the great assault on religion occurred all over, and all at once all the synagogues in Kamenets were closed, except for the "Gedalyahu Heller" synagogue. On the last Shabbat before my trip to Eretz Yisrael in the month of Elul 1936 I prayed in that synagogue, and there was no way of moving further inside. The courtyard was filled, and many stood in the nearby streets, perhaps hoping that they might hear "Barkhu" and "Kedushah."

There were no mikvaot in the whole area. In Kamenets there had been a mikveh for several years, in the bathhouse of Sara-Leah. After this bathhouse was destroyed a room was rented in the apartment of a gentile, on the ground floor of the "Brom" (city gate), and a pit was dug to serve as a mikveh, despite the real mortal risk involved. The owner of the apartment was accordingly punished for this act, and thus people were forced to steal their way into this pit to bathe, under the nose of the members of the militia who stood on the outside walls. Many people came from near and far to bathe in this mikveh in Kamenets.

Even in these especially difficult and troubled times, many people were occupied with Torah study. In the summer of 1936, several months before I left Kamenets, and before the destruction of the synagogues, I found in the "Gedaliah" synagogue, during twilight hours, large crowds of worshippers, not less than on holidays. Between the afternoon and evening services, scores of men sat and studied Mishnah, Ayn Yaakov, and Mishnah B'rurah. After the evening prayers as well there was a class in Talmud with huge attendance. There were also classes in Torah in several other synagogues. Once the synagogues were destroyed in the month of Av 1936, they began to worship in minyanim in private apartments, in secret of course.

The "Stolen" Torah Scrolls

by Rabbi Ben-Tzion Fendler

Translated by Rabbi Dov Peretz Elkins

The following occurred many years ago in Kamenets-Podolsk, during the days when the Yevsektzia in Soviet Russia persecuted religion, when houses of worship were confiscated and transformed into clubs, and religious items, including Torah Scrolls, were sent abroad for sale.

The largest and most beautiful of the sixty houses of prayer in the city was the synagogue of the tailors, that excelled in its wide and tall Holy Ark, which was coated with silver and gold, and decorated with pictures of animals and birds, fruit and flowers, and all kinds of musical instruments—beautifully crafted by talented artists. In this beautiful Holy Ark, on all three levels, stood more than one hundred Torah Scrolls.

[Page 65]

When this synagogue was destroyed and turned into a club for the city's workers, and the Torah Scrolls were plundered to be sent abroad for sale, the Gabaim (synagogue managers)—of all people the artisans—performed a daring act and "stole" thirty of the Torah Scrolls and secretly, with supreme devotion, hid them for safekeeping in the basement of one of the private houses. No one knew about this hidden space, of course, and from time to time the "thieves" went down to the basement to assure their safety, and guarded them very secretly for a long time.

At the end of the war the Soviets left the city and the Nazis entered with their servants from Romania and Galicia, and with them all the horrible, well-known results: the city was plundered and totally destroyed. Most of the Jews were taken out to be murdered in the nearby forest, and a few were able to flee to the neighboring villages and reached the border of Siberia. At the end of the war several of them were able to return to their destroyed and ruined city.

The same fate fell to the villages near Kamenets: destruction and devastation everywhere. Most of the Jewish residents were murdered, and the few who wandered away remained alive. After a period of time some of them returned to their destroyed villages, broken and dejected, and tried to renewed their former lives, and most of all they were concerned to establish for themselves quorums for prayer. This, without their sacred vessels, and especially without their Torah Scrolls.

Lo and behold, among those who returned was one of the Gabaim of the tailors' synagogue, who was among those, years before, who "stole" the Torah Scrolls, and remembered them. This Jew entered with a quorum of Jews to the secret basement, and brought out from its hiding place the "holy treasure"—all thirty complete Torah Scrolls, as if he had placed them there only yesterday. They all viewed this event as a "miracle from heaven."

These Torah Scrolls were sent as "gifts" to nearby villages—a Torah Scroll to each and every village.

[Page 65]

The Campaign of Orynyn

by Y .A. Bar-Levi

Translated by Monica Devens

The years 1917-1919 were years of severe calamities for Ukrainian Jewry. The political and military regimes, which changed with lightning speed from one season to another, did not last. Military occupation forces (Austrian, German, Polish, Czech), which acted according to the orders of the Western coalition against the forces of Bolshevik Russia, came one after the other. At the same time, the war and the struggle between Bolshevik Russia and the forces of the Ukrainian national movement (Hetman, Petliura) continued to increase.

And in all the turmoil of these days, the Jewish population was seen as the scapegoat, on whose head all the blows were poured, and the anger and rage of the masses of Ukrainian farmers found their outlet in wild riots in Israel. The pogroms in Ukraine, which cost us a hundred thousand victims, are still well remembered. Most of the disturbances took place in the southwestern part of Ukraine, bordering with

[Page 66]

Galicia, and more than other places, the Jewish settlements in this part of the Kamyanets Podilskyy region suffered both in property and in life (Proskorov= Khmelnytskyi, Felshtin=Skelevka, etc.).

But even in those days of rage, the Jews knew how to stand up for themselves, to show signs of bravery and to teach the besieging and destructive enemy a lesson. And I would like to single out one occurrence of heroism here.

* * *

On the border of Podolia and Galicia, at a distance of 17 versts (verst=about a kilometer) west of the city of Kamyanets Podilskyy (then often the capital city of the new alternating authorities), a small town stood on the Zbruch River (stood and is no more...) - Orynyn, which counted less than one hundred families. With the increasing pressure of the Red Army on the forces of Petliura in the spring of 1918, these last ones crossed the Zbruch River and moved to Galicia. Here they found a place of rest and help from the Entente and, with its financial and military help, reorganized and turned to Ukraine again. Of course, the small town of Orynyn was the first prey they encountered on their way. For three days and three nights, Petliura's gangs ran amok there, engaged in robbery and looting and even harming people, and in a little while the entire Jewish population would have been destroyed by them.

In this situation, some young people put their lives on the line and on Saturday night, May 24, 1919, they left the besieged town in the dark, and by side roads reached Kamyanets Podilskyy on foot in order to call for help. The garrison forces of the Red Army in Kamyanets were very few and this was well known to the Ukrainians. They also knew that if they "finished" with Orynyn, the road to Kamyanets Podilskyy, which had 60-70 thousand inhabitants at the time and whose conquest was then their immediate desire, was open to them because the value of this city was great, both strategically and politically as the future seat of the Petliura government.

The young people turned to the Jewish businessmen in the city and also to "Revkom" - the local Bolshevik government. They demanded quick and urgent help saying: "If you don't save us - you are also in danger." There wasn't much time left for reflections and calculations and the call went out: "Go up to Orynyn." In the blink of an eye, every good young man among the young people of Israel, for whom the honor of their people was a guiding principle, gathered and united. All partisan accounts were forgotten and everyone united, starting with the Zionists and ending with the Bolsheviks, and all those who felt in their hearts that one should not sit idly by and that the miserable town had to be saved, gathered on that Sabbath night, May 24, 1919, at Governor's Square. And these were not necessarily people who had served in the army and knew the art of fighting, but rather young people who had never known holding a gun in their hand.

After midnight, 50 to 60 soldiers left the city in a truck, with a small number of machine guns and one cannon in their hands, together with about 90 other young men under the command of an experienced commander. The company had not yet arrived at the desired district and had gone only 10 versts and then the command: "Get down from the vehicles and lie down on the ground!" At that moment, there was a loud sound of machine guns rattling from the enemy, who numbered 1200 men. Some of the Jewish youth who, as mentioned, had never held a rifle in their hand and even now were armed with primitive defensive tools, were, of course, afraid of the Ukrainians and they began to retreat crawling. However, there was one of the group, a brave and influential man, who turned to them

[Page 67]

and said: "Comrades, there is no room for retreat, if we return - then we have lost and, together with us, all those we left behind us in Kamyanets Podilskiyy; our way to victory is only in our advance towards the enemy" - and it was this call that influenced and breathed a new spirit, a spirit of heroism into hearts.

In the meantime, the one and only cannon, which was in the company's hands, managed to find out the whereabouts of the enemy forces and to hit those who fired from the machine guns and also managed to silence them. The nimble company commander took advantage of this new situation and addressed his comrades with the call: "Comrades, forward! Death to the murderers" - and the miracle happened: all the hatred towards the murderers, who had threatened Orynyn, and also the recognition that the fate of Orynyn and the rest of the towns could be foreseen for Kamyanets Podilskyy, too, all the indignation against the enemy, which had accumulated in their hearts for many months, became a driving and stimulating force, and with unprecedented enthusiasm, all of them burst forth to meet the enemy and moved from defense to attack.

The "Heidemaks" of Petliura did not stand in the battle. They retreated in panic, leaving behind them the many weapons they had in their hands: cannons, machine guns, field kitchens, and the like. Some of them knelt before the young people of Israel and asked them for mercy. The answer was - bullet or bayonet. 60 of the "Heidemaks" fell in battle and the remainder scattered in every direction. On the side of the Jews, one was killed (Avner Korman - a member of "Tse'irei Tsiyon") and two were slightly injured.

When the company continued on its way to Orynyn and was close to the town, all of its inhabitants came out of their hiding places and, with happiness and tears of joy in their eyes, met their saviors. None of them could understand how it had happened that the few stood against the many and they had only these words: "There was a miracle here"…

Indeed this was the miracle of Jewish heroism, like those miracles that we here in Israel have witnessed.

Types and Characters

by Shabbetai Kaplan

Translated by Monica Devens

A

Kamyanets, a city whose Jewish community was a typical cross-section of Russian Jewry and in relation to it - a province. It had a thin layer of the rich and a thick layer of the middle class and the poor. The layers were by nature anonymous and silent, and their expression was intelligence. In Kamyanets, there was an "elite," but not an exalted elite, like nowadays, but an elite bending down towards the masses; not of those who are lifted up from the people, but of those who lean towards them to lift them up. In contrast, there were people whose standard of measure was not that of intelligence, as possibly they were not intelligent at all, but they were characters, men of attributes whose intellectual talents were acquired in Beit Ulpana. These were inherent in them from birth.

A long gallery of characters are standing before you in remembrance of your townspeople, characters from 50 years ago, before and after the Revolution.

The new mail street, the Potschtovke, was the heart of the city and its "spiritual center." Here were the bookstores. On one side was the store of the Baynvelman brothers and across from it, my parents' store. The first was used as a club

[Page 68]

for the "Bund" and the second - for lovers of the Hebrew language and the Zionists. The identical aspect of them - vigilance. On Christmas days, when the shops were closed for three days in a row and there was only frost outside, all those who were discussing politics and looking for "tomorrow" would hang out together over a steaming bowl of potatoes. Messiahs were in things that were at the top of the world, that were in the renewal of literature and that were hidden in the bosom of the future. Serious things were seasoned with "jokes" and, cheerful with the hot potatoes and the cup of stew, someone would pull out a pamphlet and read a story from Shalom Aleichem that dealt with the "Pale of Settlement" or hidden allusions to the Japanese war. The hilarity - "pony-thief" was a stinger, the cruel and stupid tyrannical rule, and the longing for redemption was aroused with the laughter and the mockery, some for redemption in this, in the land of the diaspora, and some for redemption in the future, in the renewed Land of Israel, in the "emerging world."

So - before the revolution. After it - as if the city was flooded by a tremendous current that burst the prison of a dam. What was hidden went out into the open, what was secret went up to the top of a platform. No more conversation that was related between the walls - a loud and carried voice, a ringing and singing voice in open halls and under the dome of the sky, on the squares and when walking in the "narrow passage" called the "Dorozhka."

With the current, new faces appeared. Some of those had been hidden in the city until now and some came from afar, from the small towns in the vicinity and the metropolitan cities. Kamyanets was buffeted by strong winds, a Jewish socialist spirit from here and a Zionist spirit from here, and between them intermediate spirits, taking both of their temperaments in a fusion.

And here are some characters I remember from our city.

Moshe Kitai - squat, skinny, skin and bones and furrowed forehead. He was an old bachelor and chronically unemployed. What did he get the "necessities" from? Apparently from private lessons he had or didn't have, "we will make a living from starvation." He would wander from one "club" store to another "club" store or walk down a city street when "those looking for news" like him would join him and he would be stuck in the middle between them. His mouth was full of stories and his ears were devoted to "tales." His voice was thin and he had a high pitched laugh. This squat body - was a treasure store of folklore. He would collect in his storehouse everything that came to the ear and distribute it widely. He was a "member of the household" in our store, coming in and going out, and he had other places like that. He was a warrior against the rule of the tsar, against the haters of Israel, against the haters of Zion. A fighter with mere words and drowning them in his spit that was bursting from his lips with his gargling. He would destroy them with his witty humor. With the coming of the revolution, Moshe Kitai's life was disrupted, his weapon - mere words - was replaced by a different weapon, by speeches from stages, in open public struggles. His weapon - passed its time and rusted.

Dr. Knoping - Dr. of philology, a well-known figure in the landscape of Kamyanets. Tall, broad-shouldered and with a belly. His stomach was dreamy, dreaming of good and satisfying foods, which were apparently rare in his bowl. After the revolution, he was a Zionist businessman, mounted on a platform, unusual speech with every word lingering in his mouth before it came out, as if for cooling and the voice was muffled, drum-like. Dr. Knoping! - His entire appearance said: Dr. Knoping!

Dr. Mendel Goldstein. Every speech of his - a work of art! His speeches, more than they heard in the ears - they saw with the eyes. He was a seer of visions in his speeches and the listeners would see visions after him. His Russian language was juicy and picturesque. Regarding immigration to the Land of Israel, he would sail to the charms of song: "And here are ships being carried across the Mediterranean Sea and reaching the shores of Palestine!" The audience sat captivated by his charms, caught

[Page 69]

in the richness of his poetic language, placed in the refined palm of rhythm of the smooth words. When he finished and other speakers followed him, it seemed to you that you had fallen from the blue sky to the gray earth.

Completely different was Nachman Yakir or, as they called him, "Comrade" Nachman. He was a member of "Po'alei Tsiyon," a worker who didn't acquire an education in his youth, but later asked for it. He was an extreme Yiddishist. I don't know if he called himself "Treister" (a translation of Nachman) on his own initiative or if they stuck this name on him as a necessary nickname. One way or another, the name "Treister" was popular and displaced Nachman.

"Comrade Nachman" was devoted heart and soul to the "Po'alei Tsiyon" idea and this devotion commanded him to not pass up any opportunity to "beat" his dogma. There wasn't an assembly at which he was present where he didn't make himself heard. He was black, moustached, and a veil of sadness covered his face. He walked with a cane. He would hang his cane on his arm and give a speech. He spoke about socialism and Marxism. He had no power of expression. He spoke simply, but with self-confidence and he hung his words on "trees": Marx, Borochov, and more… They liked "Comrade Nachman" because of his honesty. They knew that he was not an "intellect" and that the knowledge of the lowercase letters was beyond him. In the heat of the debate, his opponents would sometimes cling to this weak point of his. Once when he mentioned Marx, someone from the audience asked:

- Have you read Marx?

- I've already started reading it - he replied - I haven't finished…

The audience received this answer with a forgiving and kind smile. There was no doubt that "Comrade Nachman" was indeed working diligently on Marx and was certainly "moving spasmodically" with it with the rest of his strength. They knew that he was not one to adorn himself with borrowed feathers and the honesty of his answer made up for his innocent and insecure fumbling with issues and laws. But sometimes when they made him mad, "Comrade Nachman" also knew how to attack sharply.

- Nachman, do you, Po'alei Tsiyon, have a program? They once pressured him.

- We have many programs! Who will give you "blows" like the number of our programs!

"Comrade Nachman"'s birthday was May 1st. "Po'alei Tsiyon" was a small party and in the general procession - a handful. At the head of the handful "Comrade Nachman" was marching upright, serious, holding the flag high in his hand as if holding the two Tablets of the Covenant.

Kamyanets Podilskyy was a metropolis on a small scale, a magnet for young people from the towns who came to be educated in it and seek status in life. Many who gathered in it left their mark on it, even standing at the top. The source of flowing water for Kamyanets was the town of Zhvanets. The town who gave it Shikle Salzman, the popular leader (may he rest in peace) and Shalom Altman, the organization man (may he rest in peace).

Shalom Altman was a strict man. Strict with himself and strict with others. His firmness was seen from his eyebrows. He was uncomfortable, nevertheless the people accepted the satisfaction of his firmness with love. His power was in action and not in words, but in narrowing down his opponents, from the Jewish socialists to the Zionists and celebrating the suffering of the revolutionaries in the days of the Tsar, Altman did not spare his language and spoke. And the style of his speech: We were also interested in prisons in Siberia! We were also exiled to the taiga! According to him, this was a personal cover. Shalom Altman was exiled from his town of Zhvanets for the crime of his Zionist activities. Altman's pronunciation was rough, with the letter Resh grating sharply. His thick whiskers, the width of his bones gave him an appearance that was not "of the diaspora." He looked like a farmer,

[Page 70]

A group of pioneers on their way to Israel

Taking leave of Shalom Altman for his immigration to Israel

[Page 71]

like a "Starosta," who had solid ground under his feet and was a symbol of national pride, uprightness, and decisiveness. He served as secretary of the Zionist Federation and as an activist in the Jewish community, friends as well as enemies were respectfully careful.

Shikle, the popular leader - was the opposite of Altman. Small in stature and round. Oval in body, but his tongue - knife-point. There was a row with the lions in the rival parties and he could overcome them. And this to remember: in those days, the weapon in the public struggle was the debate. A meeting of any party was open to debates. Not the format of the meetings we have in Israel, which are "individual prayer" or "solo concert" in the sense of, hear and accept! The lecturer would start, debaters continued after him, and the audience judged by clapping, by shouting out or by decisions. A meeting without a "revolution" - that was no meeting! Sometimes the disputants would change the situation completely. A "Bund" meeting would become a Zionist meeting and vice versa. The scales of the listeners would rise and fall with the argument. Shikle would captivate the audience with his strumming of the fine strings of the Jewish tradition and the infantile versions, he would strike at his characters and overcome his great rivals, like David overcame Goliath.

The political meetings in the years of the revolution were magical in their dynamism, in the grace of popularity, and in the multitude of shades that were expressed in them.

Among the leaders of the parties in the city were those of the "Bund" and of "Fareynikte," of Lithuanian origin, whose Yiddish language was eloquent and juicy, and their bag was full of parables and fables. The speeches were not "oral journalism" - they were interspersed with anecdotes whose sting spoke on their behalf. There was a rhetorical confrontation, a competition with spices. The opposing sides would come out defeated or victorious, but the audience would come out with "great assets."

Shikle, who also charmed as a student of "Herzliya" High School in Tel-Aviv, who returned and got stuck in Kamyanets, had another stage in the city, unmediated, and that was - the "evening classes" on Dolgaya Street, which gathered hundreds of young people, most of them young women, and which served as a warm nest for cultivating a Zionist atmosphere. Two won on this stage: Avraham Rosenzweig (today: Rosen) and Shikle Salzman. The first - by studying the Tanakh, the second by studying Hebrew. Aharon Ashman was later added to the two. They studied on Dolgaya Street and continued on "Mish'ol" - it is the natural promenade in Kamyanets. They would speak Hebrew, sing songs of Zion, and dream of the Land of Israel, of agriculture, of "bringing out bread from the earth," of being farmers or "colonists" in the language of the time.

The gallery of public activists in Kamyanets numbered many. There were those who stood out on stages, those who acted in the ranks. Among the first to be remembered is Munia Zak (he is M. Ezrahi z"l), whose Russian language was ringing, captivating with a polished gloss. Moshe Sister, then a member of "Fareynikte," today a lecturer in Tanach at the Kibbutzim College, the cut of whose speech was bitter and always used against the Zionists who dreamt of Buntsi Schoig and would ask reproachfully: "Un a Bulke mit Putter iz nicht gut?" (And a bun with butter isn't good?) Meaning: what is this skyrocketing to you, seeing dreams in Spain?

There was one dynamic Jew in Kamyanets, a Caspian Jew, his name was Akiva Kahana. An original person, independent, a fighter and full of humor. He did not belong to any party or rather he was a party to himself. He

[Page 72]

was also a journalist with a sharp pen and a writer for "Podolskiyy Kray." I remember a reply in the same newspaper about a "Letter to the Editor," which was signed "Kamit" and whose style indicated Akiva Kahana.

- What does "kamit" mean? They asked him.

- It's the translation of a verse of the "Little Song of Songs" using acronyms, he answered.

Two newspapers appeared in Kamyanets: "Podolskiyy Izvestia" and "Podolskiyy Kray." The editor of one of them was Fuchs. Short of stature and goose-like in his step.

"The activists in the ranks" were also manifested in special enterprises, in the organization of receptions, in election propaganda. And remember "The Palestinian week" ("Palestineskaya Nadlaya") in which the entire city was occupied by them. Tables were displayed in the street corners for the distribution of Zionist literature, ribbons were stuck in every lapel. The "attraction" of the "campaign" was Aharon Ashman (today the writer and dramaturg), who wore an Arab keffiyeh for his head that equated his brown hair and mustache to a Bedouin figure, a symbol of the Land of Israel.

This is how Kamyanets looked in the first two years of the revolution, which were stormy and dynamic. The liveliness encompassed all circles of the youth and young people. The student youth organized themselves in associations, "Kadima" to the upper stratum, "Ha-Techiya" to the lower stratum. The Brandman Choir was established, which was a huge cultural instrument for the spread of Hebrew song and musical culture, "Ha-Zamir" Drama Society was established, which staged plays in Yiddish and in Hebrew. For a certain period, Kamyanets was ashamed of the slowly flowing and deeply penetrating lectures of Alexander Heshin, one of the leaders of Po'alei Tsiyon, who came to our city and stayed there for some time. He eventually rolled into the Yevsektsiya and met his death in prison.

Later, due to the honeymoon of the revolution, the rallies decreased and the activity was concentrated in actions. Two pioneer training farms were established. The pioneers sowed wheat, buckwheat, potatoes and used to wield scythes standing proudly. Young men would volunteer, in turn, and go up to the farm to cook meals, young men would volunteer to take out potatoes.

The atmosphere became more and more sour, regime replaced regime and fears and anxieties descended on the city. The focus shifted to self-defense. Word of disturbances in Proskorov (= Khmelnytskyi) and Palestine came. On the Shavuot holiday, the Heidemaks rioted in Kamyanets and about eighty Jews were murdered. But what was this pogrom compared to Proskorov (= Khmelnytskyi) and Palestine? A minor pogrom! Indeed, a week after that, the Jews returned to their routine. The shops opened, "the narrow Mish'ol" - the boardwalk - came back to life, and there were people walking, and on Saturday nights the Potschtovke was full with couples.

A few days after the pogrom, the Petliuras sent a Jewish "messenger" to the community to collect donations for the government. The community called for a meeting in the synagogue and the "messenger," a large man with a moustached face, spoke in the audience's ears. From his words about the donation there arose a smell of contribution.

When the rumor came about the infiltration of the Heidemaks into Orynyn, a company of young men was mobilized who received weapons from the "Revkom" and went out to meet them. The Heidemaks were repulsed and the company returned except for one, Avner Korman, who was killed in battle.

When the possibilities of immigration opened - the first group of pioneers left Kamyanets for Israel, the founders of Kiryat Anavim. That morning was like a holiday in the city. Many accompanied the departing wagons

[Page 73]

The Hebrew musical organization "Kadima" in 1920

[Page 74]

up to "Podzamcze." From then they started going out in different routes, whoever was going to Galicia and who to Bessarabia, illegally crossing the border at night. The reserves were used up little by little, after them the members of the younger generation who had grown up in the meantime held on, and the outflow was stopped.

Kamyanets was tossed from regime to regime, but the Petliuras extended their stay. The city served as their temporary capital and also housed the Ministry of Jewish Affairs within the framework of personal national autonomy in the Ukrainian Republic. The Minister Pinchas Krasny - from the Folkist Party, was not involved with the public in the city. He had no interest in it and the main occupation of his office was "to photograph the past," to write reports on the pogroms, and to send memos.

B

Our yard was also across Dolgaya Street, which is the street of the market. In the morning, the children still in bed, and the cry of the first of the passers-by was heard, the bagel seller:

Frish un ayerdik
Frisch un tsafledik
Frisch un ayerdik
Frisch un tsafledik
Frisch un ayerdike baigel...

His figure stands before my eyes: his beard is light, elongated and pointed, his tone is continuous and curling and as if the taste of the bagels is in it, which stimulates the palate. He opened the "procession" of the passers-by.

Among the passers-by in the yard every morning, there were "Froike with the cymbals" and "Netta with the flute." Froike had black hair and a peg beard. Happy and making others happy, singing softly and accompanying his song with cymbals. The children would follow him and he would entertain them. This was his "hobi" (hobby) and his occupation - service to humanity. He would take out the sewage buckets and the trash baskets from the houses and in return he would receive the gift of bread or a plate of stew. Apparently, these were relations between employee and employer, service for pay - and not it. There were other motives to the service of Froike. He simply loved to serve humanity, helping women carry their baskets, and felt a special taste for helping those who needed it the most, a poor family, an old or sick woman. My father used to say of him: this Froike - a philosophical soul nests in him, a kind of Diogenes.

The women on the upper floors would be waiting for him, for Froike impatiently: - "Has Froike already passed?" "Have you seen Froike?" They would ask and Froike would carry the sewage buckets from the floors with a sense of purpose. He was never irritated, never angry, he was always kind-hearted. Froike knew how to value himself and he would publicly announce his worth. Before whom? Before the crowd of children who followed him and cheered him on.

- Who is a human being? He would ask in a loud voice, and the children would answer in chorus: Froike!

- When there is a need for a porter, who do you call?

- Froike!

- When you need a decent person, who are you inviting?

[Page 75]

- Froike!

- Who is a human being?

- Froike!

It is possible, and in his question of "who is a human being" was the intention of a demonstration, a demonstration of the "inhumanity" of others, who pretend to be civilized but distance themselves from the simple human act. It also had an appreciation of labor, which coincides with the human. And indeed, Froike was a human being, not pretending in vain.

"Netta with the flute" was different from Froike. A round face like the moon, without a beard and his chest sticks out in front of him like a pot belly. The chest was a storage room for bread. Every piece of bread he got would be stuffed there. The flute was not a flute - a scarecrow of a flute, just a reed or a stick and he would "play" with his lips, which he would tighten by inflating his cheeks. As the fee for playing, he would receive a penny or the equivalent of a penny, which he would tuck into his "pot belly."

A tragic "meshugge" was Isaac, crippled, toddling on his crutches and reaching out. He was a romantic, and princesses and countesses did not leave his mouth. He would set his eyes on beautiful girls and find evidence that they were meant for him by Providence. When they pressed him: "Why don't you finally marry one of the girls?" He would claim that it is the fault of the mothers, who fall in love with him and withhold his love from their daughters. If only they would imprison the mothers for one day, he would be saved.

Children would follow him, scratch his "wounds," and annoy him. When his anger reached its peak, he would pick up one of his crutches and chase them away. Isaac met his death in the rampages of the Shavuot holiday. The Heidemaks pierced him with swords and since then he disappeared from Kamyanets.

And there was another "exception" and they called him "Stroini Tschelobyak" (a tall man). He was thin and very tall. But that wasn't enough for him and he would stretch even more. A flexible walking stick in his hand and a narrow-brimmed straw hat for his head. He used to walk proudly on the sidewalks in the public parks and dream of romance,

A play about life in Israel during the "Eretz Israel Week" in 1918

[Page 76]

which was far from him. His clothes were ironed, spotless, and as he passed by the storefront windows, he would linger, peek in the mirror, and fix his hair and his hat.

Completely different from the previous ones was Simeon. You could talk with them. They were involved with people. Simeon was a society hater, running away and causing others to flee. In a black kapoteh, with his hands clasped behind him, he would run through the streets and his mouth would curse: May She'ol swallow you! May darkness take you!

The children would tease him and repeat his curse and he would chase after them and hit them with his fist. The nail of his madness was money. Haunted by fear lest they plot against his money, he would shout: "Das Beytele?" - a "makka!" ("My purse - fever!"). To upset him, the children would actually shout: "Simeon, das Beytele!" (Simeon, the purse!) And so it repeats, God forbid. Simeon saw all the people of the city without distinction as his enemies and would curse them.

- Simeon, why do you curse me, I didn't curse you? - They would argue against him.

- If you didn't curse me today, you will curse me tomorrow!

There were other "unusual" types, but the ones mentioned above were the most prominent.

"Tse'irei Tsiyon" During the 1917 Revolution

by H. Sharig

Translated by Monica Devens

In the last years before the 1917 revolution, a Zionist youth movement called "Tse'irei Tsiyon," which advocated the idea of work and a separate organization of working Zionists, continued to develop within the Zionist Federation. The movement preached the love of work and the working life as a foundational element in life, which they called "the work religion." The fathers of this movement and its founders were A. D. Gordon, Yosef Vitkin and others, who served as its guides, a model and an example of a life of simplicity and perfection. The movement's aspiration was to establish a reformed society in the moral sense and its goal - the creation of a "working people" in the Land of Israel.

A regiment of Scouts

[Page 77]

In cities and towns throughout Russia, organizations of "Tse'irei Tsiyon" arose, which coalesced within the framework of a faction within the Zionist movement. By nature, the youth and the workers were attracted to the organization of this faction. It brought them closer because it saw in them the natural element for action and organization.

At the end of the First World War, with the outbreak of the revolution in 1917, the "Tse'irei Tsiyon" movement became an independent working Zionist party, which operated in various areas of public life.

Also in Kamyanets, a "Tse'irei Tsiyon" federation arose, made up of the working classes and the youth, whose number of members reached hundreds and which was the most active political collective body on the Jewish street.

The "Tse'irei Tsiyon" federation devoted itself mainly to informative, organizational action, participated in the work of the community committee, managed the work of "He-Halutz," organized the immigration to Israel, and also worked in the organization "Ha-Haganah." The pioneer youth who were planning to immigrate concentrated on agricultural or professional training, so that they would adapt to working life and to shared kibbutz life. The local branch was headed by: Y. Sharir (Schreier) as chairman and H. Sharig (Schreiberman) as secretary.

In 1920, a conference was held in Kamyanets of representatives of "Tse'irei Tsiyon" branches in the cities and towns of Podolia and a district committee was chosen headed by Z. Pretkin (Porat).

At the same time, the local organization was visited by Comrade Eliezer Kaplan, who headed the All-Russian Central Committee of "Tse'irei Tsiyon."

Due to the revolution, transportation in Russia was disrupted and all the activity of the movement was handled by the local forces.

Children Fighting for Hebrew

by Shmuel, F. Barzin

Translated by Monica Devens

The hard-working "Ha-Shomer Ha-Tsa'ir" in Kamyanets Podilskyy engaged in Zionist work also among the school students. Over time, its influence among them grew and it managed to win many souls to the movement. The devotion of the boys and girls knew no bounds, and more than once they were tested and overcame.

In 1925, an incident happened that stirred up all the Jewish residents. One of the members was not admitted to the high school because of his affiliation with "Ha-Shomer Ha-Tsa'ir." This touched his heart so much that he fell ill with a fatal nervous disease, got encephalitis, and died. The Jews of the city were shocked to the core because they saw him as a victim of the arbitrariness of the authorities. His funeral was attended by crowds of Jews. From the members of the Zionist federations alone, about 2,000 people followed his coffin. We wanted to have the students of the school where the deceased attended participate in the funeral, but the school administration presented a condition, that the funeral would be "civil" with a red flag and that, instead of "El Male Rachamim," the "International" would be sung. We did not agree, of course, to these conditions. The students were not allowed to attend the funeral. But in fact, they also joined. Almost all of them, members of "Ha-Shomer Ha-Tsa'ir."

This spontaneous protest against the behavior of the Soviet school management, encouraged and strengthened

[Page 78]

the movement into a bold political act. In those days, persecution worsened against the learners of the Hebrew language and its teachers, and it was necessary to make public the Jewish public's opposition and lack of acceptance of the banning of our national language. The institutions of the "Tse'irei Tsiyon" party, the "Tarbut" society, and the main leadership of "Ha-Shomer Ha-Tsa'ir" decided to submit a petition, signed by multitudes of children, to the government institutions to permit the study of the Hebrew language in schools.

"Ha-Shomer Ha-Tsa'ir" took on the main burden for the realization of the project. It issued a proclamation to the youth and school students in which it emphasized the special status of the Hebrew language, prohibited from being used and studied, unlike the other languages of the minorities in the country, and called on all Jewish youth to demand from the government institutions to return to their national language - Hebrew - its natural right. The announcement was distributed

A group of members from "Ha-Shomer Ha-Tsa'ir" in 1923

in all parts of the city. When the students came to school in the morning, they found copies of the proclamation on the benches. The proclamation reached the youth in the nearby towns as well.

The signing of the petition began. The main points of the action were: to only have children up to the age of fourteen sign, school students; to have the petition written by a child; its content: a demand to open a Hebrew school and to allow the study of the Hebrew language in the existing schools. The action was met with great sympathy from the students. The power of "Ha-Shomer Ha-Tsa'ir" cells in the schools was evident throughout the operation. In Kamyanets alone, about 2,000 signatures were collected. First name, last name, and city name were specified. The signing was also arranged in the nearby towns.

This large action among the masses of children caused great Zionist agitation. Through the operation, "Ha-Shomer Ha-Tsa'ir" also managed to expand its ranks. The main leadership saw the need to give its branches in Kamyanets Podilskyy a blue and white flag as a sign of its excellence in the petition enterprise.

It was a time of exhilarating elation when the messenger of the main leadership handed the Zionist flag to one of the local boys in an illegal assembly outside the city.

The petition, signed by thousands of boys and girls in the cities and towns of Podolia, was sent in two copies - one to the central authorities in Ukraine and the other - to the authorities in Podolia. The Yevsektsiya did not, of course, sit idly by and began an investigation. Several signers of the petition

[Page 79]

were called to the G.P.O. and were required to cancel their signatures. It used various means of pressure on the children - threatened them that it would expel them from school, that it would imprison them. When it failed to impose its will on the children, the G.P.O. turned to the parents and demanded of them to influence their children. But that didn't help either. Not only did the children not respond to the demand of the G.P.O. rather, on their own accord, they continued to collect new signatures of those demanding permission of the Hebrew language and its study. These signatures were nothing more than an additional demonstration of the matter since the petition had already been submitted to the authorities before this.

The general Soviet press did not respond to the petition at all. Only in "Stern" from Kharkiv did a cartoon appear, depicting a typical "teacher" and a small child by his side. And the same teacher dictates: "[Yiddish sentence]." From this we understood that the petition fell into the hands of the Yevsektsiya and this is where its fate was decided.

("Naftoli Dor," Volume 1.)

The Struggle for Hebrew Among the Youth

by Pesach

Translated by Monica Devens

In 1926, the Yevsektsiya was at the pinnacle of its "national" work in Yiddish: it opened a network of Yiddish schools and invented all kinds of tricks to force the Jewish children to study in these schools. It even increased the imprisoning of teachers of Hebrew, a "clerical" counter-revolutionary language.

At the same time, a circular was received in Dunayivtsi from the district headquarters of "Ha-Shomer Ha-Tsa'ir" and the district committee of the Zionist Youth Federation with instructions to send a petition to the Soviet government, that it would allow the study of the Hebrew language. The petition had to be written in two copies, and the first and last name should be signed in clear writing.

The branch committee assigned one of its members to carry out this instruction. There were children who sacrificed themselves for this action. The "job" was difficult: on the one hand, they had to be careful about the G.P.O. And on the other hand, also of the parents, who, of course, did not have a negative attitude toward the Hebrew language, but were full of fear of the authorities.

On the day of remembrance for Taras Shevchenko, a reception of questions and answers was held at the general school. The member who was tasked with carrying out the signing was invited to the reception as a guest of one of the students. It was arranged in advance that the question of "What is Zionism" would fall to him and so it was. For his part, he rose to answer this question. The member briefly explained the essence of Zionism and its connection to the Hebrew language, and emphasized that Taras Shevchenko was recognized as a Ukrainian national poet and his language was permitted, while our national poet, Hayim Nahman Bialik, his language was forbidden because that's what the Yevsektsiya wanted. It was well known that the Hebrew language was allowed in Moscow. Possibly if they would send a petition to Moscow and ask to recognize Hebrew as a language of study, like the other languages in Russia, the government would respond positively to this request.

[Page 80]

Apparently these things had an effect on the students and one of them, Zhitomirsky, passed from student to student and got them to sign the petition. We collected over a hundred signatures that evening. (The boy did not last long at the school because after a while he was expelled from it.) On the other hand, we encountered strong opposition in the Yiddish school, which was entirely under the influence of the Yevsektsiya. Nevertheless, we collected many hundreds of signatures in a short period of time.

In 1926, there was the population census and among the other questions, there was also the question - in which languages is the citizen fluent. We organized a broad publicity campaign among the population so that they would also mention the Hebrew language. Many, many strongly demanded to register their knowledge of Hebrew, but clerks announced that they were ordered not to list this language.

In different ways, we tried to impart some knowledge of Hebrew to the youth. We organized evening lessons in groups of 2-3 children, we also established a traveling library. Under our influence, the number of parents who taught their children Hebrew increased, even though the risk of imprisonment was involved.

("Naftolei Dor," Volume 1.)

Zionist Youth in the Resistance

by Chaya Gelman Tissenbaum

Translated by Monica Devens

The "Scouts" battalion in our city was simply called the "Federation of Scouts," deliberately as regards the authorities, but the boys and girls of the battalion knew very well what and who they were. It was Zionist youth in resistance.

On the 20th of Tammuz, they would go on a regular trek to the forest and older members would come there to lecture on Zionist issues, especially on the affairs of the day. Of course, the adults would come separately and at different times.

The "Ha-Shomer Ha-Tsa'ir" battalion

[Page 81]

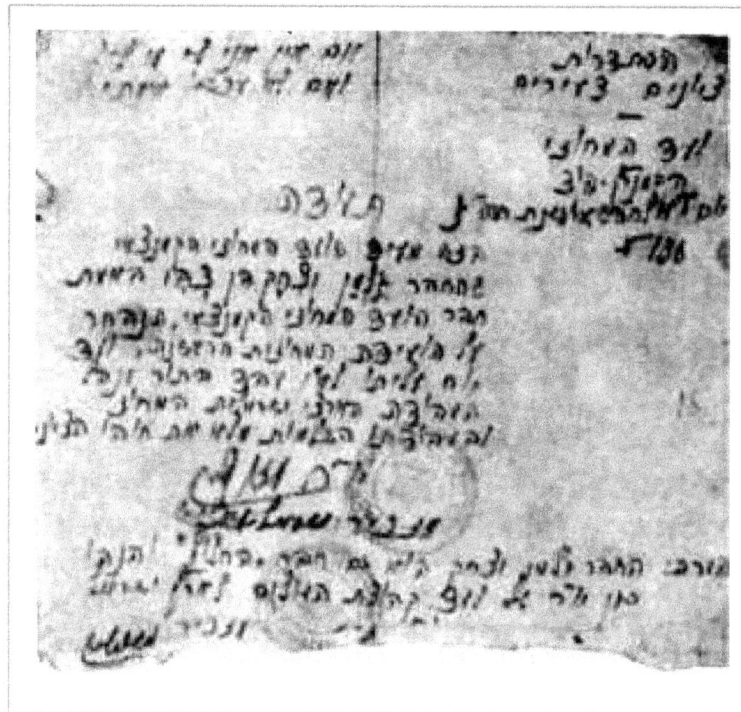

A document from the Federation of Zionists for a
member who was immigrating to Israel

On its way to the forest, the battalion would pass through the city streets to the beat of the drummer Yitzhak Beharav z"l and to the song of Y-h hai-li-li ama-li-li. At the head of the battalion marched its commander Yitzhak Gelman z"l. To many who stood on the sidelines watching the scouts, it was known that this was pioneering Zionist youth.

As the commander's friend in those days, I remember how difficult this position was. As far as the authorities were concerned, it was a kind of Gadna (youth battalion) for us. The sports instructor of the "Vase'ovoch" was also the instructor of our battalion. He knew the whole truth about us. He was a gentile who apparently did not like the authorities very much.

Many members of the battalion were captured by the authorities and exiled to Siberia. A few of them are in Israel today and many of them perished in exile. The commander and, along with him, several members were also arrested after a Zionist conference and sent to the prison in Vinnytsya after first serving out part of their crime in a "basement" in Kamyanets. The court acquitted them of any guilt and they all returned to Kamyanets.

The Kamyanets Podilskyy Ghetto

by Moshe Deutsch

Translated by Monica Devens

In the second half of July 1941, exactly one month after Nazi Germany attacked the Soviet Union, two Hungarian gendarmes appeared at my house in Teresva (Hungary) and ordered me and my wife to be ready within ten minutes to go with them. Yes, we were ordered to take provisions for the road for several days. We heard about transports of Jews from Budapest and other cities in Hungary, but

[Page 82]

we didn't know where they were being taken. In Budapest, there was a "KAUK" office to deal with foreign citizens and the authorization for these transports - lack of Hungarian citizenship.

From my apartment they led me, my wife, and my daughter to the courtyard of the town's secretariat and there we stayed until evening, when hundreds of women, children, and old people were brought there from the surrounding area. There were few young men because these had long been conscripted into forced labor camps. From this yard, we were transferred to sleep overnight at a school. The next day, my wife and daughter were released, and I and the rest of the detainees were taken to the train station, where we boarded train cars. After wandering about, we arrived in Yasinya and the gendarmes who accompanied us ordered us to sit down on our luggage. We waited for about an hour until an official from the Bureau for the Aid of the Jews arrived from Budapest, who addressed us with this language: "Everyone who has an original Hungarian citizenship card is requested to give it to me, I do not accept any other document." There were two Jews among us, one born in Transnistria with a majestic appearance whose long white beard hung down and one born in Poland who gave the requested certificate to the clerk. These were taken out of the transport and sent back home.

A Concentration Camp

From the train station in Yasinya, a Hungarian soldier led us along a path next to the railroad tracks to the town of Huashalya and put us in a camp enclosed by wire fences in the middle of which was a factory for making planks. Thousands of men, women, and children were gathered there. Hunger tormented all those who were there for a long time. Although the Bureau for the Aid of the Jews and the Jewish community in Yasinya did their best and provided food to the detainees, the handful did not satisfy the lion. The general situation in this camp was horrible, especially at night, the cries of the babies and the groans of the old and sick were unbearable.

Departure to an Unknown Location

Every day, 15 to 20 military trucks appeared in the camp and the camp residents were loaded onto them and taken to an unknown location. Rumors spread that the Jews were being settled in the houses of farmers who, due to the outbreak of the war, had abandoned their homes and joined the Red Army. Other rumors said that the Jews were being murdered in Galicia and their bodies were being thrown into the Dniester. Our turn came. One Friday evening at the end of July, we were loaded onto trucks and driven to an unknown place. We crossed the border between Hungary and Poland that had been conquered by the Germans. In the evening, we arrived at Borszczów in Galicia. In the Jewish homes, the Shabbat candles were already lit and in our hearts we prayed to join these Jews who looked at us with fear and compassion, but the cars did not stop. In the late hours, we arrived at the fortress of Kamyanets Podilskyy. There we were taken off the cars and ordered to stay put, with Hungarian gendarmes guarding us all night. The morning dawned and the men were brought into the church nearby and the gendarmes closed the door on us. Then they took us out one by one and ordered us to raise our hands, while the sergeant checked our pockets and stole the little money we had with us as well as rings and watches. Then the command was heard: "Now go ahead, anyone who dares to come back - a bullet in his head!"

In Kamyanets Podilskyy

Our procession started to climb up the street in Podzamcze. I ran into a Jew and greeted him

[Page 83]

with "Gut Shabbes" and he replied "Gut Shabbes." "Are you Jews from Hungary? - asked the Jew. "Yes, we are Jews from Hungary." "Oh my" "What happened? How did you get here" - "We have no answer, dear Jew, war is war." "Tell us R. Jew, maybe we can stay with you?" - "I am very sorry, I already have Jews from Hungary, but in the kindergarten not far from here you can find shelter."

Under the guidance of this Jew, we reached the kindergarten where we found Jews who had been expelled from Hungary sitting at small tables with the remains of onions on them, singing sweetly, "Yom Zeh Mechubad Mi-Kol Ha-Yamim."

I went to the center of the old city and there I encountered hundreds of deported Jews, among them many acquaintances. I heard from one source that there would be a meeting in one of the buildings there and that I should attend this meeting.

The Meeting and its Results

The hall where the meeting was held was full to the brim. At this meeting, three committees were chosen: one that was intended to negotiate with the German military headquarters; the second - with the Hungarian military headquarters; and the third was intended to coordinate actions in the area. The next day, the two committees returned empty-handed and only one of their members managed to contact the German commander, and he said to him: "The Jews wanted war - and here it is in all its cruelty, and they must bear all its consequences."

The Ghetto Gate

[Page 84]

The Old City as a Ghetto

We wandered around free for about a week. There were few local people, Jews and Ukrainians, whom we encountered. Very slowly, they all came out of their hiding places and the Jewish people of the place saw a good sign in the presence of Jews from Hungary and helped us as much as they could. When we went to the nearby villages to buy food, the Ukrainians, too, the "Muzhiks" and the "Hazaikas," showed understanding for our troubles and refused to accept compensation for the food items we received from them.

One day, the Germans ordered us to form a "Judenrat" within twenty-four hours and notices appeared on the streets of the city ordering all the Jews in Kamyanets Podilskyy and the surrounding area to concentrate in the old city, which was declared a ghetto. Yes, all Jews from the age of ten and older were ordered to wear a white ribbon with a blue "Star of David" on the left arm and not to leave the area of the ghetto; contact with the German headquarters should only be through the "Judenrat"; one who violates the orders mentioned above - any one, a death sentence.

The Germans promised to provide food to the ghetto residents at cheap prices. But apart from a few hundred kilograms of barley flour, we received nothing. Each head of a family put three rubles into the Judenrat coffers to finance the shopping. As a committee on behalf of the Judenrat, we were given a license to go to the market during certain hours to buy food, but we were unable to get more than one cart of cucumbers and one cart of cabbage. Once only, the three local members of the Judenrat managed to buy about two hundred kilograms of meat. The surrounding farmers occasionally entered the ghetto and took Jews from there to work, so that they could receive bread from the bakeries at their expense. Indeed, even the work we were assigned to do was not necessary at all.

The Ghetto Gate in Karvasar

[Page 85]

Forced Labor

Every day, the German army took people, especially women, to various jobs outside the ghetto areas and in exchange for their work they received food. They also brought some of the rations they received to their families in the ghetto. In the ghetto itself, hunger began to show its signs. Many people and children fell ill from hunger. Children reached out for alms, but the pennies they collected could not buy anything in the ghetto.

One day, a Hungarian officer contacted us and asked for ten craftsmen, carpenters and painters, to install road signs. Only carpenters were found and I alone took it upon myself to draw signs. And so we went to work. Before we finished the work, a Hungarian officer entered the workshop and asked who would volunteer to go to the front tomorrow on August 25th to install signs there, and if necessary, to paint more signs. No one opened their mouth. The officer added that every volunteer would stand under his protection and would receive the rations and services that a soldier deserves. I answered him that I was ready.

At dawn on August 25, 1941, I left in a truck with an officer and four soldiers in the direction of Vinnytsya and Haysyn. On the way, I made friends with the officer and one of the soldiers and we talked because they would take Hungarian Jews out of the ghetto for a suitable ransom and I took upon myself the responsibility of paying the ransom. According to the registration, ten thousand local Jews, six thousand deported from Hungary, and two thousand from Bessarabia were found in the ghetto. Many local Jews fled with the retreat of the Red Army. On our way, we passed Dunayivtsi, Proskorov (= Khmelnytskyi), Mohyliv-Podilskyy, Vinnytsya, Haysyn, and other towns. In all these places, I saw frightened and terrified Jews. In Haysyn, the Hungarian officer told the German commanding officer there that I was a sign painter and he wrote down his address on a piece of paper, so that he could send me to him in case of need. After a week, when we finished painting the signs, we returned to Kamyanets.

The Liquidation of the Ghetto

On August 29, on our way back to Kamyanets, a Hungarian soldier got on our car and told us that thirteen thousand Jews had been killed in Kamyanets. The officer didn't want to believe it, he saw it as a "horror-propaganda," but the frightened soldier apologized because he had heard it from his officer who had returned from Kamyanets. At noon that day, we arrived in the city and stopped by the army base of the Hungarians. No one was seen outside and the soldiers said that the Jews had been killed. I was ordered to hide until the Gestapo left the place. I hid in a car for a week.

After some time, an engineer from the Hungarian engineering corps appeared, sent to me by my friend, the officer mentioned above, to assist in my escape and he told me about the events in the city since I left it: "Next to the tank excavation outside the city, they dug another two large pits, and informed the Hungarian Jews that they were being taken home, but in fact they brought them to these pits and ordered them to undress. Pillars were erected from these pits and a plank formed a bridge between the top of the pillar and the edge of the pit. The Jews were ordered to get on the board backwards and a machine gun was pointed at them from the front. This is how the Jews were exterminated. Two Podkarpatska Rus soldiers refused to shoot, saying that they would not raise their guns on women and children. What befell them for disobedience is unknown to me."

[Page 86]

The Escape

The engineer left the car and went to organize my escape, but before he could return, the officer appeared in a panic: "Run for your life because the army base found out that a Jew is hiding here. Hightail it!" At my request, the officer gave me the address of that German officer from Haysyn who had invited me to work for him.

That evening, I spent the night in the attic of a peasant woman in Podzamcze. I didn't close an eye all night because of mental stress and fear and because of the barking of the dogs, which howled in a terrible voice. The smell of the blood of the victims reached their nostrils and they, the dogs of Kamyanets Podilskyy, were the only ones who eulogized the victims... The next day, I arrived in the town of Orynyn and there I learned from a Jewish boy that about 2,000 Hungarian Jews were murdered in this town, while the local Jews remained alive.

A remnant of a destroyed synagogue

On the back of the paper on which was the address of the German officer, I wrote in German in Gothic letters the following letter: "A. N. In accordance with my promise, I am sending you the man you asked for and he will do his work with complete faith to your satisfaction. With respect and admiration" and I concluded with my signature in an illegible hand and the date. On the way, I spoke only Ukrainian. Near the Russian-Polish border, near the Zbruch river, I fell into the hands of two Germans. I showed them the letter I had forged and they guided me in the direction of the border. Continuing my journey, I arrived in Galicia to the town of Skala-Podilska and from there to Borszczów. In these places I met with Jews and one of the Borszczów Jews advised me not to enter a Jewish home. This is how I passed through the towns of Tlost, Horodenka, Kolmyya, Delyatyn, Jaremcze, Mikuliczyn, and Tatarow. In all these towns I saw Jews carrying their personal belongings to ghettos. In Lubliniec, I was stopped by the Ukrainian militia, who were not satisfied with the letter in my hand, and they took me to the German headquarters on the Polish-Hungarian border. They said that there was no hindrance on their part and a German officer accompanied me to the Hungarian border guards and persuaded them to allow me to go to Hungary. However, the Hungarians ordered me to return in the same manner as I had come. I was forced to return to the village a second time and was caught by the militia. I was miraculously saved by a Jew until I arrived together with other Hungarian Jews in Hungary.

[Page 87]

Personalities

by Moshe Deutsch

Translated by Monica Devens

David Schleifer

On Shmini Atzeret 1920, one of the veteran businessmen and Zionists was shot dead by Denikin's soldiers in Kyiv - the lawyer David Ben Shabbetai Schleifer from Kamyanets Podilskyy. He left us at such a time of unrest that even his closest friends and acquaintances were unable to pay him the last kindness and almost did not eulogize him satisfactorily. And in the meantime, our heart will forget the memory of one of the good and important Zionists who sacrificed his blood and the best part of himself for more than thirty years on the altar of our national work.

D. Schleifer was born in Kamyanets Podilskyy in 1863 to poor and somewhat educated parents. He graduated from the local gymnasium and was accepted to Kharkiv University in the law faculty. Being a student, he suffered much poverty and deprivation because he had to take care of his own existence. During almost all his days studying at the university he lived only on bread and salted fish, and despite his poor material situation he gave his heart to the Bilu movement and was one of the active members who were preparing to immigrate to Eretz Israel, despite the sad news received from there after the immigration of the first group back in 1882. In the meantime, he finished the university and became a lawyer, came to Kamyanets, married a wife, and began to practice his profession and, within a short time, became famous in the city and the surrounding area as an expert in Jewish civil law and from all over the region, the Jews flocked to him to ask for advice and protection in their various cases.

After the first congress, the deceased devoted himself to the Zionist idea. His work later occupied his entire life. He founded, in his city, the first Zionist association of the intelligentsia and immediately after that - associations of middle-class men, educated young men, middle-class women, educated young women, and more. An urban center was chosen from the representatives of all the associations and the deceased was at its head.

He did not excel as a speaker. In his speeches, there was logic, a healthy mind and moderation, and his words came from his heart with excessive enthusiasm and made the strongest impression on the audience. In particular, the deceased excelled in his wonderful organization. His soul could not find rest due to his constant fear that he might not yet fulfill his duty to the idea and therefore, he organized the Zionist work in the provincial towns and, with the consent of the Central Zionist Committee, a conference of Podolia Zionists was called in 1908. The conference chose a regional committee, whose role was to organize and manage the work in the entire region, and the deceased was the head of the committee and succeeded in a short time to organize and strengthen the work by more than 100 points.

The authorities in Kamyanets related to the deceased with great trust so that the Zionist work was conducted almost legally. Without special difficulties, he often managed to hold area-wide and district conferences. And in Kamyanets itself, assemblies, lectures, receptions, and the like were held every week.

Once at the urban Zionist center, the question about an anti-Semitic play "Contrabandists," which the city theatre wanted to grant the city residents, was on the agenda. The Minister of Police knew what was happening in our camp in relation

[Page 88]

to this matter and he came to that yeshiva in his own right, participated in the debates, and finally took it upon himself to be the mediator between the Zionists and the theater - and the play was removed from the repertoire.

However, the extensive and visible work in Kamyanets and the surrounding area was not liked by another authority, and one day in 1910, the gendarmerie searched my house and took all the protocols, lists, letters, accounts, and correspondence, and the like, and after multiple investigations, turned the matter over to the area court and it was necessary already to make something out of this because they could not pass over the extensive material in silence, which showed in black and white the existence of a strong and organized illegal federation in every region with an area, national, and international center... and here even D. Schleifer could no longer cancel the matter. He mainly tried to weaken the legal material and to remove from the matter, first of all, the central institutions as well as the federations in the provincial cities. And in this regard, he was able to influence the course of affairs a lot. First of all, they bribed the legal investigator with a tip (200 rubles) and since he was a legal investigator for important matters - he accepted the gift warmly. And in 1911, D. S. gave an enthusiastic Zionist speech at the court, which was a demonstration to the outside and to the inside, and all the members of the committee were found innocent.

After the Zionist sensation at the court, D. S. wanted to raise Zionism in the eyes of the residents of his city, in spite of the opposition of his haters and opponents who thought that the end had already come to the Zionism of Kamyanets and the surrounding area as well as to Schleifer's greatness. For this purpose, he organized a large masquerade ball for the benefit of the Palestinian Committee in Odesa and at this ball an Eretz Israel market was arranged from the country's produce. The city's elite came to this ball, both Jews and Christians, and many from the nearby cities. The success of the ball was so great that they forced D. S. a few days later to an encore and the ball went by for the second time with great success.

Along with his Zionist work, D. S. participated in all public works in the city and everywhere he was one of the leading speakers. Through his efforts, a Talmud Torah with craft departments was founded in Kamyanets from the meat tax money. A "Hebrew Club" was also founded by him (the only club with such a name in the entire region) with a rich library of three thousand Hebrew and Russian volumes from the life of the Jews. In the above-mentioned institutions, D. S. was the chairman. He was also known throughout the province not only as a Zionist, but also as a general community activist.

His Zionist enthusiasm reached its peak only at the time of "Hedvah." And whoever did not see the deceased with "Zionist joy" did not see a happy person in his days. There was no limit to his devotion, either. At times like these, he sometimes even forgot his duty to the government as a lawyer and how many times was he in a situation of danger for such sins.

I remember one case at Simchat Torah in a small town "Orynyn" near Kamyanets. We arranged

a "Minyan" in a private house there for the benefit of the congregation, during the reading of the Torah, a carriage drove up to the house, and in the carriage sat D. S. and a legal investigator who traveled according to the order of the area court to the nearby village for an investigation. D. S. left the investigator in the carriage and he himself entered the "Minyan." We honored the guest with an "Aliyah" and we thought that he would hurry to go on his way. But the deceased waited until they had finished reading the Torah, gave a Zionist speech, and after

[Page 89]

"Musaf," blessed the wine together with us with singing and dancing as usual. But he wasn't satisfied with that. The Torah still needed to be brought into the synagogue. And look, the Zionists of "Orynyn" surround the whole town with songs and dances. Schleifer walks in the lead and conducts the tunes, and after him -

all the Zionists, and after them - the whole town, men, women, and children, and the "goy" sits in the carriage and waits…

A case of a different kind happened in the city of Dunayivtsi (30 km from Kamyanets). In this city, there was for a long time a conflict between the "old" and the "young" Zionists and the Zionist work suffered a lot from this. The regional committee that wanted to put an end to this quarrel came to Dunayivtsi for a special meeting to clarify the conflict. On that day, Schleifer, together with the investigator, had to visit the nearby village on behalf of the area court, and on their way to Dunayivtsi they were going to rest for a while. D. S. left the legal investigator at the hotel and went to the meeting of the local Zionists for a little while. The meetings lasted two days and two nights and D. S. had already forgotten the legal investigator and the government investigation…

D. S. was a delegate to various Zionist congresses and conferences. And after every congress, it was as if his youth was renewed. Several times he decided to visit the Land of Israel, but he could in no way come to Israel as a mere Zionist or a simple tourist and always dreamed of connecting his trip with a real Zionist enterprise, and even in 1908 he said to organize a group of fifty young men and women from Podolia and to found a cooperative settlement for them. One day I found him engrossed in a map of Eretz Israel and, while he was telling me about the details of the plan, he showed me on the map the place for the settlement (next to Motza). The deceased did not like to argue and went to work: he issued a call for proposal on this matter to all the Zionist associations in Podolia, came to talks with our central institutions (the reduced and the large Executive Committee, the Central Committee, the congregation, the Odesa committee, etc.). Also with wealthy private individuals and those who were familiar with the issues of settlement and cooperation. And he had already dreamed of the happy hour in his life that he would accompany the group immigrating to the Land of Israel. But our institutions found that the time had not yet come for such an enterprise.

It is worth mentioning that, in the same place that D. S. dreamed twenty years ago of founding the settlement there, the Kiryat Anavim collective farm is now located, ninety percent of whose members are from Podolia and most of them from Kamyanets itself.

The deceased expressed another idea also:

He came in contact with a photographer in Kamyanets for the purpose of traveling to the Land of Israel to photograph Jewish life in the cities and collective farms and later to tour Russian cities for the purpose of propaganda for the Zionist idea with the help of these photographs. This did not work out either.

When D. S. saw that all his dreams of traveling to Eretz Israel in connection with a real undertaking were not coming true, he decided to travel as a simple tourist and in 1912, when his only daughter finished her studies in Switzerland, he said to please himself and his family and to visit the Land of Israel. He said and he did: he arranged his affairs, got a passport, and everything was already ready to go. However, due to unforeseen circumstances, his trip to Israel was postponed this time, too.

With the beginning of the World War, when the Austrian armies entered Kamyanets and demanded a huge amount of contribution over twenty-four hours, D. S., along with the rest of the city's businessmen, was forced

[Page 90]

to go all night from house to house and collect money and valuables, and a few days later, when the Russian armies expelled the Austrians and began to take revenge on the Jews for the contribution (even though, according to the order of Emperor Franz Joseph, the money and belongings were returned in their entirety to their owners), the deceased decided to leave Kamyanets.

At that time Tsar Nikolai visited Kamyanets as one of the places of the war front and the local municipality gave him a festive reception with delegations of Christians, Catholics, and Jews. The Hebrew community requested that D. S. walk at the head of the Jewish delegation. It was decided not to make any speeches before the Tsar. In those days, rumors were already spreading about the Jews, that they were spies for Germany, etc., etc. These rumors had already caused the expulsion of Jews from towns near the border and there was a similar incident in the town of "Kutni." D. S. could not suppress his pain and go through these events in complete silence, and when he presented the Tsar with bread and salt, he addressed him with these words: "If you, Your Highness the Emperor, do not believe in the incident of "Kutni" - accept from the Jewish residents bread and salt"… The Emperor extended his hand to him and said: "I accept" …

A few days later, Schleifer left Kamyanets and from then on began his wanderings with his family members from Kamyanets to Vinnytsya, from there to Ekaterinoslav (=Dnipro), to Kyiv and again to Kamyanets, Ekaterinoslav (=Dnipro) until the end of the war… At the beginning of the revolution, he returned to Kamyanets and, although he found there a strong Zionist federation, especially of young men and women, he could no longer live in the city that had become the nest of the Petliura supporters and decided to settle in Kyiv where, according to the efforts of the Zionists, he was appointed a peace judge and also found an extensive field for public and Zionist work. At that time, Kyiv became an important Zionist and public center, and the local Zionists cherished the deeds of the deceased. He was elected vice-chairman of the first democratic Hebrew congregation, a member of the municipal Zionist committee, a member of the "Jewish National Assembly," a member of various committees of the Zionist Center in Ukraine, and published articles in the Jewish newspaper "Telegraph," which was then published in Kyiv and around "the world," in "Al Ha-Mishmar" and more.

With the change of regimes, D. S. remained without work and, together with other businessmen and Zionists, refugees and those affected by the war and the revolution - suffered poverty and deprivation.

His mood became depressed from day to day and the man always full of life and enthusiasm, hopes and dreams, fell into an abyss of despair.

When Denikin's men entered Kyiv and began to abuse the Jews and their property, the deceased was not able to hide in the attic or in the basement. And went out into the courtyard to influence the wild soldiers. But upon his appearance in the courtyard, they shot him and he fell to the ground covered in his blood.

Israel Goldman

[Page 91]

Israel Goldman

Born on Tuesday, October 20, 1879, in the town of Orynyn, Kamyanets Podilskyy district, to his father, the ritual slaughterer, R. Yeshayahu Goldman. He received a traditional Torah education in the "Cheder" and the "Yeshiva," as was customary in those days.

After becoming an orphan at a young age, he moved to his grandfather's house in Kamyanets Podilskyy and continued his Torah studies. Together with these, he glanced at the Hebrew and Yiddish Enlightenment literature, fell in love, and was caught up in the stirrings of new times and the Zionist idea. When he grew up, he learned Russian and received a teacher's certificate.

Gifted with the talent for writing, he began to write poems and stories in Yiddish and even published a collection of poems called "Ideal and Life," which was printed in Vilnius. Over time, he devoted himself mainly to Zionist-public work in Kamyanets Podilskyy and the cities of the region.

I. Goldman was a friendly man and soon stood out in the Zionist movement, and the leader of the Zionists in Kamyanets Podilskyy, the lawyer D. Schleifer, brought him closer to him and chose him as secretary of the Zionist federation in Podolia.

He also knew how to wage war with opponents and to stand his ground in a war of opinions out of a fair attitude towards his opponents.

Despite being entirely immersed in teaching and in public-Zionist engagement, he began to publish articles in newspapers and over time became a significant journalist who knew how to faithfully describe the life of the Jews and their problems in Podolia. For many years, he was a regular correspondent of the Odesa newspaper "Gut Margen" and also participated in the local press in Kamyanets Podilskyy in the Russian language.

When Jewish immigration from Russia to North and South America increased and the ICA (Jewish Colonization Association) opened an information bureau in Kamyanets Podilskyy, I. Goldman was appointed the bureau's secretary and over time also to the administration. Thanks to his humane attitude towards immigrants, he was liked by them, who saw him as a friend ready to help them with heart and soul.

From his intimate knowledge of the wishes and troubles of the immigrants, he gave them faithful expression in his "Gut Margen" articles.

On the eve of the outbreak of the First World War, I. Goldman moved to Kyiv and was appointed secretary of the area committee of the Jewish National Fund.

In 1917, after the February coup, he was counted among the members of the "Jewish National Assembly" and served as vice chairman of the Jewish community in Kyiv.

When power passed to the Bolsheviks and the Zionist movement in Ukraine went underground, he continued his illegal Zionist work and was imprisoned in 1922, along with a number of other activists in the illegal Zionist conference in Kyiv, for two years.

[Page 92]

In 1925, when the authorities made certain concessions to the prisoners of Zion by expelling them from Russia, I. Goldman chose "expulsion" to Israel.

Upon his arrival in Israel, he devoted himself again to public work and together with A. Mazza initiated the establishment of the organization, "Brit Rishonim," and served as its secretary and the living spirit in all its activities. Thus, G. saw his main role in Israel as creating a constant connection between himself and the Jews of Ukraine through an exchange of letters with his acquaintances and friends about the resurrection of the homeland and its building and the life of the Jews behind the Iron Curtain. His letters served as a great encouragement in the diaspora to the Zionists suffering there, and their letters were published in Israel in most of the newspapers.

At the end of World War II, when the bad news arrived about the Holocaust that befell the Jews of Europe, including the Jews of Kamyanets Podilskyy, I. Goldman initiated the establishment of "The Organization of Expatriates of Kamyanets Podilskyy and its Surroundings" and devoted much of his energy and time to it.

Y. A. Bar-Levi (Weisman)

Zalman Porat (Pretkin)

A native of Pryluky in Ukraine. He arrived in our city at an advanced age on the eve of the Russian Revolution of 1917 and immediately entered into public-Zionist action as a member of "Tse'irei Tsiyon." His talents and his ways with people immediately placed him in the front ranks of the movement. With the outbreak of the revolution and the change of regimes, he was included with the other members in a big fight, both with the authorities and with our opponents in the Jewish street.

Gifted with a talent for acquiring languages and for building relationships with people, he was nominated by our friends and those close to us from the other parties in the city at the head of the Jewish community during the time of the Ukrainian government and the Jewish Ministry led by Minister Pinchas Krasny; he excelled in his ability to organize and in his accuracy in managing affairs. He was among the initiators of the creation of the first consumer cooperative in our place and was the head of its management.

When the Bolsheviks entered Kamyanets Podilskyy for the second time in 1920, he was forced, like the rest of our friends, to leave the city and cross the border into Romania. There, too, he quickly found his place in the Zionist work in Kishinev (=Chisinau) and for many years was active on behalf of the national committee of Keren Ha-Yesod throughout Bessarabia and Romania. He soon acquired the Romanian language, which allowed him to work for Keren Ha-Yesod among the Jews of Romania. In Kishinev (=Chisinau), he wrote in the Jewish press and was one of the participants in the "Unser Zeit" newspaper.

Twenty-five years ago, he immigrated to Israel and started working at the supervisory union for the agricultural cooperative next to the agricultural center and he continued in this job until the day he died.

Y. A. W–n

[Page 93]

Balin
(Balin, Ukraine)
48°52' 26°41'

A town in the district of Kamyanets Podilskyy, 15 kilometers away. The Jewish community there counted about one hundred families, which supported itself principally through small trade and crafts.

In the town, there was a synagogue, "Cheders" of the old type, an "Improved Cheder" and also a Zionist organization and a "Linat Zedek" group.

After the First World War, five of the townspeople immigrated to Israel.

\

[Page 94]Blank[Page95]

The Hero in My Town

by A. Ashman

Translated by Monica Devens

My small hometown - fifty-sixty houses among dozens of Ukrainian villages on their fields and their gardens and their forests - what will I mention about you?

You didn't have great men - many great scholars, famous rabbis, cantors whose names were known. Famous artists did not emerge from you; the routine life of a small congregation in the Pale of Settlement flowed through you; Jews, simple "Amcha," engaged in small trade, in poor shops. And your craftsmen - tailors and cobblers - made a living sewing furs and boots for the peasants in the area. Weddings and the visits of the Hasidic "rebbes" were the only events that breathed life and sent waves of awakening and enthusiasm.

However, one exceptional, rare, and extreme thing was found in the town of Balin. Something that had no precedent in other towns and cities in the vicinity and perhaps not only in this vicinity: Balin was blessed to have a Jewish hero live there, a wonderful hero who seemed to be a direct continuation of a chain of legendary ancient heroes and whose image captivates from remote generations.

I will tell, therefore, what is stored in my memory of the character and misdeeds of this hero and may these matters please be a headstone for the grave of my town - a small community that perished in the flood of blood and destruction.

Israel Nettes was his name (his father's name was, apparently, "Nette" or "Natan"), his height was a little below average, broad shoulders, solid, muscular, well-shaped, light, and flexible. His facial expression was intense, alert, but his eyes were full of mischief and laughter. He had five or six children and he lived in the back of the town in a house rented from an old non-Jewish woman - a scion of a privileged Polish family that had declined. This house was different from all the houses in the town as it had a spacious yard surrounded by a fence of boards standing next to each other vertically, many of them leaning diagonally, black and rotten. In the yard, there were a few fruit trees, a large stable - a low and dilapidated wooden hut - and a deep well whose source was dry.

Israel's occupation was not fixed and, from time to time, he tried his hand at different livelihoods. He was a tailor, then a hatter, and finally - during the period when I left my childhood and gave my opinion about him - a grain merchant. In those years, the years of the first decade of the twentieth century, many of the townspeople in Podolia were drawn to the grain trade: they would wander through the surrounding villages in light carts, drawn by one horse or two, and buy from the farmers the harvest of their land.

Israel Nettes made a partnership with Shmuel the ragman and they became merchants. Their flimsy cart resembled a large poultry cage with wheels attached to it and their pair of horses were called "retarded cats" by the townspeople. Israel himself, who was a witty "joker" and whose thought was always amusing, would say

[Page 96]

that at the incline of the mountain, he and his partner Shmuel would load the horses on the cart and push it up until they reached the slope.

They would tell of a miracle in the town, how Israel Nettes managed to save himself and his partner from robbers who had a regular resting place in the large forest of the village of "Tskiva (=Snitivka)" and terrorized the surrounding villages. Armed with axes, those robbers once chased after the two merchants who were traveling in their cart. It was on a summer day in the twilight after sunset. The "cats" harnessed to the cart could not save their owners and the distance between the pursuers and the pursued kept shrinking. So Israel stopped the horses, stood in the cart in a firm stance, and pulled out of his pants pocket the hand scales that weigh light packages. He pointed the tool with a vigorous movement towards the pursuers: "Go away, and no - I shoot! one, two …"

In the gloom of the twilight, the copper of the number board glistened and the hook on which the weighed package was hung was tilted forward… Before Israel counted "three," the robbers jumped into the bushes and disappeared into the thick of the forest.

Israel was full of vitality and antics. At Simchat Torah and welcoming the "Rebbe" - he was at the head of those who were happy and making others happy, dancing and singing tirelessly and sweeping the entire crowd after him. He was involved with the young people of the town who liked him because of his stories. Israel used to narrate with rare talent about his adventures in travels and wanderings, exaggerating and tying incident to incident and incident within incident, fascinating his listeners and bringing them sometimes to laughter and sometimes to gaping mouths and widening eyes from so much tension - and in the end, when he reached the peak of intrigue and life-threatening danger, he would finish: "And of course I would not have remained alive, were it not that the whole tale was one big lie from beginning to end …"

Twice Israel saved the entire town from holocaust and destruction. The first time occurred during the period of disturbances after the Russian war of 1905. A number of disturbances had already passed over many communities in the Pale of Settlement and now unrest had also begun in the vicinity of the town of Balin. One day - it was market day - the town was flooded with an unusual amount of farmers from the surrounding villages who came in their carts - they, their wives, their sons and daughters. An ominous sign was evident in the fact that they brought almost nothing with them to sell - the carts were full of empty sacks intended to receive the loot … They wandered through the shops, harassed the shopkeepers, and any other Jew they encountered. Then they appeared in the middle of the market on the pile of sacks of one of the tall carts, two or three speakers who incited the audience to get rid of the Zhyds, "the murderers of the Messiah and the bloodsuckers of poor and innocent farmers"… The crowd became heated and burst into shouts of rage in a moment and the evil began.

At that moment Israelik, Israel Nettes, jumped on the orators' wagon. He waved his hand and called aloud: "Listen to me, farmers, respectable proprietors!"

The sight of the only Jew who dared to appear in the heart of the roaring crowd (all the Jews of the town were already hidden in their locked houses) astonished the farmers and they quieted.

Israel continued: "Look, I am the only Jew standing here among you. You have it in your power - of course - to eliminate me in an instant and also to destroy the entire town. Those who are locked inside their homes -

[Page 97]

old men, women and children - will not stand against you. But where are the young men, every good young man, who are strong? - they are not in the town, they were already ready for this hour of turmoil. They are now spread out in the surrounding villages, lurking in hiding places next to your houses, your granaries, your barns… each of them is equipped with something full of kerosene and worn, dry rags. As soon as the cry of the robbed town is raised, the fire will take hold in your villages, the flames will spread from house to house, from granary to granary, from barn to barn, and when you return with the spoils, you will find in front of you only smoky wood. And now - the choice is yours! Do as you wish!"

He jumped from the cart and disappeared before the crowd awoke from its astonishment. And when they awoke - they were all gripped by the spirit of escape, a stampede. The whips lashed the horses' backs, the carts rattled, pushed each other out of an excess of haste, tangled with each other, and were left to the sides amid the sounds of swearing. The market emptied out and the town was saved.

A second act of rescue was carried out by Israel several years later and this time he proved not only the courage of his spirit, but also the ease of his arm. I was already an adult at the time and the event remains etched in my memory in all its details. To a certain extent, I even participated in it, although - like other young people like me - only passive participation.

It was a late winter Saturday. The snow was still falling in a thick layer and the sky was low, full of dark gray clouds, the air was humid. It was in the afternoon, the time of the Shabbat nap.

At that hour, a large convoy of sledges, loaded with quarry stones, appeared in the town. A sugar factory was then being built in the village of "Makovo" and the stones for the building were supplied by the quarry in the village of "Zalenchi"; the road between the two villages passed by the outskirts of the town of Balin. For some reason this time, the peasants, the stone carriers, parked inside the town itself and the large caravan of forty sledges stretched from the entrance of the town to its end. The peasants - tall, muscular men - tied the bags of fodder to the necks of their horses and some of them started knocking on the shutters of the closed shops; they demanded to sell them smoking tobacco, matches, edibles - and when they didn't respond, they knocked over a shutter here and a shutter there with a shout and sent their hand in looting. A wild debauchery immediately broke out among the rest of the group and from the houses that had been broken into were sent screams of fear.

I was then with my elder brother, Yirmiyahu, in Uncle Fischel's house. At the sound of the shouts, we dashed outside and at the sight of the rampaging gentiles, we immediately ran to Israel Nettes. He lay down on the wide oven cornice - a typical oven for gentile homes in Ukraine - and slept peacefully.

- Goyim are rioting in the town! - we shouted.

He shook off the fur he was covered with and quickly jumped on top of the oven. He didn't wear his outer clothes, just put on a light winter coat, put the fur hat on his head, and took out some object from the desk drawer with his back turned towards us. We did not see what this object was even when he turned towards us because the hand holding it was pulled inside the sleeve. (Later it turned out that it was the riveted iron plate that is worn on the palm.) He ran to the center of the town, we lagged behind him. We saw in the distance that he stopped by Moshe Tabachnik's kiosk and the peasants immediately surrounded him in a tight ring and started

[Page 98]

to beat him with the gun butts that were in their hands. It was as if he sank and was swallowed up in the dense crowds, but suddenly the ring broke, the peasants recoiled to the sides wailing and screaming and began to run away, with their faces and skulls dripping blood. Now the doors on both sides of the street opened and people who were encouraged stood in the doorways and threw wood chips at the fleeing goyim, taken from the stockpile of wood used for heating in the winter.

- Idiots! - Israel rebuked them - Do not throw pieces of wood! Do you want to give the goyim better weapons than the whips in their hands?

He stood bareheaded (the fur hat had disappeared), his face and scalp scribbled with red stripes, swollen, from the blows of the whips, but he was in a good mood.

- I'm not asking you for any help - he said with a laugh - only that you run fast after the escapees and cover up the blood that was spilled on the snow.

Large and dense blood stains reddened in the snow by the kiosk, the place of the skirmish, and along the escape route. We ran and obliterated them by rubbing with the soles of our shoes and by piling fresh snow from the sides.

- And now, untie the horses from the sleds and bring them into my courtyard, - Israel commanded - I will not return the horses until they return my fur hat, one of them knocked it off my head during the commotion.

This order was also carried out immediately. Israel's courtyard filled with horses, the abandoned sleighs stood outside, and the defeated wagoneers gathered near the "cloister," the Christian house of worship located some distance from the town. They dressed their wounds and held a council until the evening. In the evening, a delegation came from them to Israel, asked for pardon and forgiveness, and returned the hat. Israel returned the horses to them and, after a sip of reconciliation at the expense of the coachmen, the caravan set off on its way.

A few years later, Israel emigrated with his family to his relatives in London and nothing has been heard of him since. I heard that one of his sons visited Israel after the establishment of the state and met with one of the Balin expatriates who are here. He said that his father was no longer alive, but I don't know if he died before World War II or after the war or perished during the "Blitz" on London.

Please let his memory be - a memorial candle for all of the small town that sheltered in his shadow until the terrible shadow came, the shadow of the complete extinction from which there was no escape again.

[Page 99]

Personalities

Aharon Ashman

by A. Rosen

Translated by Monica Devens

Born in 1896. He received a traditional education with a secondary educational level and attended lectures in philology at the University of Kamyanets Podilskyy. In this city, he taught Hebrew for several years, participated in varied cultural work, and for two years (1919-1920) he even served as the president of the Jewish community within it. He was also active in the Jewish self-defense organization and went with a company of fighters to the battle in the nearby town of Orynyn against the Petliura army, which was about to invade Kamyanets Podilskyy.

In 1921, Ashman immigrated to Israel and, in addition to his work in teaching, devoted himself a lot to literary creation. He wrote stories and songs, translated about thirty operas and oratorios for the musical stages in Israel, and became especially famous as the author of original plays on Biblical themes and on the Israeli way of life from the beginning of the agricultural settlement in Israel to the present day.

In his plays, Ashman revealed the talent and natural sense of a talented playwright who stays as far away from external effects as possible and strives towards discovering the intricacies of the human soul. The plays, ten in number, were presented with great success by "Ha-Matate," "Ha-Ohel," and "Habima" (this last presented "Michal Bat Shaul"), among them also at the International Theater Festival in Paris and by troupes of amateur and professional actors in various places in Israel and abroad (the United States, France, Canada, Argentina, and others). Two of the plays, "This Land" and the trilogy "Michal Bat Shaul," won the Keren Govinska Prize and the Zemach Prize by means of the "Habima" theater.

In addition to operas and operettas, Ashman translated several plays from foreign languages into Hebrew and dramatized "The Travels of Benjamin III" by Mendele Mocher Sefarim and "Menachem Mendel the Dreamer" by Shalom Aleichem. He also authored textbooks and anthologies, and these several years he serves as the chairman of the Association of Composers and Authors (ACUM) in Israel and devotes much of his time and energy to the protection of creator's rights ("copyright").

[Page 100]Blank[Page 101]

Dunavitz
(Dunayivtsi, Ukraine)
48°54' 26°50'

In Russian: Dunayivtsi, a town on the Tarnov River, 32 versts away from the county town, Nova-Ushytsya, and about 30 versts from the regional city of Kamyanets Podilskyy. During the rule of the Poles, in 1765, the town had a Jewish settlement of 1,129 people and in the immediate vicinity another 1,598. After the Heidemak attacks, the number of Jews in the area decreased and in 1775 it reached 884 in the town and 849 in the area. In 1784, the number rose again and reached 748 in the town and 1,221 in the surrounding area. About 3 years later, one must note, the number dropped again: 568 in the town and 1,133 in the surrounding area.

With the annexation of Podolia to the Russian Empire after the division of Poland and as a result of the settlement of Germans in the town and in the surrounding area, a period of development and prosperity began. The general number of residents reached 11,000 and the number of Jews also rose. At the beginning of the twentieth century, there were textile factories, a place for dyeing cloth, a flour mill, two hospitals and general schools. In the area, there were many fruit gardens and a well-developed branch raising sheep.

[Page 102]Blank{page103]

Dunavitz[a]

by Avraham Rosen

Translated by Monica Devens

A

The city of Dunavitz (in the national language: Dunajewzi) was located on the slope of one of the flat mountains on the edge of the Carpathians at a distance of 40 kilometers from the regional city of Kamyanets Podilskyy and belonged to the jurisdiction of the district city of Nova-Ushytsya. It was divided into two: the old city and the new city. The latter stretched on both sides of the main road, which was an important transportation artery between the district city of Proskorov (= Khmelnytskyi) and Kamyanets Podilskyy, and was connected to the old city by a long street, the "Main Street," which ran along the entire city and closed it off from end to end.

The old city included two large markets (the shop market and the cattle market), Butcher Street, Tailor Street, Synagogue Street, and several other streets and alleys. In the shop market were concentrated most of the wholesale and retail stores for food, for haberdashery, for manufacturing, for clothing and footwear, for household appliances and building materials, for furniture and more. In its center stood about 40 wooden huts, in which there were small shops for selling sewing notions, agricultural tools, foodstuffs, tobacco and more. For the most part, these huts were equipped with shutters that opened outward and some of the goods were placed on them for display. Behind the huts were located the Christian pork butchers who came there every day in their carts and sold their merchandise from there. On the days of the "fairs" (usually every Tuesday), the market-shops were filled with a lot of farmers who came from the surrounding area and brought in their carts the crops of their land for sale and bought the supplies they needed in return. In front of the huts, on a spacious lot, dozens of peddlers' and craftsmen's counters (tinsmiths, glaziers) crowded together, and the gentile women from the suburbs and nearby villages put on the ground for themselves the farm products they brought for sale: fruits, vegetables, dairy products, and the like. Not far from them were spread out the tent stores of the Katsafs who came from the interior of Russia and sold mainly "icons" and other Christian religious objects.

The livestock market, also large and spacious, was used to sell rough and fine animals and poultry. Most days of the week it was empty and deserted, but on the day of the "fair" it was crowded with many people and animals.

The houses in the old city were mostly one or two stories and resembled each other in their appearance and exterior structure. Not so the two churches, the Catholic and the Pravoslav, which shone, the first in the center of the shopping market and the second up the main street, and stood out for their size and their special architectural form. An ancient building with three floors and an arched passage, which stood on the border between the two

[Page 104]

markets and served as a kind of common house for many tenants, was also unusual in this sense. The Gentiles called the house "Ratosh" (council house, which apparently was used formerly for this purpose), while the Jews called it "History"(?).

The inhabitants of the old city, excluding the suburbs within its borders, were mostly Jews, with the exception of a few hundred gentiles, Poles and Ukrainians, who made a living in the city and lived at its edges.

The new city excelled with its straight and clean streets, with its beautiful houses sunken in the greenery of gardens of ornamentation and fruit, and all of it, with the exception of a large market with a Protestant church and a large German school in its center, was also a beautiful public garden, which the Germans, most of the inhabitants of this part of the city and its founders, planted and set aside for their own use only. Indeed, the main importance of the new city was in its industrial establishments: about 50 textile factories that employed and supported, either directly or indirectly, a large part of its residents.

At the beginning of the nineteenth century, after Alexander I, the king of Russia, made a "holy alliance" with Austria and Prussia, many Germans immigrated to Russia and developed various industries there. According to what the elders of the city said, several families of these immigrants, weavers by profession, arrived in Dunavitz with their wives and children transported in carts drawn by dogs. They brought with them hand-operated looms, opened small workshops, and began primitive textile production. Over time, they brought steam-powered machines, established large factories, and turned the remote town at the edge of Podolia, which until then had barely made a living from handicrafts and small trade, into a place of important textile industry, the only one in all of Ukraine, competing with the production of the large industrial cities of Lodz and Bialystok.

During the First World War, the government expelled most of the Germans from the city, who were foreign nationals, to the interior of the country, from the machines of the factories it cast cannons and bullets and turned their buildings into barracks. This is how it destroyed the "Dunavitz textiles" industry by itself, which had served them to a considerable extent to clothe the army and whose lack was most felt during the war. Of course, this also had a negative effect on the economic situation of the entire city and led to considerable depletion.

B

The number of residents in Dunavitz was estimated at 15,000, of which about 10,000 were Jews and the rest Ukrainians, Poles, and Germans. According to what is recorded in the district archives, there were 1,129 Jews in the city in 1765, besides the Jews of the surrounding villages, who also belonged to the Dunavitz community. In the days of Bohdan Khmelnytsky when the Cossacks attacked the Jewish communities and carried out brutal pogroms there (decrees of 1648 and 1649), and after the massacre they carried out in Uman in 1768, many of the city's residents fled and only 484 people remained. Over time, their number increased and, according to a census conducted before 1900, there were 5,000 Jewish families in the city, including 800 artisans, 200 shopkeepers, 296 grain merchants, 200 textile merchants, and the rest small peddlers and merchants.

As mentioned above, the industry, which was founded in the city, changed its economic system. Many of the Jews became close to the German industrialists, learned their trade from them, and worked in their factories as weavers, dyers, shearers (cutters of the wool from the hides), mechanics and more. They also served as clerks and suppliers who brought them the wool and other raw materials from the primary sources, such as Bessarabia, Crimea,

[Page 105]

Caucasus, and even Australia. Agile agents and merchants also arose who distributed the textiles all over Russia and found extensive markets for them. Over time, several Jewish factories were also established and a large part of the inhabitants of the old city actually participated in the development of the industry and lived off of it.

Besides those engaged in the industry, there were in the city various craftsmen and artisans (tailors, shoemakers, furriers, hatters, carpenters, blacksmiths, tinsmiths, goldsmiths, watchmakers, and others), merchants (mainly grain merchants for export), shopkeepers, clerks, pimps, moneylenders, and more. Compared to the other surrounding cities, the economic situation of Dunavitz was quite good and established and left its mark in all areas of life in the city.

C

As is known, Podolia was the cradle of Hasidism and the place of its first growth and flowering. Of course, this popular movement struck deep roots in Dunavitz as well and in the early days even made it an important center for it. In "The Book of Argument" of Rabbi Yisrael Leibel and in the anthology of documents, "Criminal Fracture," from the period between

From views of the city (A)

1798 and 1800, the names of the great righteous men of those days were brought, among them the first, R. Levi Yitzchak of Berdychiv, the second, R. Wolf of Zhitomir, and the third, R. Isaiah of Dunavitz. In his book "Or Torah" ("Torah Clues"), he collected the sayings of the Magid, Dov Ber of Mezeritch. There was also R. Pinchas of Dunavitz, one of the students of R. Yehoshua Heschel of Afteh, and even he published a book of Torah collections called "Siftei Zaddikim."

Over the years, as everywhere else, different Hasidic sects arose in the city, each of which believed only in its own "Tzaddik" and criticized that of others, which led to quarrels and sometimes even hand-to-hand fights. In Dunavitz, there were the Hasidim of Sadigura, Husyatyn, Chortkiv, Zinkiv (these split into the followers of R. Moshe and the followers of R. Pinchas, his brother, and were hostile to one another) and more. The dedication and loyalty of the Dunavitz Hasidim to "their tzaddiks" is evidenced by the following incident:

In 1838, two Jewish whistleblowers ("mosrim") who were bothering the surrounding Jewish communities a lot by reporting on them to the authorities were killed in the district town of Nova-Ushytsya. According to what was told, it was imposed

[Page 106]

upon one of them to be brought alive into the burning furnace of the bath house in Dunavitz and to be burned there. The authorities saw this murder as the work of the nearby communities and delivered community leaders to a military trial. The tzaddik, R. Israel of Ruzhin (Kyiv Region) was also imprisoned as a suspect of incitement to murder and was taken under heavy guard to the trial in Nova-Ushytsya. On the way there, he was brought to spend the night in one of the houses in the courtyard of the Pravoslav church in Dunavitz. What did the Hasidim of the city do? They put on shrouds and lay in ambush behind the tombstones in one of the cemeteries by the road that goes up to Nova-Ushytsya. The next day, when the guard with the prisoner passed near the place, the imaginary dead jumped out of their hiding place, attacked the guards with wild shrieks and screams, until they were frightened, left the prisoner, and fled for their lives. So the tzaddik was brought across the border to Austria, settled in Sadigura, which is in Bukovina, and founded the Sadigurite dynasty.

D

There were three rabbis in Dunavitz and each of them had his own circle of "householders" who seated him on the throne of the rabbinate and took care of his livelihood, even in a very limited way. In order to fill, even if only a little, the shortage of her home, the Rebbetzin would sometimes be forced to try her hand at small household trade, such as selling yeast and the like. Sometimes the rabbis would quarrel with each other over various religious questions and severe quarrels broke out between the people who shared their same ideas. It so happened that due to the matter of the "mikvah," which was found to be illegal in the eyes of one of the rabbis and kosher in the eyes of the other, a great quarrel broke out between the Jewish residents and the whole city was in turmoil for an entire year. Similarly, each rabbi had his own butcher, only his butchery was faithful to the men of the rabbi's flock. Of course, this also caused quite a few divisions and conflicts in the city, in addition to those which came because of Hasidism and its sects.

The affairs of the community were managed by the gabbaim of the synagogues and its budget came from the meat and candle taxes. Besides a large general synagogue, small synagogues for artisans (tailors, cobblers), and "enclaves" for different Hasidim, there were several other public institutions in the city, such as: "Talmud Torah" for poor children, a shelter for the poor ("Hekdesh"), a bath house, "Bikur Cholim," "Chevra Kadisha," Chevra for Shas, a psalm reciting group, and a volunteer fire brigade company. The last was founded about sixty years ago after a big fire that broke out in the city and burned about 20 houses. With the funds received from the municipality and with various donations, the city purchased the necessary equipment and also built a large house in the city center with warehouses for the various fire fighting equipment and a large and spacious hall for meetings, lectures, plays, and the like.

E

The trade in the textiles of the local industry ("Dunavitz textiles") brought those involved in it, the merchants and the traveling salesmen of all kinds, in close contact with the wider world and was an important factor in the spread of education in the city and in its cultural progress. There arose, in addition to the teachers and the "Cheders" of the old type, expert teachers of Tanakh, of Hebrew and its grammar, of the state language, and of general studies. Many of the children of the affluent and wealthy were even able to be accepted as students in the government high schools in nearby Kamyanets Podilskyy and to finish their studies there or be examined as externs.

When the Zionist movement began to spread among the Jews of Russia, Dunavitz claimed a prominent place. The best of the educated in it, led by those who later became known as long-time Zionist leaders: Yosef Blank,

[Page 107]

Elia Rubinstein (both dealers in "Dunavitz textiles"), Mordechai Rosen (writes articles in "Ha-Melitz," "Ha-Tsfira," and "Ha-Shilo'ah" and afterwards also in "Ha-Doar" in the United States). And many others founded the first Zionist association in the city of "Dorshei-Tsiyon" and developed many activities of great initiative and scope in all areas of the national revival. Information and Zionist propaganda were advanced, members were acquired for the Zionist Federation by selling membership certificates, donations were collected for the benefit of the settlement of Eretz Yisrael by the Hovevei Zion committee in Odesa, and quite a few shares of the "The Treasury of Jewish Settlement" were even sold. During the days of the Zionist congresses, the association would send a delegation and the account that it gave later in public brought the hearts of the residents even closer to the Zionist idea.

Education in the city was also given a distinctly Zionist-nationalist character. At the initiative of "Dorshei-Tsiyon," a Hebrew school (the first in the city) was founded, whose curriculum included both Hebrew and general studies.

The influence of the Zionists grew, especially on the younger generation. A Zionist youth emerged imbued with a deep national consciousness, who saw their main role in reviving their people, their country, and their language. The "spiritual Zionism" of Ahad Ha'am also gained many supporters among them and the association of young Zionists, "Ha-Techiya," headed by its founder's son, Rabbi Avraham Lerner (immigrated to Israel and died there during the First World War), advocated this method. Between the two associations, it is true, for a while there was a spirit of rivalry and bickering to a certain extent, but this only added energy and activity to both. Over time, several public and private schools for boys and girls were founded by the young Zionist businessmen, and the renewed Hebrew language (including speaking Hebrew) was the property of many. Hundreds of young people were diligent about reading the new Hebrew literature and the Hebrew newspapers of that time, "Ha-Melitz," "Ha-Tsfira," "Ha-Zman," "Ha-Tsofe" and more, acquired many subscribers and readers among them. The monthly "Ha-Shilo'ah" had 35 subscribers in Dunavitz, which, according to its editor, Dr. Yosef Klausner, there was not as many as this number in any other city in all of Russia, except perhaps for Odesa (the city where the monthly was published) itself. Of course, the number of readers of "Ha-Shilo'ah" far exceeded that of its subscribers.

The organization "Pirchei Tsiyon," founded in 1908

[Page 108]

In 1903, a large Zionist conference was held in Dunavitz and among the lecturers at it was the authorized member of the Zionist Federation, Menachem Sheinkin. The conference, held in a large hall and with a large audience, made a great impression on its participants and the name of the city became known as an important Zionist point.

Indeed, the nationalist-Zionist education, which opened the gates of its institutions to all strata of the people (there were also "Shabbat classes" for studying the weekly Torah for artisans out of a nationalistic-free viewpoint), brought a lot of praise. Over time, the city raised a whole generation of Jews of national standing who embraced the idea of redemption, including the writers: Dr. Yehezkel Koifman (author of "Gola ve-Nechar" and "Toldot Ha-Emunah Ha-Yisraelit"), Prof. Zvi Sharfstein (writer and educator), S. L. Blank (novelist), M. Michaeli (author for children and educator), L. Y. Riklis (writer and educator) and more.

Apart from the Zionist organizations, there were almost no other parties in the city. The "Po'alei Tsiyon" organization was called by this name only because its members were craftsmen without any connection or affiliation to the world party known by this name.

F

Neighborly relations between the city's Jews and the rest of its citizens were reasonably normal until the First World War. In particular, the closeness that arose over the years between the Jews and the German industrialists on the occasion of their trade connections should be noted. Many of the latter even adopted Yiddish and there were also among them those who knew how to write commercial notes in this language.

In 1903, after the pogroms in Kishinev, an anti-Semitic agitation was felt in the vicinity of Dunavitz and the firemen, most of them young men, ruffians and courageous, took the defense of the city upon themselves. And here at one of the "fairs," when all the markets of the city were filled with lots of carts and peasants from the surrounding area, a fight broke out in one of the Jewish taverns between drunken Katsafs from the road construction workers there, and the voice came out as if they were shouting: "Beat the Jews!" (a known password for pogroms). Immediately the firemen's alarm was heard and they appeared on the spot with their equipment and their ears and showed their strength. A commotion and confusion arose, and the peasants were very frightened at the sight of the heroes wearing uniforms and copper helmets and they fled from the city. A legal complaint was later filed on the part of the authorities against the fire chief for the occurrence, but he was acquitted and the city returned to peace.

G

With the First World War, there was a change for the worse in the city's situation. The destruction of its industry by the military authorities (see section A), a wave of pogroms during the days of Petliura, which passed through several of the Jewish communities in Ukraine and did not skip that of Dunavitz, as well as the frequent regime changes from 1917 onwards - all these caused the diminution of both its material and spiritual strength. Many of its Jewish residents, especially the younger generation, left and immigrated to different countries, a significant part of them immigrated to Israel to share in building it. Nevertheless, the Jewish community of Dunavitz continued to exist, albeit in a poor way, until the Second World War came and brought the Nazi oppressor upon it as well. After several difficult edicts,

[Page 109]

there came brutal abuses and mass incarceration in the ghetto, as in the other cities and towns in the Ukraine, the "Final Solution": some of the Jews of Dunavitz were shot and buried in one of its central markets, and most of them were executed outside the city and buried there in one large mass grave.

Thus was destroyed the Jewish community of Dunavitz, a prominent city in Israel, known for praise, both for its past in the field of the nation's tradition and for its actions towards its future.

Original footnote:

    a.   With the kind permission of "Yad va-Shem," the memorial authority of the Holocaust and heroism.

My Native City[a]

by Zvi Scharfstein

Translated by Monica Devens

Our town was not busy, but life and movement flowed through it. There were a large number of people coming to buy or sell and a large number of people going out for business purposes. The one walking down the street - generally he has a goal and a purpose. In the town, there was also a stratum of affluent people who were not so careful with their pennies and their clothes were nice and their table was full and rich. The Jews of our city had additional sources of income beyond the usual sources in the Pale of Settlement. They supplied the German manufacturers with wool from Bessarabia, from Crimea, from the Caucasus, and even from abroad, from far away Australia. The plant fibers, jute, were brought from Nizhny-Novgorod and the dyes from Lithuania and Germany. At the railway station in Proskorov (= Khmelnytskyi), we loaded heavy freight cars and transported them by horses to our town. And the Jewish citizens of our city were also the traveling agents who passed through all the cities of Russia, far and wide, from city to city and region to region, to sell the product, either at the expense of the factory or at their own expense. Our agents also reached the interior regions of Russia and even cold Siberia. A guest who came to our city was recognized as a stranger, but no one was surprised by him and the stranger did not serve as a wall for conversation and they did not wait to hear from him unknown secrets.

The negotiations with the cities of the great country broadened the horizons of the educated people of our city and brought them to generosity and to activity. The citizens of our city were not so strict and precise in their zealousness and they were not killed for every old custom. The merchants and agents would wear semi-modern and modern clothes, hard and soft hats on their heads according to the fashion, use pince-nez spectacles with black ribbons, silk ribbons, hanging down to connect with the clothing. They read daily and weekly newspapers, mostly Hebrew and sometimes Russian, and knew what was going on in the world. During their travels, they would meet with the leaders of Judaism and its wheeler-dealers in Russia and talk with them. Therefore, our travelers and merchants were influenced by the movements and social currents that prevailed in our world at that time and, on their return, they would bring new ideas and preach to them. None of the young people in our town was forced to fight for an education, whether Hebrew or general - because it did not occur to anyone to interfere and to prevent, and the reader of Mapu and Smolenskin did not do his reading in secret and did not go up to the attic for that purpose. Newspapers and books were available and the parents also look favorably on them. Even the rabbi of the city, whose two sons were among the educated, did not prevent his sons from reading

[Page 110]

in the new literature and no one protested to the rabbi about letting his sons go to "bad culture." We had teachers for Hebrew studies and also teachers for general studies who would prepare the youth to pass the Gymnasium exam. There was hardly a young man in our city from a good family and learned in Torah who has not read the new Hebrew literature. A guy with large sidelocks and dressed in long clothes was "not to be seen." When Zionism spread in Russia, our town was the center for the whole area and voiced its opinion in the newspapers in due course and at times of disagreements and gained a reputation, and the leaders of the movement presented it as an example until it was considered to be the Jerusalem of Podolia.

In a part of the "new city" that was in our city, there was a special neighborhood, somewhat remote and isolated, where the factories and residences of their German owners were built. The houses on both sides of the road were the residences of the Russian clerks and of rich and affluent Jews, and in the "old city" there was the market, the tents of "Amcha" and their dwellings, mostly shopkeepers, grain merchants, craftsmen, and agents. Only a few of the rich and affluent lived in the old city.

In the German colony were the factories and residences of their owners and managers and clerks. This neighborhood excelled in splendor - in those days. The houses were not large, most of them one story, but their construction was solid and they shone with their whitewash and were sunk in the greenery of ornamental and fruit trees. In general, the complacency of well-informed and confident people was felt in that neighborhood. The buildings were separate, building by building by itself, with its yard and lot, with its beautiful roof and with the wide relaxing benches and with its fence and colorful flowers. From the glass

From views of the city (B)

of the polished windows, transparent curtains could be seen. A pleasant stillness. If you happened to come there in the evening, after work in the factories had stopped, the silence enveloped you. Sometimes the sounds of a piano could be heard from one of the houses. Sometimes a guy or a girl was seen riding a bicycle - a vehicle that was not found among the rest of the residents.

As I strolled through those quiet streets, I brought to my mind the sight of the "old city" with its houses

[Page 111]

crowded together, leaning against each other, with their crooked walls and looking like they might fall, I compared before my eyes its narrow and polluted alleys, I remembered the great outcropping of dusty ground.

And not just the external purity. The life of the German community was organized and orderly.

They had a public garden where they gathered on their holidays and on summer nights to enjoy their time over rich food and a glass of beer talking, singing, and dancing. In our childhood days, we would stand outside the fence during such celebrations and watch what was going on with somewhat astonished faces. We saw robust and healthy men sitting with their wives, with broad shoulders and bulging breasts, in front of large and heavy tables, tables made of oak, eating fat sausages and drinking beer from large clay pitchers with moderation and deliberateness, and singing and enjoying the pleasures of the world. Who is the Jewish family man who will get up one evening and forget his worries and sit his wife to his right and they will drink beer or wine and open their mouths in song?

The Jewish community, large in number, had almost no public buildings, except for synagogues and various Beit Midrash - and even these were somewhat neglected and did not excel in splendor. Although there were quite a few educated people in our town, among them distinguished merchants who were members of the community, they did not have much influence on the administration of the community. Most of the townspeople - their public awareness was dormant. Who were the official community leaders? - These were the gabbaim of the prayer houses, diaspora Jews who lacked independence and had provincial ideas, without imagination, without courage. The community of Israel had a considerable income from the meat tax - and it was partly wasted and partly remained in the government treasury without use. Every year the gabbaim were called to a meeting to consult on the needs of the city and the meetings were in the presence of the chief of police. Then the gabbaim remembered poor needs: the roof of the prayer house that was leaking and in need of repair, the fence of the Beit Midrash that was broken, and the walls of the Beit Midrash that were prone to fall and required the support of girders, and the like. The sums allotted for the inspection of the houses were small, so the chief of police came and proposed to allocate large sums for general needs that did not fall within the scope of the concern of the Jewish community, such as for paving roads, for the construction of latrines in the open areas, and the like, and the real needs of the community, such as the education of the children of the poor and the treatment of poor patients - they paid no attention. The rabbis of the city, for example - and their number at my time was three - made a living with great difficulty from meager salaries and were in need of side incomes of low value and great shame, such as from the sale of yeast and from gifts from homeowners for holidays and festivals such as Hanukkah and Purim. Charitable institutions were at the bottom of the ladder. In the Talmud Torah for the children of the poor there was disorder and in the "charity hospital" the sick lay in neglect without good nutrition and without medical treatment. And the gabbaim who for the most part did not speak Russian properly and it was difficult for them to express their thoughts in the language of the state - sat in front of the clerk almost trembling, nodding their heads and not daring to oppose his suggestions.

But little by little, with the infiltration of the national idea, social awareness arose and criticisms were heard about the gabbaim and the community leaders who were neglecting the charitable institutions.

One of the signs of awakening in my town was the founding of the "volunteer fire company."

The firemen's association in the German neighborhood had complete equipment, organized wagons and ladders and large rubber hoses and huge water barrels and axes and explosive devices. The firefighters were experts in fighting fire because from time to time they were given firefighting training. Wearing their uniforms and putting on their heads their copper hats

[Page 112]

and throwing the great jets of water - the terror subsided. But when a fire broke out in the Jewish streets and the bells of the prayer houses rang and alerted the townspeople - the German firemen would sit down considering as to whether it was worth it to them to go and they waited for the messengers and those who begged them to come and rescue them, and when they were so kind as to come out of the fire station and took their equipment with them - and arrived at the scene of the fire - they would do their work unhurriedly and with extreme restraint, as those enjoying the loss of the Jews' property. The residents of the town saw this and complained about the evil - but no one listened. Then the young people of Israel woke up, led by a young fighter and dreamer, Haim Hirsch Wissotzky, and founded a new firemen's association, in which there were strong young men, the sons of butchers and tailors and cobblers, strong-muscled and well-versed in work. They added some of the Ukrainian young men and, with the municipality's money, they built a large and spacious firehouse, bought all the equipment, and began to practice firefighting. From then on, the Jews were freed from the "kindness" of the Germans. And in the municipal fire station there was a large and spacious hall available for public meetings and celebrations, and the Jewish doctor, Dr. Marmor, tried and did allocate three thousand rubles a year from the meat tax money for the upkeep of the station and for the other needs of the association.

The foundation of the association was the first signal for the improvement of public affairs in the city. Then the Zionists, especially the younger ones, began to pay attention to the reform of education - and improved it. But this is a special case, a cautionary case in the history of the town.

Apart from the merchants and agents who were engaged in supplying the raw materials to the factories and distributing the textiles in the cities of the country - the rest of the townspeople were mainly engaged in trade and crafts, and the trade - was mostly insignificant. Except for twenty or twenty-five large or medium-sized stores, the rest of the stores were very poor, very small (four by four), and some were found in wooden huts that they put in the market place. The capital invested in these stores was very small - two or three hundred rubles, and even this was not the shopkeeper's property, but rather goods acquired on credit. The rest of the merchants were kind of peddlers - keeping their goods in their homes and taking them out in the morning to their territory on shelves in the market and in the evening, putting their goods either in baskets or in sacks and returning to their homes.

On most days of the week, the small shops were almost empty of people and there was a gap of time between customers and the shopkeepers sat idly in front of their shops and neighbors and agents and just idle walkers who were in the streets came up to them to chat about trivial matters and when the conversation flared up and its contents got lost, boredom and yawns would come. This hour of emptiness was fit for gossip, to discuss the state of the townspeople, who rises to greatness in commerce and who approaches bankruptcy, who - negotiates with faith and who - has fraudulent scales, who gets lucky with a decent match and who marries his daughter to a fool or a failure, who is deprived because of miserliness and who squanders more than a fifth on delicacies and sends his wife to abundant happiness and healing, and similar destructive conversations.

Because of the bad economic situation - the number of the poor was large even in our successful town - the competition was enormous and did not breed peace. There used to be about three hundred merchants in our town who would buy field grain from the farmers and sell it at a small margin to wholesalers who would export the wheat, rye, and buckwheat abroad. On market day, the farmer would bring his cart loaded with grains, vegetables, fruits, chickens, geese, swans, and eggs. Rows and rows of carts went by,

[Page 113]

one after the other. The grain merchants would gather at the market and ask the farmer, "What did you bring?" "How much does it cost?" And so on, and the farmer scratches his forehead, considers the matter, and it is difficult for him to come to a decision what to ask for and he does not want to sell until a second and third buyer comes before him and he hears their offers. What did the merchants who were eager to buy do? They outsmarted their competitors and went out of the city to the roads to greet the farmers and to buy their grain from them even before they entered the town. As such the competition began in the greeting of the farmers. Even the competitor went outside the city and went farther than his friend, the third came and went even further, so each tried to get ahead of his friend, and the farmer seeing this great eagerness became suspicious that all these Jews had eyes for his grain only to buy it from him at half the price. And the more the buyer raised his price, the more suspicious the farmer grew, and the more he pondered the Jew's intentions until he drove the buyer out of his sight and went to the market to see what he would get there. And if the merchant managed to buy a sack of rye or other grain on the way, he would load the sack on his shoulder and carry it to the wholesaler and sell it to him at a margin of pennies.

Mostly there were craftsmen in our town - about eight hundred in number - and from all professions. Tailors for men's clothes and tailors for women's clothes, shoemakers and carpenters, furriers, hatters and leather workers, also coopers, tinsmiths, and blacksmiths, house painters and sign painters, watchmakers and goldsmiths, bakers and bagel makers and apple canners - and every craft that had any demand whatsoever. They were artisans, but most of them could not earn the name artisan because they did not know their craft properly. Where did they learn from? There were apprenticeships with craftsmen, but at the beginning of their studies they were enslaved to two masters: the craftsman and his wife: carrying the food basket from the market, sweeping the floor, taking out the chamber pots, and doing other services

[Page 114]

that are important in and of themselves, but do not bring about progress in the craft. Their teachers and instructors were also not of the type of Bezalel ben Uri and their work did not earn the title of "work of art." The demand for beautiful work was not very widespread because they did not value it nor could the majority of those who ordered it pay for it. Only the rich and affluent asked for nice and appropriate clothing and the majority of the community looks down on this and sees no fault in a lack of beauty. The main thing is "the purpose." We don't sew a garment except to cover the nakedness of the body and to warm it when it's cold and we don't make a shoe except to protect the feet from harm, injury, and damage, and what is the problem if the garment is too big? I remember that my father owned a hat workshop and we had one worker, his name was Neta, a guy who depended on his desk and lived in one of our rooms in our house. And this guy was meticulous about his clothes: his robe was white and ironed, and before he went to bed he would straighten his pants and hang them on a hanger so that they wouldn't crease, and when he went out for a walk he would be dressed elegantly - and he would be a subject of laughter. Please see how this guy is adorning himself! And if the pants are wrinkled - what does that mean? Why all this hassle?

Apprentices and artisans were considered the elite of the city. The minority learn the craft of their forefathers and for them the saying is true: "The deeds of fathers are a sign to the sons," however, most of them train in a different craft. For every craftsman felt the suffering of his art and the "distant fields looked green." These apprentices well knew what was in store for them in the future so they would not be able to say, "My legacy was good for me," but they would not hesitate on the question of what "the day would bring." And since they knew that when they went out on their own after marrying a woman, they would taste the taste of poverty, they decided to enjoy life as long as it was in their hands. That's why the sound of happiness and the sound of joy was heard from the workshops, the voice of the apprentices singing holy songs and secular songs, songs of love and songs of ridicule, and telling jokes to each other, and laughter did not stop from their mouths all day long.

Those learning a trade did not hope for greatness, but their path was clear before them. This was not the way of the children of the house owners, the minority would study in the Beit Midrash and study the Talmud and the majority would study "Haskalah" at home, that is: they read the new Hebrew literature and learn the state language and secular knowledge from teachers or they learn by themselves and often go on trips and have bad conversations. Few have prepared for a certain profession, such as to engage in pharmacy or medicine or religion and law, and the majority just study because it is not good for a child from a good family not to study. When the boy reaches puberty, the matchmakers would come and present an "appropriate" match to his parents, and when the matter came to fruition, the father-in-law would set a dowry of several hundred rubles and guarantee maintenance for a year or two, and even more than that, each according to his status, until the newlywed man found his way in life. The groom took the girl as a wife for good luck, handed over the dowry in the hands of a "safe person," and received interest. But the months of serenity or "honeymoon" passed quickly. The father-in-law promised what he promised on the basis of the saying, "Man Di-hiv Chai Yahiv Mazoni" (God who gives life will also give food), and waited for a miracle. The miracle did not happen, the saying was not confirmed. The young couple was a burden on the hard-pressed parents.

In the first days after the wedding, the newlywed groom would curl his clothes and his hair, go to the Beit Midrash, meet with friends and debate with them, and return to his baked bread and his poured glass, and the father-in-law and mother-in-law would treat him with respect and hide their distress from him and not talk about their worries in front of him. But the distress was not hidden in the dishes and the time came for it to be revealed, sooner or later, sighs and complaints about

[Page 115]

the hard times burst from the heart and entered into the heart of the newlywed yeshiva student. The foods that were given to him in abundance at first gradually decreased in quantity and quality and the time came when they stopped being nice to him, gave him a subtle or rough hint that he won't feel good at their expense. So the student was faced with a sharp question, the question of "what to do." The one lost in the ways of life did not know where to turn. The choices were few: to take his money out of the hands of the "secure" and give it to the favored and the small traders at a high interest rate - and lose because who knows if they will succeed at repaying the loan; to partner himself with the merchant who needs money - and lose. All roads would lead to loss. And in the end, he was another one added to the congregation who prayed with conviction: Help the poor, please save!

A number of rich people made a living from interest businesses or mainly from interest. They would lend small sums, from fifty rubles to several hundred, to each person according to their worth, and the borrower undertook to pay the principal at fixed rates every week and to add the interest to it and to complete the payment of the entire debt within a year. Every Friday afternoon, men and women, boys and girls, would flock to the house of the lender to bring him the week's wages. The lender would sit in the courtyard next to his table, count the bills and coins with consideration and with great intent, as one doing the holy service, check and write in his notebook. These rich people who lend at interest reached the level of stinginess on the occasion of their rolling in pennies of interest. Like mice, they would lie on their dinars and some would deprive their souls of goodness. And there was one lender who was admittedly not one of the great rich who brought the degree of avarice to great perfection, and yet was not very successful. His body did not withstand the test and his soul swelled with hunger.

* * *

The relationship between neighbors and acquaintances was good in general. Every day the owners of the houses would meet in the prayer house and the Beit Midrash and spend an hour talking about the issues at hand and tell each other news about the affairs of the city and the world. In the winter, neighbors would enter one another's houses for a chat over a cup of tea. Every Shabbat and festival, relatives and friends visited each other, as well as on Saturday evenings. The Hanukkah holiday was a time for family celebrations. Then the woman would fry pancakes filled with porridge or potatoes, add a little fat to them, bring up the good cherry wine from the cellar, and the neighbors who are called or who come of their own accord, sit at the set table in the well-lit and well-heated dining room and eat and listen to the stories of the tales or the miraculous deeds of the Hasidim, and the soul is lifted and the hearts grow closer and friendship increases.

In those days of my youth, close to 1895, the custom of reading in a group spread. And the reason for this was the popular writer Shalom Aleichem, who brought the light of life and joy of heart to the sad dwellings of Israel. In those days, his monologues and short stories appeared in small pamphlets and were sold very cheaply, a pamphlet for an agora or five kopecks. These small pamphlets were disseminated to many. I remember that these pamphlets came to our store in packages of hundreds and the interested customers fought over them and they were sold in a few days. The pamphlets would be read at house parties and over every joke and conversation and idiom and quarrel between a woman with a tongue and a man with ideas, the company would burst out laughing and the listeners would praise the writer extensively.

* * *

[Page 116]

The regimen of life in our town was fixed and specific. All its inhabitants were enslaved to one tradition. They followed a paved path and held to accepted customs and a fixed practice without many changes. The year was divided into weeks, and the week into days, and the most beloved day was the Sabbath day, a day of pleasure - therefore all of the weekdays were subject to it and subordinate to it. When the woman went out to buy a chicken, even though it was Tuesday of the week, she did not buy the chicken or the goose for the weekday, but for the Sabbath.

The peak of pleasure for the youth on Shabbat was the trek. On Friday night, after the feast, on a moonlit night, the young men and women, even those who choose each other, went out to the road, which is the King's Road, beautifully dressed, each young man with his robe collar shining white and his eye-catching, colorful silk tie and his hair beautifully made and his pince nez on his eyes and his modern hat placed on his head in a foppish way, and every girl - her hair is washed and combed and her black mane shining with a silken luster and a light perfume emanates from her. And the young men and women join in groups of three, four, and five, and walk together and see what is in front of them and meet friends and acquaintances and ask how they're doing and talk pleasantly and with joy of heart. And immediately they move on to words of literature and wisdom. If boys, they will talk about the last poem and the last story and the last article in "Ha-Shilo'ah," and if girls join them, the conversation will turn to Tolstoy and Turgenev and Dostoyevsky, and from them to Gorky and the other new writers who are opening new worlds and new types for their readers. The Friday night trek was second only to the big trek that took place the next day on Saturday in the early evening. So the road was blackened by the quantity of the trekkers. Not only the youth went out then, but also the owners of houses with their wives and every man who had not yet died created life in his soul. Overly worried merchants and shopkeepers, hard-pressed in their livelihood, apprentices in workshops, seamstresses who sit all day bent over their machines and their needles, cooks and maids who hear insults from the mouths of their mistresses - all of these dissolved the cares of their day and the wrinkles on their faces straightened and a cloud of grief rose from their eyes and they walked satisfied and with a feeling of affection and fondness and they felt the pleasure of the world and of life. A boy who came of age and wore an ironed gown and a hard collar and a colorful silk tie for the first time - he would look at the passers-by to see if they thought about him and his clothes and if they knew he was coming to take a place in the company of the adults. A girl who is coming to puberty, washed hair with a long braid and adorned with ribbon and an anxious heart - examines the passers-by with her eyes, the young people, to see who will notice her and give his opinion about her, and every look given to her - will arouse in her pleasant reflections. Young couples after their marriage show everyone the cuteness of their clothes and homeowners who are level-headed - talk about the affairs of the city and the state of commerce. The crowds get closer and closer, rows rise and fall, and elbow reaches elbow, and everyone feels that he is a part of the whole, that the bigger the crowd - the greater the confidence in the heart.

The young people, the members of the new generation, no longer differentiated so much between the holy and the profane. And they no longer believed that all the days of the week were created only to serve the Sabbath day. They seek the pleasures of life whenever they find them. Here comes a new baker and opened a new shop in the new city - a shop of sweet cakes, the likes of which can only be found in the large city, cakes made of layers and layers of chocolate and on top of them a kind of whipped egg yolk and a strawberry or cherry stuck in it. There are young people who come there every evening to eat and enjoy themselves. They do it almost modestly, first because there is extravagance in it and second because who will testify about

[Page 117]

the kashrut of the cakes? They enter at the hour of neither day nor night and from there they set out on the big trek, sometimes young men and maidens together, and they will go far to go outside the city. And the parents will no longer object, they close their eyes and will not see wickedness, if only they observe the condition of going with the daughter of a decent householder, according to his honor and the honor of his family and status. And there is that on a snow day, a frosty day, we, a group of young men and women, will rent a fancy snow cart drawn by brave horses and we will go on a journey of an hour or two on the patch of snow on the King's Road, the cold urging us on and strengthening us, and we are happy and rejoicing from so much joy and joie de vivre.

This is how old and new are used in a mix. The old order still rules and determines life, but a new custom is standing at its door and it creeps inside the house and stakes out its place. There is no great resistance and no outbreak and no rebellion. The young people live in peace with their parents and put on tefillin and pray,

A school for girls that was founded in 1902

and go to the synagogue on the Sabbath and on holidays and observe all the customs of Israel, even a custom that is not of great importance, but is respected in the eyes of women and the simple people, such as the custom of making atonements and the like. Even the young man lifts the rooster that is given to him above his head, turns it around and says, "This rooster will die and I will enter a good life" - and laughs good-naturedly, but does not feel the holy duty that the yeshiva boy felt who went into a bad culture to fight "superstitions." The parents see their sons learning secular studies and reading books of knowledge and shortening their clothes and their sidecurls and sometimes even disobeying a specific law and shaving the corners of their beards and going out for walks with girls, and they don't protest. This is the new time and these are its demands. On the contrary, education is a jewel for the new generation and the Russian language is necessary for life and commerce and the boy who has these - he is a glory to his parents.

* * *

In their physical development, the residents of the city as a whole, and the middle-aged and the very old in particular, were typical diaspora Jewish types: faltering in their gait, thin, stooped, and worn out. And two factors

[Page 118]

were the main points about this: most of them were tent dwellers and shop dwellers, scholars and businessmen, people with crafts that require constant sitting, such as tailors and cobblers - without physical exercise in the fresh air. Sport was "not to be found." As a child - he would compete with his friends in a race, play the game of sticks - to throw a stick at a small twig placed on top of two separate stones from a distance without missing, swim in the river in the summer, and skate on the ice in the winter. But even in those childhood days, the game was a kind of sin, spending time without a "purpose." A respectable Jew when he passed by and saw a child at his games - he would fulfill his duty and observe the mitzvah of "rebuke"; "You are a boy of five years and why do you spend your time in vanities?" And once the boy began to study Gemara - and the beginner was six or seven years old - everyone began to be strict with him and watch over him, and the opinion of the majority influenced the children to be ashamed of this stupid act, and when they succumbed to temptation - they would feel themselves to be sinners, playing and flicking their eyes back and forth lest an older person see them. And as he grew older - so did his seriousness, his awareness of his duty to engage in things of learning and purpose. After the days of marriage came the days of worry: the face was wrinkled, in the depressed mind thoughts run all day long to find a source of livelihood. Under the burden of the poor household economy, the newlywed fell and, in a short time, poverty left its mark on his face and body and made him "a broken Jew."

And yet the youths were well developed. The desire for life worked. A good mother - her eye was watching over her son and daughter that they eat and drink, and pleasant friends sweetened life and introduced games and laughter and sometimes joy. But here came the twentieth year, the year of the crisis, and discriminated against the good-looking, well-educated and healthy-bodied young man. A twenty-one-year-old was obliged to serve in the army - unless he was the only son of his parents or was weak or had a disability and was not successful for war. There were few only sons - in those days people did not ask to know the secret of prevention. Sons were considered a blessing and not a curse and blessed was the mother who had many sons. But they didn't want to be inducted. And this is understandable; they trained in the army for three years - during this time the boys were torn from their parents, from their studies, from their businesses, from their training for life. Why would this young man go to do the work of the Russian army - out of loyalty to the monarchy? Out of feelings of gratitude for the decrees that the Evil Kingdom frequently brought upon Israel? Because of the restrictions that limited their places of residence and their occupations and their visits to schools? And what will the Jewish youth do in the army? He will be found among the sons of Israel-hating peasants who will abuse him and surrender to evil-hearted officials. And even the question of kosher food was not an easy question. To make oneself impure with pork and disgusting foods - both the parents and the sons despised it.

Therefore, the parents and sons looked for ways to get rid of this obligation. And the ways were different: a few months before conscription, the young men who were called to the army would join groups in order "to suffer." They would eat less and when they did eat - they would choose foods that led to diarrhea, sleep less, spend entire nights in the Beit Midrash and friends' houses, without rest, in order to lose weight and reduce body weight. After a few weeks of hardship and self-denial, the face turned pale and resembled that of a dead person, and the young man was skinny and declining in life and swayed in his walk. But if a young man who was weak like that was not released completely and when he was tested, he was given an extension for a year, and after the end of the year, he was tested again and he was again given a one year extension and only in the third year, if they saw that his weakness was greater and he had no hope - they let him go. For three years

[Page 119]

the young man was tortured and austere until he undermined the foundations of his health for the rest of his life. He was released with a damaged stomach, weak nerves, and as a candidate for all kinds of diseases of exhaustion. "Happy" he married a wife like that and entered the war of life as a broken plow.

And worse was the situation of those who mutilated themselves. Some "experts" were found who knew how to inflict defects on healthy humans. Someone injected some kind of drug into the eye, which has put a cloud over it and the victim could not see. Someone dripped strong drugs in the ears and pierced the eardrum and an abscess that converged and leaked, and the hearing was disturbed and for every wind present and not present, the infected person would have a cold in his ear. Some would dislocate the leg from the knee and the guy become lame and a cripple, and some would have the "expert" cut the tendons of the arm and connect them to the joint and the guy couldn't stretch his arm. Some would inject the candidate for the army with various drugs and the drinker's face and eyes turned yellow as if struck by greensickness, and other kinds of deformities and diseases. Of course, the expert promised that the deformity was only temporary and that, after a short time, the cataract would disappear and the boy's vision would return as before, and the ear would heal and his hearing would return to normal, and the dislocated leg would return to its place and go straight, and the tendons of the arm would expand and the hand would be stretch out to receive and to work, and the greensickness would turn red-white - but the promises were not always fulfilled. And I have known such unfortunate people for the most part: the son of one teacher in our city whose hand was shortened and did not recover and out of no choice he also chose teaching for a living. And I also knew one of my relatives who became deaf because of the drugs they dripped in his ears.

The army doctors and the members of the commissions examining recruits knew about all these tricks, but they accepted bribes and turned a blind eye and the majority of those accepted into the army were the sons of craftsmen and poor people who were not afraid of this work. These were young men from the working class used to hard work, and they went

A school for girls that was founded by the Zionists in the city

[Page 120]

to serving in the army willingly. They hoped that they would eat there to satiety and that the government would provide them with good clothing, and that they would also find free hours to do whatever their heart desires after the work day. But these were very few and most of the young men of Israel tried to avoid serving the hostile government, and this effort increased the number of the weak and disabled.

The Jews living in the cities, without contact with nature, gave them the character of being powerless, fearful and afraid of every barking dog and every animal. Every gentile from the suburbs - he had a dog to guard his yard in case a stranger came in, but no Jew raised a dog in his house and the child who plays with the dog and caresses it - is a naughty child and it is a mitzvah to warn him and keep him away from this evil deed. The Jew was therefore always afraid and when he saw a dog approaching him, his face would turn pale and his heart would throb, and he would look for ways to escape from the evil animal and save his soul. Therefore, the farmer from the village and the Christian from the city treated the Jew as a weak creature and was not afraid to harm him.

And yet among the Jews there were mighty men of strength and men of arms who did not fear nor were they afraid to speak to an enemy at the gate. These were the craftsmen who worked with large and rough tools, like carpenters and beam sawers and woodcutters, butchers and cart owners, accustomed to outdoor life and walking on roads and knowing how to hold a whip and train horses. In particular, butchers acquired a reputation as strong men. They would split the thighs of oxen and cows with their axes on their anvils and hold a coil and a knife, and a drop of blood did not shake their nerves or squeeze their hearts and did not make them faint. And when there was a danger of rioting in Israel, such as on the day a fight broke out between a farmer and a Jew in the market, if the Jew accused the farmer of theft and the matter came to a fist fight or when the farmer accused the Jew of fraud and the fight broke out, and farmers gathered on market day to help their co-religionist and to beat the Jews, and the townspeople panicked and hurried to lock their shops and to lower the blinds on the windows - then the butchers came out of their butcher shops, armed with their axes, each one of them tall and with large limbs, and when they raised their tools above the heads of the quarreling men ready for war, wisdom came to the hearts of the farmers and they scattered, and the two disputants went to a respected Jew to bring before him the matter of their quarrel and the community was saved from bloodshed.

Original footnote:

   a.   From the book "Dunavitz, My Native City," published by the Bnei Dunavitz Aid Society (Podolia) in America.

[Page 121]

A Jewish Metropolis[a]

by S. L. Blank

Translated by Monica Devens

My birthplace and the cradle of my childhood, Dunayivtsi, which is in Ukraine, was divided into two - the new city and the old city.

The new city

Many years ago, a decent number of German families settled here, they founded textile factories for themselves ("Arig Dunayivtsi"), built themselves beautiful stone houses, planted gardens and nurseries, and all with great precision in the German fashion. The men were strong and lithe and the women were fat and stout. Their sons and daughters rode bicycles and engaged in all kinds of sports. On Sundays and other days, they would go out in carriages drawn by knightly horses. And their firemen's association, which is conducted in a kind of military discipline.

There the streets are paved and order and cleanliness prevail.

Your entrance to the new city, indeed far away, far away their church building rises in glory, all drowned in greenery and two rows of tall oaks, protecting it from this and that. Healthy yellow-haired and blue-eyed boys and girls play on the wide green velvet-like bed. As a frame for the church, charming houses shine in their paleness and their fierce dogs lie in their doorways lest a stranger approach.

It is a German colony unto itself, with its manners and its arrangements and its institutions.

The high chimneys of the factories, those on the main street and those in the nearby entrances rise up like black giants and emit their smoke towards the blue sky. The weavers and the mechanics of all types, the vast majority of them are of their own and the minority are local residents. -

And there are also of our brothers, Jews - textile merchants, agents, and accountants and their agents, and travelers in foreign languages of all kinds. Jews, on whom the stamp of the largest cities in the country where they wander because of their trade, is engraved. Among them are the readers of "Ha-Melitz" and "Ha-Tsofeh" and "Ha-Shilo'ah," community activists and significant lovers of Zion. Well-being and the "spirit of the times" is in their dwellings. Their riding and kindly daughters play the piano and speak Russian and German. Their sons are in universities in the country and they have good relations with the German industrialists. And there is a Midrash legend that many of the German industrialists even trained their hands to write Yiddish and in the typical Jewish style: "To my dear and honorable friend," and "Peace be upon Israel."

* * *

As in every city and town, the education in the city was mainly based on the "cheders" and the most famous of them at the time was that of a teacher of young children and his name was Hirsch "Calf." Why was his name Calf? Because he was small and squat and "his belly was between his teeth." And there is a Midrashic legend that he would butt the head of the slow students. When he would go over a lesson with the little children, a pot full of steaming potatoes stood in front of him, that he would swallow them both the insides and the skins, one by one and with extra purpose, and review and butt at the same time. This school would start with the alphabet and end with a "little" Chumash. He would teach not only mechanical reading in the prayer book,

[Page 122]

but also with the Onkelos translation - and from left to right. He reached "gvurot" (=80 years old) and was still engaged in teaching. Not for nothing would they say in self-praise that all had the privilege of passing before him as "sons of Meron" (=a battalion) - from the rabbi to the bathhouse attendant. This school, a dilapidated clay house on the street of the synagogues was on the slope of a hill, so to speak, which sprouts all kinds of thorny plants and brambles and grows all kinds of disgusting things and bugs. On clear summer days, the babies of this school of their teacher would graze there, happy in front of "Moshe Rabbenu's mare," playing various games or singing a psalm to Holy One Blessed Be He that He would water the earth thanks to the babies of their teacher's house.

From Hirsch "Calf" the child passed to the authority of the Chumash and Gemara teacher. I remember the teacher from "Kitarid" (=Kytaihorod). This person had a poetic soul, was handsome, his face covered with a short black beard and his black eyes shone with the joy of life, lover of beauty and cleanliness and order. While he taught his lesson, he would draw "playing cards" for Hanukkah in colors and give them to the students and for Shavu'ot, he would cut out paper drawings to stick on the windows. And he had a passionate imagination and would tell his students stories and fables from "Sefer Ha-Yashar" and more. The students loved this rabbi and would learn out of love. His knowledge of the Talmud was scant and he had to learn from a teacher greater than him in the Torah to prepare for his lessons.

There were also "educated" teachers. One of them was Ephraim Leonansky, a man from Yarmolyntsi, who came to our city to establish a "position" for himself and he acquired students from among the wealthy.

He instructed his students in the Bible, Gemara, and grammar. He reads books of the Haskalah and requires them to write pieces in a flowery style. And anyone who abounds in flowery phrases and fragments of verses is praiseworthy. This teacher was fluent in reading novels in Yiddish. Where did he get these novels from? There was a Jewish man in our city whose name was Avraham "Bletter Id," about whom the grandfather R. Mendele Mocher Sefarim z"l used to say that his hair was enough for a dozen Jews to have a beard and wigs and that in the fringes of his long coat, there were pomegranates, pomegranates dripping all year round. And this Avraham "Bletter Id" receives newspapers and novels and lends them to read for a small fee; Ephraim Leonansky would borrow the novels from him and read them with great desire.

The "cheder" of Shammai Weissman is worth mentioning. This teacher was an extraordinary scholar, a lover of new Hebrew literature, one of the distinct dreamers of Zion, with style and decent measurements. He had all the virtues counted for a decent teacher (many of the best Hebrews in our city were among his students, among them the great writer and educator Prof. Zvi Sharfstein and the Hebrew poet Avraham Rosenzweig, now: Rosen). In his small and clean apartment, a group of well-to-do boys, about eighteen years old, some who were grooms or intended to be grooms, studied. They studied Tanach and Talmud and Haskalah. They had to learn the words of the latter prophets and many of the Psalms by heart, as well as the poems of Adam HaCohen. Micah Joseph Lebensohn and Judah Leib Gordon. Shammai Weissmann was inclined to research and philosophy. Therefore, he used to teach them to his students as light thoughts of Gemara, Poskim, and Tshuvot, even the eight chapters of Rambam, "Moreh Nevuchim," "Hovat Ha-Levavot," the "Ikarim," and even the articles of philosophy and research, which were published in the Hebrew collections. Shammai Weissman would often write articles on the questions of the time and pushed them to "Ha-Melitz," but they never saw the light of day, except for "Torah innovations," which he would publish from time to time in one rabbinical collection called "Ha-Pisgah." In the drawer of his desk were accumulated many articles written on long yellow pages in small and bright letters.

During his time the "Free School" was founded, where in addition to Hebrew and Tanach

[Page 123]

and history, the students were also taught general knowledge. Most of the teachers were volunteers, from among the well-to-do and novices in teaching, but they try to do this job of theirs as a faith out of the holy ideal - to spread Haskalah and a love of Zion among the people. This educational institution, most of whose students were girls, made an impression at the time and caused a stir and agitation in the old city. There was a kind of innovation in it, Hebrew speech rang a little here, a little there, in the mouths of the younger generation, boys and girls from Butchers' Street, Tailors' Street, etc. There were also instigators and spreaders of bad news, of course, like the various teachers who were wary of being deprived of a livelihood, just annoyed at their own jealousy, and also jealous with the jealousy of the Lord of Hosts. The faithful supporters of this institution

Avraham Lerner and those accompanying him on his immigration to Israel

were craftsmen, from those who were relegated to narrow and shabby hallways, headed by their powerlessness, Hirsch Kalashnik and Itzik the bookbinder, "Eldad and Medad" in the camp.

* * *

The Hebrew youth in our city! There was movement and action and agitation, from the lower classes, from the "poor," to the affluent and the rich, who were in the new city - all were imbued with the spirit of nationalism and Zionism. General Zionists, "Tse'irei Tsiyon" and "Po'alei Tsiyon," just enthusiasts, educated and on duty and "simple readers," "potential writers" fighting with all the systems. and Hebrew speakers of all types. A single spirit throbbed in both parts of our city - a single devotion to all that is dear and holy to our people. And households in our city, glory to them and glory to their people, aka the Blank family (not from my family) and the Sharfsteins, the Cheifezes, and more, who provided for our country, the land of the ancestors, enough human material of top quality in all walks of life there. And there were "Beit Midrash" schools in our city for Torah and Hebrew literature and for the love of Zion. One of them was headed by M. Rosen, the author of "Letters from Russia," which appeared in "Ha-Do'ar," and the notebook "Privacy." His house was a youth council house, young people from righteous and wholesome houses, sons of R. Shevach, the local rabbi, Avraham and Zusya,

[Page 124]

both teachers, Levi Riklis, the well-known educator and writer in the Land of Israel, Mordechai Michaeli, the educator and writer in the Land of Israel, the poet Avraham Rosenzweig-Rosen, the writer of these columns, and more. M. Rosen was the living spirit of his "Beit Midrash," a scholar and a clear Zionist, a Jew "whose every bone would say." He is the one who initiates the conversation and is crucial in the debates, whether about a new poem by Bialik, an article by Ahad Ha'am, a new story - everything served as material for debate. I will see them as if living - those nice boys, in their unique styles and in their stature, the young Zion dreamers, who used to come to the "Beit Midrash" of M. Rosen to taste "forbidden bread" unbeknownst to the ancestors. Most of them are sons of the Sadigura and Chortkiv Hasidim and pray in the Sadigura synagogue. The Sadigura synagogue in our city, where the best and the brightest of the two parts of our city prayed. There were the three outstanding scholars, the rabbi R. Shevach, "Yisra'el the Black," Hirschel Hana Rozhes (my father writes these columns) are seriously arguing with the Maharsha; there were Hasidim and men of action making a public celebration with singing and dancing, with all their 248 body parts and their 365 sinews; there were the God-fearing crowning the master of the world with holy melody; there were the Toranim and the educated arguing about "Ibn Ezra." And there was the young writer, Zvi Sharfstein, and his friend, Ya'akov Wasserman z"l, a famous Hebrew educator, the representatives of their "Beit Midrash" arguing in the hallway during the reading of the Torah with the representatives of the other "Beit Midrash" over the laws of Zionism and literature, and names such as Borochov, Sirkin, Herzl, Nordau, Bialik, Y. L. Gordon, Ahad Ha'am, Tschernichovsky, and Brenner flourish in the air.

May those Shabbats, holidays, and festivals be blessed!

* * *

The Talmud Torah in our city was neglected and the Zionists took it upon themselves to repair and improve it. So Ya'akov Fichman was brought to teach there and a new period opened in the life of the youth of our city - the Fichman period. The poet instructed not only the little ones, but also the young people who had literary ambitions. Around him congregated every young man in our city in whose heart the jealousy of writers percolated, and "potential writers" whether in poetry and in fiction or in journalism, and he, the young and lyrical poet and gracious critic, would teach them a lesson in the theory of writing, drawing a line in criticism, encouraging and strengthening soft hearts and tastes, until - until "the sparks of talents" did not rise to the flame and were naturally extinguished.

There was a Jewish man in our city, "Velvel Brieftreger" by name. Why was his name "Brieftreger"? Because he would receive the mail and distribute it to each person by name, since there was not the name of a single Jew in our city unknown to him, even a poor man in the crowd who is in a meager dwelling near the "poorhouse." A long and thin Jew with a brown beard, taciturn and gathered into himself by the nature of his creation. He would enter the house with a weak greeting, lick the head of his thumb with his mouth, leisurely sort through the package of letters, give the owner of the house his, receive a fee of a penny or two, all according to the giver and the letter, and slip the coin into his coat pocket, kiss the mezuzah and depart with a blessing.

The home of this letter carrier was a youth welfare center in our city. Until Velvel came with the post, Ya'akov Fichman would read his poems in front of his young fans in the meantime and give his opinion on writers and literature. Fichman was early to come here, sitting and reading the newspapers "Ha-Melitz" and "Ha-Tsofeh."

[Page 125]

In those days, a firemen's association was founded in our city, headed by Haim Hirsch Wissotzky, a young man full of life and initiative. Every good young man joins it, especially from the sons of Butchers' Street and Tailors' Street. And really, could we expect the kindness of the German firefighters? Are they alone, may their name be obliterated, likely to put out the frequent fires in the old city and its suburbs? Isn't the young Israel talented for this? And not only that, but they stood and built a walled house for glory, with two floors, put in there all the devices necessary for this, even huge barrels full of water, and they had leaders and clerks and exemplary discipline. Anyone who hasn't seen our firemen with the shiny copper hats on their heads and with their uniforms put out a fire hasn't seen a great spectacle in his day, by the time "the idiot" arrived at the scene of the fire, it was already after the fact. It was not for nothing that "Michal" was secretly resentful and angry because he was always "out

Firefighters

of work." He will split open from jealousy - who cares? Lest you say that the firemen's house was built in the first place only to put out fires in Israel, you are wrong. On the upper floor there was a spacious hall for gatherings of all kinds and even a "theater" was used for playing bands, the "wandering stars" of Shalom Aleichem z"l, which would widen the eyes of the Jews of the old city with the plays, "The Witch" and "Two Kuni Lemels," and the like, and please their ears with singing and music.

[Page 126]

Ahh, the firemen's house in our city! -

And please, may Ya'akov Wasserman, mentioned above, be a light matter in your eyes! After years, though, when he married a wife and fathered sons, he calmed down and he gained a reputation as an excellent Hebrew educator. He is the one who headed an educational institution in Odesa in the days of Mendele Mocher Sfarim and Bialik and Ussishkin, may their memory be blessed. However, when he was a boy, he would curl his hair and play with [unreadable word]. He was beautiful to praise and the women were captivated by him. His clothing was not according to the state custom - he wore a frock and his shoes were always shiny. He was full of youthful enthusiasm and had wonderful talents. In particular, he would amaze his listeners with his enthusiastic speeches. The hour is the hour of awakening, the clash of the various currents in Zionism, the clash of tongues, the revival of the national language and its literature, etc., and the time to do for our people, to educate the lower classes in our city. After all, what did Ya'akovke do (Ya'akov Wasserman was called such out of affection)? He founded an actors' organization (actiyorim in the language of the people) to develop "Amcha"'s taste in drama. Who were the members of the association? Obviously from among the sons of the affluent and the daughters of the rich, these thin, beautiful young women who spoke Russian and German, who wanted to come down from the heights of their dwelling places, from the new city, from near the piano among an atmosphere of well-being and lack of worry, to the old city to show the poor their beauty, their grace, and their culture. What did they perform first? "Uriel Acosta." "Ya'akovke" played the main role - Uriel Acosta.

Ah, who will recount the impression made by that show in our city! -

May those days be blessed.

Original footnote:

a.   From "Sefer Sharfstein," published by the "Shvilei Hinuch" committee, New York, 1944.

My Stay in Dunayivtsi (Dunavitz)

by Yaakov Fichman

Translated by Monica Devens

One day I happened upon Yosef Blank, a kind man and a Zionist businessman from Dunayivtsi, a town of commerce and industry in Podolia. I liked the man and that was enough for me to agree to his offer and to accept a job as a teacher in his city. It's necessary to do something! I was never very diligent. But I hated emptiness. My hometown at the beginning of the century was an empty city. My friends had scattered and there remained there only two or three weaklings who were close to literature, but left both their trade and their attempts at creation in a state of despair and they were unable to strengthen the hands of the novice "that he succeed." It was a kind of warning to me: don't freeze here in the emptiness. And perhaps unwittingly, I had a purpose to make Dunayivtsi, which paid well, a shortcut to Warsaw.

I left Blazowa immediately after Passover. I remember, sitting on the train, comparing what was in front of me to the Podolia town where I had to read the Torah, I heard the conversation of a priest who told the passengers - most of them from the village - with frank joy about the massacre of the Jews of Kishinev (=Chisinau). It was from his mouth that I first learned about the horrifying event and from the joy of the wretched priest at the calamity, I was first exposed to Russian hooliganism in all its ugliness.

[Page 127]

- That's fitting for them! The Christian shepherd with the big cross on his chest finished and none of the listeners became aroused by the defamatory words.

This conversation shocked me. I was unsophisticated and the poets of Russia and its tellers had instilled in me a love for the Russian villagers and the Russian people in general, and here I saw them eye to eye, among whom I sit! I breathed a sigh of relief when I left this stupid company and sat in the cart, which took me through Kamyanets Podilskyy to my desired district; and perhaps then the thought had already taken root in me that not only Dunayivtsi, but rather all of Russia is nothing but a corridor to my future life.

We lingered for a little while in Kamyanets Podilskyy. And it was strange the peace that was over this city of beautiful gardens, which apparently did not yet know about the disaster. There the wounded still quivered and every alleyway was filled with anxiety and here, "the sun shone and the plants flourished"... Indeed, I was surprised by the delight of the city, which lies alone far from the King's Road, surrounded by green meadows and wild fields. And remembering that Mendele once stayed here, Gotlober stayed, I felt as if their spirits still floated over the quiet, clean streets, and I prayed that Dunayivtsi would please me no less than this city, which I have not returned to see since.

Yosef Blank with his family in Israel in 1914

In the evening I came to Dunayivtsi. The place, unfortunately, did not capture my heart much, but its people were very kind and they came close to me all the time I stayed with them. In this town I first met the young generation who were different from my townspeople. I met those who became my dear friends, friends of Hebrew literature and its fighters always. Closest to me was the house of Yosef Blank (a member of this family was later, as I learned from Shlomo Hillels' autobiography, the narrator S. L. Blank, who got to know the Bessarabian way of life as a man in Bessarabia from birth). I taught his nice little daughters Hebrew and they have been living in this country for a long time.

Dunayivtsi was a short stop on the road of my wanderings. But I remembered it all my days as a good stop. The town, when we do not dwell in it for a long time, is a blessing to its inhabitants. Here you acquire friends. Here you get to know the Jewish way of life up close. And it is possible that, in this city, I understood Jewish existence more than I understood it in the city

[Page 128]

in which I was born. And indeed, it was a very typical Jewish town. It had faces that stood out and I remember some of them, as if I had left them yesterday. Here there was something turbulent, boiling, and those who do not remember what Dunayivtsi was like in the days of the Uganda controversy do not know what fanaticism for Herzl, for the Zionist Federation (there was a strong group of "Federation defenders" here) is. It gave the same signs as Podolia Hasidism, which believed in the rabbi as an angel of God; and the reincarnation of such a "rabbi" was Herzl to the people of Dunayivtsi. It was forbidden to insult him!

Here I insisted on it, what Herzl was to the masses of Israel whose soul was consumed by a man of miracles, by a redeemer. Since I had already published several poems in "Ha-Dor," the young men of the town approached me, with whom I would walk and talk and dream in the reddish fields at sunset on the way up to Yarmolyntsi. Of them, I remember Zvi Sharfstein the most, who was then a soft-spoken man with beautiful eyes and who already showed productive literary talent. His articles in "Ha-Melitz" under the name of Even Hadah were published with amazing frequency. There was not, as it were, a subject that did not need him and his style was clear; and it was like a wonder in my eyes that a boy, a town boy, had such quick perception. All the paths of literature, all the problems of the time, were understood by him while I was still entirely immersed in the little poems. We have been friends since then for the rest of our lives; and he is also the one who published the first assessment of my poetry in "Ha-Yarden" and it is written with affection and understanding - and there are few critics among us to this day who understand poetry. And how good it is for a person who has dealt with education problems all his life (and also wrote an important book on the history of education) that his heart is open to poetry, which is the most reliable key to understanding the child's soul.

A few more spirited young people approached me who brightened up my monotonous life in my short time in this town. Among them I will also mention the witty Ya'akov Wasserman, a significant pedagogue and active Zionist businessman; and one of the Blank family, a pure-hearted young man, who would stand and wait near my residence for my departure almost every evening to accompany me for a short time on a walk before bed. There are very few people, whose souls were connected to mine like he was. And he perished in the spring of his life (in the October riots that took place in Proskorov (= Khmelnytskyi) in 1905). To this day my heart will rejoice at his memory.

My City, Dunayivtsi (Dunavitz)[a]

by Shlomo Rosen

Translated by Monica Devens

Many years have passed since I left our home in Dunayivtsi. For one, success shone brightly and he climbed the social and economic ladder, and for the other, we were called by twists of fate...many of us visited big cities, others live in New York, the largest of the metropolitan cities of the world, and the life of wealth and pleasures even intoxicated them, nevertheless, the memory of our old home lives in the hearts of all of us. We cannot forget our quiet and humble city of Dunayivtsi. About twelve thousand Jews, laborers, before the Holocaust, filled the streets of the city. All weekdays, the streets were full of noise and tumult, merchants, shopkeepers, and craftsmen. If a stranger would happen to be there

[Page 129]

on such a day, he got the impression that, apart from livelihood issues and livelihood concerns, the Jews of the town have nothing in their world and only the war for existence concerns them all the time. However, this impression was completely wrong. Although they were very busy and embodied the verse, "By the sweat of your brow, you shall eat bread," some less and some more, each according to his luck, but in all of them beat a warm Hebrew heart and one spirit surrounded them, a spirit of Torah and good deeds - each according to his achievement. And just as they gave their minds to commerce and work, so they gave their hearts to dreaming and creating spiritual values. The people had dreams and their ambition was always to educate their children in the Torah and wisdom. Immersed all their days in their small shops, they were always longing for another world, beautiful and sublime, for the resurrection of their people in the land of their ancestors, to the revival of the Hebrew language. When Beryl Sharfstein's store was filled with all types, bursting with endless buyers, Zvi, the son, would sit in a hidden corner or in a special room and weave threads for the enrichment of the new Hebrew education. And when my grandfather's shop was full of merchants and bills, my father, Mordechai Rosin (may he rest in peace), wrote articles for "Ha-Shilo'ah," "Ha-Zman," and "Ha-Tsfira." Avraham Rosenzweig (A. Rosen) found in Dunayivtsi treasures of poetry and over time earned himself a reputation as an important Hebrew poet in the Land of Israel. And the small, dark house on the street of the butcher shops gave us the well-known Hebrew writer, S. L. Blank. If a person thought that Dunayivtsi did not have a favorable atmosphere for talents in the field of art and painting, he would be wrong. Dunayivtsi gave us the gifted painter, Branzi Blank, and the important sculptor, Deutschman, the daughter of Shalom ben Aharon Ha-"Adom" and the sister of our active businessman, Yitzhak Deutschman. An artist or a poet was given the opportunity to receive inspiration in Dunayivtsi. The city excelled in its beautiful girls who were blessed with Jewish grace and human radiance.

Our town was divided into two parts: the old city and the new city, and into different classes with special streets: the synagogue street, the mill street, the butchers' street, the tailors' street, etc. were found in a part of the old city, which differed from the new city both in terms of its appearance and in terms of the composition of the residents. In the old part of our city, a spirit of true democracy prevailed and all the residents of this part saw each other as brothers and sisters, members of one big family, and a feeling of brotherhood and devotion filled all hearts. Whereas in the new part, where the wealthy homeowners lived, it had a completely different character.

The family feeling was missing there. These were dear Jews, but - a bit cold and disapproving, and sometimes they didn't even allow their children to play with the children of the old city... nevertheless, despite these spots of pride and arrogance that were seen here and there, our town in general, both the old city and the new city, shone with the traditional Jewish life that was our pride.

Here standing in front of my eyes are the precious streets and alleys of our unforgettable town of Dunayivtsi: the commercial lot (Targavitse), the market with the stores, the huts, the street of the butcher shops, the synagogue street, the enclave of the Zinkov Hasidim, the Beit Midrash, that throughout the hours of the day they did not cease reading and prayer - one "minyan" ends and the other begins. I see in my mind's eye the great synagogue and feel still today the terror that struck the child's heart when we, who are now here, used to pass there in the silence of the night and whisper a secret to each other about the dead standing there, inside, wrapped in tallits and praying...

and image chases after image.

Here I enter the enclave of the Sedigura Hasidim and see in front of me an image shrouded in holiness and awe in the precious and beautiful figure of R. Yisraelikel R. Arkis. The owner of the eyes that produce wisdom and the kind smile that flows

[Page 130]

on the face of his white beard. I see him wrapped in his large tallit that covers his shiny silk kapoteh with its multitude of colors as he walks between a "column" and the Holy Ark, praying with devotion and repeating each word 5-6 times, and with burning looks of love, respect, and reverence accompanying him.

And here is the market, the center of small and large shops, the huts, the tinsmiths, Nachman Cantor's store. Itzi Freezman's store full of ready-made clothes for the "goyim," Sevi's grocery and kerosene store, Simcha Yossel Meirchis's hardware store, Beryl Sharfstein's department store where you could find: needles, hats, violins, hammers, saws and also prayer books, Chumashim, and so on. And here is the small shop of Feivel's wife, where we bought a piece of salted fish for one kopeck.

A special place in the life of our town was occupied by the house of Hana Leibeles on the street of the butcher shops, a place where we, the little ones, could have excellent meals: for one kopeck you could buy a piece of liver, half a roasted chicken leg, and the merchants in the town, who had the means, went there by "stealth" and with care to get a delicious meal, fresh bread rolls, stuffed fish, roasted livers, etc., as the owner of the "restaurant" greets them: "Bon Appetit!"

And here I see in front of my eyes the tailor, Yehuda'leh, from Frompil, a squat and cheerful Jew whose mouth did not stop singing and joking. On summer days, the doors and windows in his house would be opened and the sounds of the workers singing, accompanied by the calling of the numbers, would emanate from them. And here walks and enters the market the tall, angry Yankel, the bathhouse attendant. And in his hand is a basket full of fresh loaves of bread with the smell of cumin wafting from them. Standing before my eyes are the few taverns of Jews, and I see the "goyim" when they leave their "cloister" (church) on their holidays and go straight into the taverns and leave their money there and go out drunk again and call for calamities...

And the wonderful winter nights of Dunayivtsi! We, the students, return home from the "Cheder," lanterns in our hands and song in our mouths.

My ears are still ringing with the voices of songs that emanate, on hot summer days, from the open windows of the houses of teachers Izikel, Eli Ya'akov, Yitzhak Meir Hirsch and others.

* * *

Where are you, dear Jews of Dunayivtsi! It's over, the dear people have been cut off; only their good deeds remain engraved in our hearts. The good deeds of our saints; only the memories of our childhood remain. Who told and who believed possible that this town, rooted in Judaism for generations, would one day be obliterated from under the heavens of G-d.

"The Master Race" brought destruction upon it. But the Jew comes back to life and builds the State of Israel.

Original footnote:

1. From the book, "Dunayivtsi, The City of My Birth," by Zvi Sharfstein, published by the Aid Society of Bnei Dunayivtsi (Podolia) in America.

[Page 131]

From the Atmosphere in Our City

by B. Blank-Bokser

Translated by Monica Devens

In countries and cities through which I passed on my long wanderings over many years, they asked me: Where are you from? I would answer: I was born in Dunayivtsi, where the mothers used to tell their children on cold winter nights, lying in a clean bed and covered with a warm blanket, that there are poor children in the city freezing cold and hungry. In my city, it was customary to give old clothes and shoes to the poor and they would mend a torn shirt before it was given to them. This is how they used to invite a guest to the Shabbat meal and to set aside bread and challahs from the bakery for the poor. The townspeople were used to looking down and not up, and jealousy was forbidden. When one of the "lords" married off a son or daughter, he would make a feast for the poor. Otherwise, the joy would not be complete. A poor woman giving birth would be given a sheet, a chicken, a cup of jam, and the like. When a poor daughter of Israel entered puberty, they would collect donations for her dowry and wedding expenses. And mothers used to tell us that, with the coming of the Messiah, all the holidays will be cancelled except Purim because Purim is the only holiday dedicated to charity and sending food to the poor. Everyone felt that it was their duty to help others in their time of need.

I remember that my aunt, Riva, for whom giving charity was a major part of her life, was once offended because her husband, as they sat at a meal, prevented her from giving a whole gold coin to a poor man. She got up from the table angrily, went into the kitchen, and said: If I am not allowed to give charity with a full hand, why should I sit around the table with the master of the house?

All her days, the Shamash and Gabbai Blimele would go around seeking "donations" and, in a basket under her bath, she would collect "hidden things" for the poor: fat, sugar, jam, underwear, and clothes. While walking, she would knit socks with her short, crooked fingers.

Pasia bat Chaim Avraham assigned herself a unique mission: "giving in secret." She would wear a silk scarf on her head and, in half-holiday clothing, she would visit her "Hasidot" and whisper to them the word of her coming and, after receiving what she received, she would kiss the mezuzah and leave satisfied.

It also happened that the owners of "houses" would wear the Shabbat "kapotehs" on weekdays and collect donations for the benefit of "one who was burned out" or who had become impoverished. The teachers would also teach the children of poverty for free. Not only the needs of the body were taken care of in our city. Many of the teachers devoted time to spreading Torah and education among the children of the poor by giving free lessons. I believe that there is no need to remind us, the children of these noble ones who brought us up in this spirit, of the terrible disaster of our people, of the destruction of our relatives that is unparalleled in the annals of mankind. In this country, there are many mothers who do not allow themselves to hug their children because of the bereaved parents who lost their children in the Holocaust.

The Institutions of Our City

by M. B.

Translated by Monica Devens

In our city, which lies 50 kilometers from the Austrian border, according to the laws of the Tsarist government, only Jews born in this area were allowed to live. Jews who were born outside the "Pale" and tried to settle there were punished and deported. Thanks to its special geographical situation - Dunayivtsi occupied an important place in trade and industry.

At the beginning of the 19th century, a group of German immigrants from Austria and Germany settled in this town.

[Page 132]

These immigrants were poor and wretched when they arrived. They arrived in the town in carts drawn by dogs, but they brought weaving machines with them. Over the course of time, these weaving machines became 35 textile factories (fabric and cotton) and 2 steel smelting factories. Thanks to this industrial development, Jews began to flow from near and far places beyond the Pale. The Tsarist police persecuted these Jews, lacking residence permission, and many of them were likely to be deported from the city. A struggle began between the Jews and the police, and in this struggle, Mr. Yonah Bokser was active. As a private lawyer, he fought against threats of deportation. The struggle was long and difficult, and only after many years did they manage to remove Dunayivtsi from the framework of the laws of the Pale and the trials against the Jews were eliminated.

In actions of this kind, Yonah Bokser endangered his position in the city. The danger of deportation and imprisonment threatened him frequently. As was mentioned, the German immigrants enjoyed economic prosperity and many of them became rich and this prosperity drew many of their countrymen to Dunayivtsi. Over time, a large German colony arose in the city. They developed their own social life: they established a German school, an evangelical church, a club where meetings were held, and even their own fire department. The contact of the Germans with the other Christian residents of the city was very loose. While their contact with the Jews focused only in the economic area, in other areas the Germans showed implied and sometimes overt anti-Semitism.

Permission to enter the public garden of the Germans, which surrounded their fire station, was given to all residents of the city, except for the Jews. And only when various celebrations were held in this garden - were the Jews also allowed to buy tickets for entry. The German fire brigade was required to help all residents of the city in the event of a fire. For these services, they received a certain amount of money from the district city of "Nova-Ushytsya." And the Jewish community also contributed from its budget to the German fire brigade.

Firefighters next to fire trucks

[Page 133]

latter would fabricate different types of revenue, including arson attempts. For this purpose, they would choose a house of an affluent Jew, attach the ladders to it, climb on the roof and, with hammers, they would destroy the wooden shingles and splash jets of water on the walls and cause great damage to the house. To get out of these "experiences" - the owners of the houses would "donate" for the benefit of the firefighters. However, when a real fire broke out in a Jewish house in the Jewish quarter - they did not rush to come and put out the fire. And here it once happened that a fire broke out in a quarter where the Jews lived densely. The firefighters arrived very late and more than 20 houses went up in flames. Many families were left homeless. This disaster provoked the Jewish public figures to take measures. Through the initiative of the businessmen Yonah Bokser, Eli Rubinstein, Yosef Blank and others, a Jewish fire brigade company was established in the city. The Jewish youth and many other respected Jews participated in this society

Chief of the Fire Brigade

and after a rather short time, this company of the fire brigade became a huge public factor, which gathered around it various groups from the Jewish public in the city. Over time, this company became extremely important when it assumed a role of "self-defense." After the pogrom in Kishinev, active anti-Semitic agitation began in all the cities and towns within the Pale of Settlement. The Jews of Dunayivtsi sent a delegation to the governor of the region in Kamyanets Podilskyy. The leaders of the businessmen in the city, who wanted to ask

[Page 134]

the governor to take deterrent measures by force against the violators, participated in this delegation. However, the governor did not want to accept the delegation and they returned home with a few vague promises from the secretary of the region. It was decided to rely solely on their own forces, that is: on the organized youth within the framework of the fire department. The opportunity for a clash was not long in coming. One bright Sunday, when the market was full of peasants from the area, the people of the "Black Hundred" incited the peasants who began to destroy the shacks of the Jewish shops and destroy the goods.

The firefighters in uniform, with copper hats - equipped with all kinds of devices, appeared at the place where the pogrom started. The rioters were frightened and began to retreat and run away, and the town was saved. This lesson saved Dunayivtsi from riots many years later during the Petliura period. But this rescue came at a rather high price. The "Black Hundred" did not sit idly by. They misrepresented the events in the market on the aforementioned Sunday and, in a distorted and exaggerated form, submitted a memorandum to the governor of the region who ordered the liquidation of the Jewish fire brigade company. The German colony helped the "Black Hundred" both openly and secretly. A few of the leaders of the company such as Dr. Marmur did not stay long in prison. An appeal was filed with the court against the governor's order of elimination, and in addition to the local lawyer, Yonah Bokser, the Zionist prosecutor, Schleifer, from Kamyanets Podilskyy, and the famous lawyer, A. Gruzenberg from Sankt-Peterburg appeared in court. The trial lasted about two years and in the end, the fire brigade company was re-established. It should be noted that the initiators of the fire brigade company along with other businessmen also helped to establish a loan and savings bank, the first of its kind in the area.

The main initiators were: Israel Rabinowitz, Chaim Meir Rosenblatt, Chaim Schneider, Yonah Bokser, Yosef Blank, Aaron Perlmutter, and others.

The purpose of the fund was to create cheap credit for artisans and small traders. The credit was limited to 300 rubles, given with weekly and monthly payments. This institution somewhat raised the economic situation of the lower classes and the poor of means and enjoyed much support from the population. The Jews of the city also brought their savings to the fund. This institution existed until the end of 1914, when the First World War broke out.

Our City 1920-1935

by Feige Tauchner

Translated by Monica Devens

After the disturbances of Petliura in 1919 and after the regime changed several times, the Bolsheviks captured our city on Monday, Kislev 5, TRP"A (15 October 1920). The occupying army lacked everything and as soon as they entered the city, they began "to take" from the residents everything that came into their hands; life in the city was completely silent, the shopkeepers did not open their shops and the villagers did not bring their wares for sale - the rumors of the confiscations and the "takings" by the soldiers reached them, too - the city dwellers achieved with great efforts the minimum necessities of life. The connection between cities was cut off; the mail, the telephone, and the telegraph did not work; newspapers did not arrive and the few who wanted to travel from place to place could indeed do so because

[Page 135]

the roads remained open for a while, but for that they had to rent a special vehicle. Thus, some residents were given the opportunity to leave the city, and Russia in general, thanks to the fact that the Polish border - which was about fifty kilometers from our city - could be crossed without many difficulties. Many of our citizens crossed the border into Galicia and from there dispersed to all parts of the world; a large part of them also immigrated to Israel. A few months later, the border was completely closed and intercity traffic was also restricted, and even to travel to Kamyanets, which is close to Dunayivtsi, a special license was needed. With the closure of the roads also began the period of the searches. The Bolsheviks looked for anything and everything under the pretext of looking for weapons, but they took everything that was close at hand, especially clocks. After a few months the tune changed - not weapons, but goods. The citizens did hide everything, but the soldiers nevertheless discovered the goods with their meticulous searches that were carried out every night and every day in a different place. The goods that were found were confiscated and their owner was arrested and brought before a military tribunal and, more than once, given a death sentence, which was usually carried out without mercy and with excessive haste. This period was called the period of war communism.

After the confiscation of the goods came the period which was called the period of "surpluses." It was terrible. During the day they asked let it be evening and at night they prayed for morning. The curfew and the searches were nerve-racking. In fact, all classes of the people suffered, but it was most difficult for the rich because they lived in constant fear of search, of confiscation, of imprisonment, and of death. It was clear to everyone that the goal of the regime was to eliminate them and remove them from the world. The middle class suffered from confiscations and lack of livelihood; the craftsmen - from lack of work; and the poor always suffer. When they got up in the morning, they immediately heard the night news, even without the help of a newspaper and radio, as if an intelligence bureau immediately spread the rumors and news about confiscation and imprisonment.

The only way they got the food they needed was through barter. The world returned to the primitive method of barter. For the most part, the women and children would go - and of course on foot - to the nearby villages and bring the villagers what they lacked and, in return, receive food. About two years passed like this.

In October 1922, the "N.A.P.," the initials of "A New Economic Policy," was announced, and it symbolized a period of light in the government of darkness. Freedom of trade was restored to a certain extent and the situation improved. Commerce and industry began to develop, everyone returned to their profession, and everyone earned a living. Some of the townspeople, a very small part, also became rich. But this enrichment was their destruction. Had it not been for the N.A.P., a large part of them would have immigrated to Israel because most of them were Zionists. I always thought that the N.A.P. was - from this point of view - a great disaster for the Jews of Russia.

At the end of 1926, they began "to smell" that the N.A.P. was approaching its end and its days were numbered, and truly, in 1927 the lid was closed on this period. The method used to eliminate the remains of the N.A.P. were: the imposition of such a large income tax, which was inevitably followed by the confiscation of the merchants' property. On the first of January 1928, there was no private business again. The remnants managed in several factories that were organized in the form of cooperatives. In the days of the N.A.P., the factory owners equipped their factories with modern machinery and prepared a large inventory of raw material so that there was something to confiscate. At the time of the confiscation, the owners were jailed and exiled to Siberia for periods of three to five years. The one who was able to overcome the back-breaking work and the difficult conditions and finally returned - the law called the "minus law" applied to him, according to which he was called "a former prisoner" for a period of time

[Page 136]

equal to the time he had spent in Siberia. The following restrictions applied to him: he was not allowed to return to his place of residence before the expulsion; he was not allowed to live within one hundred kilometers of the cities of Moscow, Leningrad, Kharkiv, and Kyiv; he was not allowed to live within a radius of one hundred kilometers from an industrial center, as well as from a border point. As a result of these instructions, the fate of our townspeople who returned from expulsion was very difficult. Even though Russia is big and wide, it was almost impossible to find a place where it was allowed to get established and to start all over again. While the head of the family suffered in his exile, the rest of the family lived in very difficult conditions in the city itself. The houses they lived in were taken over by a government office whose job it was to monitor the property. Such a family lived in a shabby room in a remote corner of the city and waited for the release of the father or the husband; and when he returned, if he returned, they took the wandering stick with them and went to look for a new place.

At the time of the N.A.P. the situation was quite good, and when those who are profiting want to enjoy life, this sometimes results in ignoring the past, not considering the present or what may come in the future. Such people bought jewelry, fur coats, silverware; everything that was buried in the ground rose as if resurrected.

On December 31, 1928, they organized a "legal" robbery throughout the length and breadth of Russia and that night was called the "Golden Night." The government emissaries went from house to house and confiscated jewelry, silverware, furs, and the like. They even removed rings from the women's hands and earrings from their ears and took with them anything worth money. The "Golden Night" was actually the drastic end of the N.A.P. period.

At the beginning of 1929, a new period began in which people tried to get by in government work, sometimes out of desire and sometimes out of necessity. This period can be called a period of transition from trade to crafts and clerical work. Anyone who was a merchant or suspected of being a merchant or a factory owner was denied the right to vote. People who were disenfranchised were not accepted into any enterprise or state office. One could only get a job through the labor bureau; the bureau did not register a disenfranchised person on the list of job seekers. And the right to vote was received only after three years of work in a factory. Now go and find the beginning and the end of this vicious cycle and learn how to switch from a merchant to a worker…During this period, the concern for finding a job was not only because of the need for a living, but mainly for the sake of receiving the certificate, otherwise known as the internship certificate, that granted the desired right of voting.

When the season for gathering the harvest and its transfer to the government approached, they needed many workers that the bureau could not provide because this was the first year that the entire harvest was transferred to the government. They opened grain delivery stations and began to also get clerks not through the bureau. The work went on in a flash. They worked day and night. After the grain came the season of potatoes, and then the season of beets, which were transferred to factories for sugar. At the end of 1929, many of our people had in their pockets a certificate of six months of work. Throughout the year they kept all kinds of lists and statistics - they worked a month here and a month there and thus they attached certificate to certificate and the number of internship months kept increasing and everyone hoped to be able to pass the necessary minimum number of months. The pace of work was so intense that private life was forgotten entirely and family life was disrupted by the hard work. My husband, for example, worked at the Dunayivtsi train station and it had been weeks since I heard anything from him. Once I was somehow free and I went to visit him at night and here I found him late at night working and with a long beard. I was very scared because

[Page 137]

I thought he was in prison, but he told me quietly that they just worked day and night without a break and there was no time to shave. At such a pace and in such a way of life, the people worked for about two or three years until they got the right to vote and managed more or less to become government clerks and, in the course of time, they were also accepted into the association.

I was reminded of a story that in itself is quite sad, but that clearly shows the eagerness after getting a government job. In the winter of 1932-33, the Russian government made a commercial deal with Germany and, among other goods, also sold feathers. My husband then worked as a clerk in the export department. Once, coming back from work, he told me that he had invited all the butchers of our city to our house that evening. They all came and my husband told them that they could be accepted as government clerks under certain conditions: a poultry slaughterhouse would be opened for them which, until then, had not officially existed; the slaughterhouse would be equipped with the best modern devices; the money they would receive for slaughtering the birds would belong to them and the government would buy the feathers from them and pay them in addition a symbolic salary. In exchange for this, the slaughterers must announce publicly and officially (by means of an advertisement in the newspaper) that they give up filling any role in religious life, that is - they will cease to pass in front of the ark, to serve as circumcisers and as gabbais in the synagogue, which then still existed and continued to exist until 1936, and will not arrange a canopy and wedding. The decision was very difficult for these respected Jews. On the one hand, they were out of work and deprived of any means of livelihood and, on the other hand, this work would have helped them in their financial distress. It is not easy for such people to give up their position in religious life and it was particularly difficult to give up circumcision. They asked for a 24-hour stay to give their answer. The next day they came back and their answer was positive. I sat down and wrote the declarations for them and they signed them. I often remember the look on the faces of these five Jews when they took the pen from me to sign.

But despite the solemn declaration, none of them refused when they were called to fulfill the commandment of bringing a child into the covenant of our father Abraham. In most cases, the circumcision took place in the presence of the grandmother and the mother without the father.

The grandmother allegedly stole the baby without the parents' knowledge and, in the event that this was discovered, she bore the responsibility for the matter; the baby's parents also handed the grandmother over for trial for the crime of stealing the child. The boy's father never participated in the ceremony - for fear of being kicked out of the party.

Except for the slaughter of chickens, there was no other slaughtering work because they did not allow the slaughter of animals that were not sick or infected and these latter would be killed.

In the conditions listed above of arduous work accompanied by constant fear, the people lived to between the ages of 25 and 45. Young people below this age would study and become competent in professions. There was an elementary school where studying was compulsory. When the children finished elementary school, the government made sure to teach them a trade. The talented among the children of the workers moved to a vocational high school. Next to every factory there was a school where they studied for 4 hours and worked for 4 hours. At graduation from a school like this, the boys were about eighteen years old. A high school graduate could, if he was the son of someone who had the right to vote, enter the university. In contrast, it was not possible to attend a high school for the children of the disenfranchised, even for the most talented. Such boys went to work in the mines because after a year of such work they were given the right to vote. The girls left the city and engaged in all kinds of jobs, even the most difficult. Regarding such young people there was a "Numerus Clausus,"

[Page 138]

even after they had already obtained the right to vote because the children of the party members were accepted first, followed by the children of the kolkhoz, and only then did their turn come. Even after they started studying, their situation was difficult and only if the parents could help their son with a few rubles a month could he finish his studies under humane conditions without being affected by any disease; but if not, then the son usually brought with him, in addition to the diploma, also tuberculosis. The son of one of the teachers, for example, did not receive any help from his father and he did graduate as a doctor, but after a short time he died of tuberculosis that he brought with him from his studies.

Perhaps I should tell about one of the election "promotions" that I also had the honor of taking part in. In the winter of 32-33, they announced the holding of elections. They organized the elections in such a way that each trade union chose separately and on a different date. On the day that the factory where I worked got the right to vote, we were informed at the break at ten (immediately after the siren of the start of the break) that we had to get dressed and go down to the "parade" ground. When I got there I found that all the workers were arranged and, together with them, the orchestra. We arranged ourselves as an army during drilling exercises because we were all arranged in foursomes. We were a crowd of over a thousand people there. The orchestra began to play and the procession moved from its position in an organized march. Although none of us knew the purpose of our march and where we were headed, no one dared to ask anything. That's how we got to the theater (it was in the Germans' municipal garden). After we were all seated, the curtain above the stage, on which sat five leaders, opened. One of them stood up and addressed us with these words: Friends, I want to explain to you the purpose for which we have gathered here today. Continuing on, he explained to us that we were about to elect the democratic government of the Russian people. He took out a piece of paper from his pocket and read from it the names of people and explained to us that the party committee had checked these people and found them worthy of being elected and that we could trust the party committee... Then he said: Let those who oppose the election of these people raise their hands. Of course, no one raised their hand... The speaker waited a moment and announced in a festive voice that there was no objection and the candidates were unanimously elected. He commanded the orchestra and we had to arrange ourselves. The orchestra started playing marches again and we marched in foursomes back to work despite the frost and deep snow outside. Many of us understood then for the first time the "exact meaning" of the word democracy. I was not the only one to hide the tears of shame and humiliation we felt because we were seen as a flock of sheep subject to the shepherd's staff.

The situation of the people aged between sixty and seventy was extremely difficult. Some of them were supported by the children and some made a living by selling their belongings, but almost all of them lived in poverty and waited for death... Those who were in the early sixties were legally entitled to get a job, but their chances of getting it were extremely slim. The few who had enough physical strength worked as night guards in government warehouses. Those who did not work were, as I said above, deprived of the right to vote and this law was also true for the elderly and those deprived of the right to vote could not continue to live in their apartments, which in the meantime had become government property. This was a period of continuous eviction orders.

Most of our people between the ages of 45 and 60 also made a living by selling things. The years passed and the household items were used up. Only a few of the people of this age succeeded to manage.

The Sabbath, or rather the desecration of the Sabbath, was a very painful problem. When there was a purge in the government apparatus, Jews were removed from their jobs because they refused to work on Saturdays and holidays and then they lived in want.

[Page 139]

It is deeply engraved in my memory of how, on many mornings on my way to work, I would meet a Jew with his tallith under his armpit and this was a sign to me that that day was Shabbat or a holiday and we would look at each other and be both ashamed, although for different reasons: I was ashamed that he was going to pray while I was going to work and he was ashamed that he did not earn his bread. There was someone who said that it is better for him to die of hunger than to work on Shabbat. And once I heard a Jew say to his friend: "It's good that your wife can work, but what will I do if my partner is sick?" Neither of them had children. The first wife's work was extremely lucrative. As we know, all the holidays of all religions were canceled and two holidays were established a year and they are: "Revolution Day" celebrated on November 7th and 8th and "International Workers' Day" celebrated on the first of May. At that time, there was no weekly day of rest except according to the calendar, that is, the days of rest were the days: 6, 12, 18, 24, and 30 of each month. The aforementioned holidays were celebrated for three days each time. November 6 is a day of rest and the seventh and eighth were the days of the holiday. In order for the people to feel the holiday, they would allocate fairly large sums to each factory to hold banquets and distribute refreshments to the workers and their families. The aforementioned woman was the "chief mother-in-law" in these celebrations and the "Tsav Fareven Di Smaches" (meaning: to be the cook) fell upon her, she also had satisfaction when they told her that the "borscht" was tasty. I remember a joke on the topic of arranging the celebrations. For one of the holidays, a million rubles were allocated for holding the celebration, but a condition was made that the person who would take arranging the festivity upon himself had to commit to doing it in such a way that the whole nation would be happy and would enjoy it and remember it forever. No one wanted to take on the difficult task.

In the winter of 1932-33, the economic situation was terrible. The cold was very strong and it was difficult to get food and heating material. We all suffered. On the eve of Passover the "Torgsin" opened and the situation improved somewhat. "Torgsin" - these are government stores that sell for dollars and gold and it was possible

Volunteer nurses from among the daughters of the city during the World War

[Page 140]

to get there usually things that had not been seen on the market until then. We started receiving checks from abroad. The atmosphere changed with the opening of these stores because, while in 1928-29 those found with gold or dollars were deported to Siberia without trial, suddenly on one fine day, when the "Torgsin" shops opened, everything became kosher. Those who still had foreign currency deep in the ground took it out and exchanged it for necessities.

In our city there were three schools in the three official languages at that time: Ukrainian, Polish, and Yiddish. We sent our sons to the Ukrainian because in it they hardly mentioned religion, neither good nor bad, while in the Yiddish schools, they did everything to remove religion from the children's hearts. They did many things to cause anger, such as on the night of the "Seder," they arranged a special celebration where they let the children eat bread, of course, or on the night of Yom Kippur, instead of "Kol Nidre," they held a feast and banquet for the children. On Yom Kippur itself we had to go to work and the child went to school. But in the Ukrainian no one cared if the child didn't eat, in contrast to that in the Yiddish, they checked all the children to see if they had brought food and the child whose backpack was found without food, his fate was to be sent home to bring food (on other days they didn't care if the children were not eating…).

After the N.A.P. was over, it was clear that the merchants had money left over. As I already mentioned, the end was very drastic and they confiscated the property of a large part of the merchants, and even the household furniture, against the excessive debts to the income tax.

The things they confiscated were valued at such a cheap price that it almost never covered the amount of the tax they set and, in addition to the fact that they were left with no property, there was another debt registered against their account. They did not waive this debt, God forbid, but started doing trials in which they handed out years of imprisonment generously. There was no prison in Dunayivtsi, so they sent everyone to Kamyanets. Those of the prisoners who were able to work, and who worked to the satisfaction of the authorities, were released from prison after two-thirds of the time. The prisons had all kinds of workshops and the people worked as hard as they could to enjoy an early release.

Despite all the high taxes, there were still a few people everywhere who paid all the payments and still had money left over with which they bought dollars and gold and hid them in the ground. It goes without saying that everything was known to our brothers the Jews who worked in the service of the G.P.O. And one fine day they started inviting people to G.P.O. and demanded that they hand over the foreign currency and gold in their possession because the country was in dire straits and needed these means of payment to buy essential commodities abroad. Later they talked to the heart of the people, that it is better for the state to use it than for it to lie in the ground. These beautiful explanations only found a listening ear among a few professors in Kyiv, but not among "Amcha"... In the small towns, the "explanation" was less intelligent and more "convincing" because they came suddenly at night, arrested the people, and started "to explain" to them. The people were put in a prison and tortured with unbelievable torture. The torture was according to a scientific method... First of all, the housing was "ideal" because they put over a hundred people in a cell with the capacity of 20. Of course, the crowding was so great that the people remained standing the whole time until they started falling over each other. The cell door was opened only once a day and the people did their business in the cell. Behind the door, they put up machines that made noise throughout the day and night. Some of the "prisoners" went mad, literally, others weakened to death, and some died. In the end, everyone handed over their money, the question was only

[Page 141]

after how much time. There were those who did not last more than a day and there were also those who kept their secret for up to six weeks; no one lasted more than that. When the interrogator was Jewish, the matter became even more complicated because the Jews used various tricks, such as: during the interrogation of the prisoner, they asked him details about all the family members, even from previous generations. After they already knew the details, the investigator went to the prisoner's wife and told her that her husband told her to hand over all the money and, as a sign, the investigator gave the prisoner's wife the date of the death, the names of the family members, etc.

In thirty-three, there was a famine and people fell dead in the streets. The cause of the famine was not, God forbid, a bad harvest, but politics. Apparently, they sent all the grains for export. At that time, things that only a short time before could still be obtained were not attainable, even in "Torgsin" (I only sometimes received for me and for the two children a kilo and 100 grams of bread per day). We were forced to take out of the house the silverware and rings that were still left after the "Golden Night" and, in exchange for them, we bought in "Torgsin" the food we could get. With my own eyes, I saw women coming to the dentist for her to remove the gold teeth she had once put in to buy a little food.

One of those days I happened to enter the house of one of the townspeople during dinner and saw that they were eating soup with wooden spoons. Of course I looked. So the man turned to me and said: Are you looking? Our soup spoons have been in "Torgsin" for a long time, I wish I had more. The poor people had not had silver and gold implements forever so that they could not even enjoy the relief in "Torgsin" and, in truth, most of the victims of the famine came from this part of the people.

We left Dunayivtsi on October 27, 1935. The last few days before our trip were full of excitement. The news about our immigration to Israel took flight and within a few hours spread to all corners of the city. An unceasing stream of people started flocking to our house to say goodbye to us and to send regards through us to their relatives in Israel. We willingly accepted all these missions, we hoped to be messengers of good deeds.

Tombstone

by Avraham Rosen

Translated by Monica Devens

I was burned with my brothers in the furnaces of death,
My ashes fertilized fields the hands of injustice had sowed,
But a tombstone, my shadow was erected in full dignity
Over the grave of the anonymous martyrs of blessed memory.

The wind will caress the two eyes of the tombstone,
Until from afar the black pupils lit up: Pe Nun (=here lies),
The two arms, carved by the hands of the sledgehammer craftsman,
Will hold on to what is written as a father holds a beloved son.

But no one will be able to decipher the heart of the tombstone:
Who is the martyr who died without a name and an age?
Day by day the sun will polish the closure of my shadow
And it never revealed: when, who, and where.

[Page 142]

This memorial monument was erected above a cave into which three thousand of our brothers, men, women, and children, young and old, toddlers and nursing babies, were thrown alive by the German fascists, on Saturday, the 15th of Iyyar TSh"B (May 2, 1942), were shut in, every exit closed and blocked, until they suffocated and died of hunger. The sound of screams and heart-breaking moans were heard in the distance from within the earth over several weeks.

"And it will be with the treading of their feet in this place, you shall remember the souls of the martyrs who were killed in strange and cruel deaths for the sanctification of God's name, and you will say: May their souls be bound up in the bundle of life. Amen."

(Copied from the text on the back of this photograph, which was sent by a native of our city, Meir Pecherskiy.)

An eternal memorial to the martyrs of our city,
Dunayivtsi

[Page 143]

Personalities

Translated by Monica Devens

Professor Yehezkel Kaufmann

Yehezkel Kaufmann was born in 1889 to observant parents. His father was a cloth merchant and brought his son, as was the custom, to the "Cheder" and when the boy grew up, he studied Talmud and Poskim in the Beit Midrash. In addition to this, he studied Hebrew grammar and some new Hebrew literature from a private Hebrew teacher. Even at the dawn of his days he showed a tendency to write essays. His first article was published in "Ha-Shilo'ah" on Ahad Ha'am.

When the family moved to Odesa, Kaufmann entered the "Rav Tsa'ir" yeshiva and heard lectures by Bialik and Klausner. It was in this Ulpan that he heard for the first time about the existence of Biblical criticism and he was particularly impressed by this scientific discipline, without agreeing to the content of the lectures he heard at the time. In the meantime, Kaufmann began to study general sciences and went to Bern in Switzerland and took classes in philosophy, history, Bible, and Semitic languages. There he was awarded the title of Doctor of Philosophy. From there, he moved to Berlin and engaged in philosophy. But over time, he devoted his work to the study of Judaism and the Bible.

In 1919 Kaufmann immigrated to Israel and taught Tanakh at the Reali School in Haifa and, after a while, he was invited to lecture at the university in Jerusalem and was appointed professor of Bible there. He served in this position until 1957. He participated in almost all Hebrew periodicals with his articles and research in the field of Judaism, its history and problems, and twice won the Bialik Prize. Of all his many writings, Kaufmann achieved recognition mainly through two books: "Exile and Estrangement" and "The Religion of Israel, from its Beginnings to the Babylonian Exile."

In his book "Exile and Estrangement," Kaufmann lays the foundations for his view of the philosophy of history in general, and of the Jewish people in particular, and insists on the explanation of the uniqueness of Israel. In his opinion, the religious factor alone served to shape the unity and merger of the Jewish nation. A most original work is his great book, "The Religion of Israel, from its Beginnings to the Babylonian Exile." Through this monumental composition, he brought redemption to biblical science, which until then was in the hands of foreign scholars or in the hands of Israeli scholars who were influenced by non-Jewish scholars.

As is known, biblical science was dominated by the view of the Wellhausen school, according to which the belief in unity in Israel developed from idolatry. Kaufmann proves on the basis of studies and evidence from the Bible itself that this view is fundamentally wrong and that the idea of the unity of the Godhead is what distinguishes Judaism and that it developed from the beginning of its appearance on the stage of history without the element of idolatry. This idea is a novelty in the literature of biblical science and, just as the idea is a novelty, so is the originality of his method and his way of proof to strengthen his position.

In the twilight of his life, he began writing commentaries on the book of first prophets and managed to publish commentaries on the book of Joshua and the book of Judges.

Kaufmann was a researcher who expressed the thought of Israel from the beginning of its existence as a people. He reflected on the spiritual beginning of the nation in order to discover its cultural cradle. In this research, he saw the purpose of his life and plowed deep into the depths of the spiritual genesis of the nation.

Dr. M. Z. Sola

[Page 144]

Professor Zvi Sharfstein

Zvi Sharfstein's literary writing is rich and varied. There seems to be no problem in education that has not been illuminated in his many books. His theory is short and sweet. He presents his ideas in copious amounts when the matter requires it, but also in brief when the purpose is clear. And another sentence only for necessity. Law and practice are bound together for him. There is no thought without an action next to it and there is no action without a theoretical clarification.

Zvi Sharfstein has many honors in many areas of our cultural system, credits of originality. The first involves his sincere and serious concern for small children in the diaspora by his writing textbooks for them that opened an era in this field.

These books were liked by teachers and students alike in different countries in the diaspora and were widely distributed.

Sharfstein was one of the first, it seems, to write a book for learning the language for adults. While he was still in Galicia, before coming to the United States, he wrote such a book together with Raphael Soferman z"l. He was the first in explaining the methodical side of the acquisition of the language. The name of the book - "Methods of Learning Our Language." He was also one of the first to illuminate "methods of learning the Tanakh."

He was also first in formulating problems and their clarifications mainly in other areas of our educational literature and among the first in reviving the language and speaking it in the diaspora. He was the first among the educated people of our city for whom the language was fluent and his fresh and sharp Hebrew speech led to the fact that, in other cities near and far also, the language would live on in speech, such that our small city was known for its influence on other cities in matters of Zionism.

L"Y Riklis

* * *

Zvi Sharfstein: An educator with every fiber of his being. Not a professional, but for whom education is a lofty national-human moral mission. The educator begins in him from the model of his outstanding personality and continues to be embodied over decades in the act of teaching and authoring textbooks for children. In everything he wrote, even in things that are apparently far from the issue of education, an educational purpose is concealed. But since the virtue of his education is a result of the foundation of the love that is in him, from the poetry in his personality - the educational purposefulness in his writings, often unconscious and therefore also indirect, wrapped always in poetic moral values, an atmosphere of a high moral level with deep religious feeling, and within everything and above everything - an essence of love. A triple love that is one: for man in general, for the people of Israel, and for the culture of Israel. The humanistic tone in which his words are incorporated comes from here. Broad-minded humanism, which accepts the problems of the Jewish people as a general human issue.

[Page 145]

Zvi Sharfstein, as mentioned, wrote a lot. In addition to the many textbooks, whose successors have passed through ages and countries, he also authored several foundational books, which add serious weight to any Hebrew pedagogical library ("The History of Education in Israel in Recent Generations"; "Education in the Land of Israel").

Most visible are his autobiography books: "It Was Spring in the Land" and its sequel - "Forty Years in America." To these can be added two more books, which also complement each other: "A Teacher's Lifestyle" and "A Conversation with the Teachers." These books belong to the field of fine literature and in them, his personality is fully realized.

Yaakov Khurgin

S. L. Blank

S. L. Blank lived his first eighteen years in my hometown, Dunayivtsi; then he lived in Bessarabia for about 14 years and in the United States for about forty years.

Most of his stories are taken from the collection of his trials and experiences during his fourteen years of residence in Bessarabia and they are Bessarabian stories and types; and even when he described Jewish immigrants in America - he went back over the Jews of Bessarabia.

He was a son of nature, rooted in it and living with it. And in Bessarabia, in the communities and towns where he served as a teacher, he found his soul's place: the fields, the trees, and the streams; the expanses of the prairie and the flocks of sheep, and the shepherd who was part of the landscape. He was a poet of the landscape and its creatures, a poet of nature in all its manifestations.

In Dunayivtsi whose inhabitants were, like in all the towns, peddlers and shopkeepers, agents and craftsmen and Beit Midrash students - Blank did not find his world. The Jews there were mostly cut off from nature. It was somewhat different in Bessarabia - some of its Jewish residents were villagers, close to the land, breathing fresh air and earning a living through hard work. Blank chose them. He depicted their lives as he saw them with his artistic eye.

Bessarabia produced several important Hebrew writers such as Yehuda Steinberg and S. Ben-Zion, who spent most of their lives in Bessarabia, and even so the types they described were not different from the types described by Hebrew writers from other districts. However, Blank did not deal with these types much. In his works, there are not many of the peddlers and shopkeepers, the agents and the learned and the educated. If he mentions them - it is nothing more than a cursory impression.

[Page 146]

Blank chose for his works the shepherd and the tillers of the land, even an American immigrant - if he were a Bessarabian Jew and lived in the city - he longs for the earth, establishes a farm for himself, and turns to the field and to the chicken coop and to the barn. As a son of nature who understands his alternatives, Blank paints him from both sides - on the side of his serenity and his beauty and on the side of his storms and destructive forces, "sheep," "colony," "land," "inheritance" - these creations of his were mainly subject to the sublime quiet, the silence of its tranquilities, its charm, its landscape, and the changes of nature's wrath. The animal is also part of the landscape. The dog, the cow, the cat, the calf, the bird, and the chick - they were all in the grasp of his eye and the whispers of his heart. He was perhaps the only Hebrew writer in the diaspora whose dog was his friend - an intimate friend - the dog, Torik, in the poetic story "Eve."

His great pleasure was to paint, with the warmth of his heart, the great peace that reigned over the expanses, the abundance of the earth that nourished its creatures. In the book "Sheep," he begins with a depiction of a plot of land, which Boaz leased after his wedding on which to raise sheep. He started with five sheep and a dog to guard the sheep. The depictions are pastoral. The whole atmosphere is full of happiness. When Boaz sees his flock grazing on the grass, he says: Eat, my dears, and let it be palatable. And when he sees them drinking from the river water, he whispers, drink nice. And a flute for the shepherd and he plays the song of the uniqueness of the meadow and thinks about his young wife who is beloved by him. And the Shabbat in the house of this shepherd, a simple person who does not know how to read the prayer book, is described as a day of great pleasure. The entire book is an idyll, an idyll, which also includes the building of life, like the story of Knut Hamsun, "The Blessing of the Earth." The story, "Sheep," and his other books of this type - "Moshava," "Inheritance," "Land" - are the only ones in our literature that are based on the poetry of the land (except for the stories of Mapu and Buki Ben Yagli, who preceded him). Even in the Land of Israel, where the religion of labor developed and its pioneers gave their souls to revive the wilderness, no idyll was created, it was not created and it could not be created.

Blank's Boaz was the innocent united with nature, son of mother earth who nursed from her breasts, and the pioneers were the sons of the cities, people saturated with culture who approached the land not as its descendants, but as broad-minded idealists who, due to their wisdom and understanding of the history of the nations, came to the general conclusion that the land is the mother of all life and that through work, the nation of Israel would be resurrected.

The other side of nature - its tremendous eruption in storm and tempest, and the inner storm in the human soul. In Blank's books there is a description of storms and horrors and angry rains. The black clouds, the thunders, the lightning, and the violent whirlwind of leaves and branches and trees being uprooted - the whole vision of nature diverging from its framework to break and to explode and to destroy - all these were described with great power. And he also painted with vigor the turmoil of the soul, the eruption of lust for the flesh, the terror of revenge, and the feelings of murder, and the thirst for blood. And since Jewish types were not the most suitable for mental turmoil and the outburst of desire - to use knives and rifles - Blank went with black people, Italians, and Romanians - Romanians during the riots against the Jews. These depictions are full of power and talent. He forces us to believe in these outbursts, their climaxes that reach a high level, that they are found in life, and that they are the obligation of reality, complicated results in the soul.

"A Man, a Woman, and a Monkey" is a wonderful story about a disabled Italian who fights with his young and healthy wife

[Page 147]

who cheated on him and was about to strangle him, and the woman killed him with a pistol bullet. The book, "During the Emergency," is full of acts of sadism and murder by Romanians and their abuse of the Jews - their victims. In his story, "The Haters," the heavy atmosphere is felt, the atmosphere of savagery in the Moldavian villages. The scene of the war fought by a Jewish boy who returned from the army and defended the honor of his mother and the honor of his fiancÃ©e - a work of thought. The boy's attack on his enemy, Akseno the Romanian, is a great artistic achievement. Blank wrote a lot about the life of the Jewish immigrants here - actually one could say: the immigrants in Philadelphia and its surroundings. He described the changes that occurred in the immigrants because of their desire to adapt or because of the necessity of adaptation, because of their desire to climb the class ladder. The descriptions are written in a sociological spirit and whoever comes to write in the future about the changes in the lives of the immigrants, the first and second generation in America, their transition from crafting and from small peddling to shops, and from shops to wealth, and the ways of imitation and human and social relations - will find what they are looking for in Blank.

Zvi Sharfstein

Avraham Rosen (Rosenzweig)

I saw his name for the first time in one of the last volumes of "Ha-Tekufa" and the things, the words of poetry, made an impression on me. I remember something new in their way of expression, new and unusual and original. I was amazed at that natural nakedness, that extreme lack of flowery language that is so rare in any poetry and least of all in our Hebrew poetry. And at the same time - what simplicity they are and what special devotion.

His basic tone - longings, longings of a child left to his own devices in the big world, "soft and graceful as the silk of a dream and joy." I still remember "sad father-mother, grandmothers knit meager socks." Fields wrapped in wildness and a variety of flowers and greenery, a river gladdening from his days as babies on holiday, a garden drowning in a sea of sunflowers and poppies - the sights of the Ukrainian landscape.

The poet is a villager and it is the village that set the boundaries of his world, but in the meantime, he went out and wandered in the big world and behold, he was captured and lost in the city. From it he strays and is drawn from his framework to nature and to the perfection in nature and complains over human beings who closed their souls in the city. And there is that, in his longing for nature, a sudden realization of illusion will come and illuminate for the poet in the suburbs of the city and he hears the following as a kind of whisper: "Man will return again to the earth and to God and somewhere the fields' harvest will still wait for us." A pure, simple, and human expression of the main prayer of his life.

[Page 148]

And in this state of mind of standing in prayer, behold he gives us gentle homeland songs. He gave us a melodic poem, "Did you hear the sound in the ravine?" The ending: "From afar, the echo still sings - is the trembling still sounding?" Or the poem, "Naked and Scorched by Sands," in which he says to his country:

> See,
> At the edge of your horizon, the tent was built.
> Did you know perhaps?
> Command pleasantness nightly and at ease
>
> In the bosom of a woman and in the lamb's pen,
> And with a burst of light in the cracks

> Rise up and engrave the destiny of my name
> Like the purity of your clods of earth.

Was the poet in real life among the true pioneers? It is impossible for those who have not tasted the taste of their lives to feel what he feels and expresses.

> And with the sprouting of my first buds
> The leaves of the tenderness of your skin
> I will hide my face and cry with joy:
> My seed, the seed of the homeland.

The secret of the homeland is revealed to the poet, if he can feel in the poem, "In the Spring," what he put, in his humility, in the mouth of the one walking in amazement wondering in the meadow (the p' has a kamatz vowel): "The walker wondered in the meadow/Who took root in the landscape?/To the tree top of a birch above the blue/He will focus his eye/The flower of happiness."

A hint of spring - and also a hint of love. Among the pearls of the dream - he tells us - there is one full of grace still illuminating the path of his life from then until now: "Aviv. Valley and forest. Light and blue sky. Paths and paths wander up the mountain. A girl runs in the wild so stormily happy. After her - he, the young poet.

> Suddenly a flash of light lit a fire in the eyes.
> A storming wave of blood is aroused.
> Like the gold of bells silently the lips sounded,
> The girl cries - and I love, love.

This last verse, full of simplicity and wonderful beauty, gives us more about love than we have found in some long and great love songs.

Dr. Shimon Ginzburg

* * *

His first steps into Hebrew poetry were encouraged and he immediately entered the most excellent literary quarters of those days, "Ha-Tekufa" edited by Ya'akov Cohen, and since then we have indeed seen his poems in all the periodicals, "Mozna'im" and "Gilyonot," "Davar" and "Ha-Aretz," "Bustanai" and "Ha-Po'el Ha-Tsa'ir," "Ha-Do'ar" and more, and he also published several lyrical and epic poetry books.

[Page 149]

Twenty-five years ago, the poet Avraham Rosen immigrated to Israel and his first meeting with the homeland was an experience for him that mostly nursed an ancient vision and his first poems that he wrote in Israel are filled with imagination, dream, and admiration. Morning light like the gold of a dream danced his first step in the sand on the beach of Jaffa and Tel Aviv seemed to him like a queen's daughter, her sides the charms of the moon and her heartbeat "dreaming of the azure of the sea and the height." And whenever he went out on the paths of the homeland and his eye encounters the high mountains on its border, he will feel that "the ancient world in the mountain is still standing before his eyes and the sleep of thousands of generations still weaves the dream." The sound of his country, if he heard it in the ravine, seemed to him smooth and soft like the silk of a dream and he felt that all this was a commotion in his soul. Thus his being clung to all the gentleness, the light, and the landscape in the land, and his soul sunk in the dream of his land. Nothingness is never a dream, the time of awakening also comes, and the poet sees the stillness of the landscape of the homeland as a life force and, if the homeland is also "naked and charred sands," indeed he will believe in her fate that days will still come when buds will germinate on "the softness of her skin."

And the longer the poet's residence in Israel, the more his poetry absorbed the land's vitality. The place of the dream was taken by reality and he sings about a poor clump of earth, about a plow and a horse, about an asphalt path and a poor shack, and the people of honest work. Avraham Rosen moved from the sounds of a homeland of pleasures sunk in paradise and dreams to the poetry of reality and also wrote about the days of great suffering and terror, of bloody events, and, as was his way, without raging tones, his voice restrained, nothing in it from the storm or the cry, but every word of his is from the poetry of the time, the war, the Holocaust - saturated with pain.

The landscapes of the homeland, Jerusalem, Tel Aviv, villages and farms, labor and building, mothers and children - all those manifestations of life with its ups and downs - are echoed in Rosen's poems, but the center of his poetry is his individual lyricism. In this area, too, it will be revealed to us in his clear and polished idiom without the drag of shiny words and without over-polishing. Rosen opens for us in his singular poem windows to peek through them into his soul, his thoughts, his emotions, the quiet sorrow that stirs in him, to loneliness, to the reconciliation that comes after difficulties following an inner awakening. The poet knows that there is no companion in dreaming and he must go on in his life alone, but the paths are various and many and they lead to heights, to the abyss, to hell, and therefore it is good to rise up out of the abyss of his life, even if he deprives himself of all. And it does happen often that our footprints on the paths of life fade and disappear and there are those anxious to continue the march, but our poet knows that the dream, even in vain, was better than waking up and that, beyond the secular, it is good to hope for a miracle because the window to the next day is open and through it one can see the "radiance of space."

Avraham Rosen's lyrical poetry is therefore caught between two poles: the pole of pain and the abysses of human existence and the pole of the reconciliation and the purification of the heart.

Avraham Rosen also created epic poetry, with his long poems and folk tales such as "Three in the Homeland," "The Penitent," "Shabbat Candles," "The Miraculous," and more - we see not only control over the material, but also a poetic, folk, essential rhythm.

Natan Goren

[Page 150]

Mordechai Michaeli

Mordechai Michaeli (Frizant) was born in TRN"D (=1893-94). His father was a rich merchant who became impoverished and, being literate and observant, tried to give his sons a traditional Torah education as well. The family lived for a time in a village close to the city and the boy, Mordechai, spent most of the weekdays at his family's old house in the city and studied in the "Cheder." On Friday nights, he would return to his father's house and on Sundays, when he could not afford to pay the fare to the city - and this happened quite often - he would walk to the city (a distance of 7-8 km) so that he did not abandon his Torah study.

When the boy turned fifteen and his father's situation collapsed completely, he was forced to stop his studies in the "Cheder" and he immersed himself entirely in reading the new Hebrew literature. Along with that, he studied a lot of Tanakh and the "Ein Ya'akov" legends that one of the teachers taught him not for personal gain, and under their influence, the spirit of creation began to beat inside him. He began to write tales from his imagination and even managed to publish some of them in children's magazines. He even edited and published, with the help of his friends, a literary collection for youth called "Ba-Gina."

The Zionist environment in which he grew up and worked during his teenage years instilled in him a strong desire for a Hebrew life in the land of the ancestors and in his twentieth year, he immigrated to the Land of Israel. There he felt as if he had returned home and the mental contrasts between dream and reality no longer existed for him. The Land of Israel, the land of his yearning ever since, received him with love and he was happy there even in his great suffering. He finished his studies at the Beit Midrash for teachers and at the Hebrew University in Jerusalem and became a teacher at the "Tahkemoni" school. The fountain of his literary work also increased over the years and he wrote many stories and legends for children that excelled in their originality and special biblical style.

He died in the year TShY"Z (=1956-1957) in his beloved city of Jerusalem, which he did not leave from the day he immigrated to Israel until his last day.

A. R.

* * *

I met Mordechai Michaeli in Jerusalem. He came there as a young man to become a student at the Beit Midrash for teachers founded by "Ezra." In this institution, where the "rebellion of the Hebrew language" against "Ezra" was announced, his national feeling was also strengthened and his love for the Torah in general, and Israeli culture in particular, deepened. Add to this the serious spirit of the eternal city as well as the degree of his natural diligence and the honesty of his thinking - and you have the general outlines of Michaeli's character and spiritual essence. But this is not sufficient. A special softness of modesty, almost feminine, was spread over him. His soul abhorred all ugliness, all harsh and coarse speech.

[Page 151]

At the university he devoted himself to studying history and literature, and even published a few monographs. But the place of his life and satisfaction was the world of legend. In this world, he sunk into spiritual closeness out of the enthusiasm of intoxication and in it, his original creative power was revealed.

This world of wonder, of miracles, of supernatural occurrences, became in his creation a reality with its own logic, with moral legitimacy. Michaeli's legend is not a matter of amusement, of entertainment, of amusing "tricks." It is serious, it is imbued with serious emotions. And another fundamental quality is found in it: it is not ethereal, it does not blossom in the air of a rootless imagination, but finds its roots in some reality of being and a Jewish way of life. There is no religion, mitzvot, or tradition at its core, and even so it has the smell of "Judaism," and it is infused with a Jewish atmosphere and saturated with Jewish folk innocence.

Michaeli chose the language and the style for his creation in the field of legend out of a special sense. Not an everyday language, secular language, but the language of the ancients with the grace of purity and innocence in it. The clear biblical language - without frills and embellishments - matches the design of his legends and is organic and adheres to their subject matter and their inner quality.

S. Shafan

Yosef Blank

One of the most prominent figures in public, national, and cultural life in Dunayivtsi was Yosef Blank z"l. A multi-sided and multi-faceted personality, a dreamer and a realist; a scholar and a man of action. Gifted with great personal charm, which attracted the best forces from all strata of the people to the current of national revival.

Not only did Zionism give him fantasies and national pride, vision and hope; not only the "Hovevei Zion" movement whose center was the Odesa Committee found in him one of the most enthusiastic and active personalities - but also in the field of education and culture was he the central dynamic force in Dunayivtsi.

Not only his friends from "Bnei Tsiyon," but also the youth from all the radical factions in Zionism, came to hear his reviews on the course of the Zionist congresses in which he participated starting with the second of them. He was a gracious speaker. Gifted with a sense of subtle humor and delicate irony. With his enthusiasm and his deep faith on behalf of which he worked, he saturated the youth with his dreams of Zion.

He was the initiator and organizer of the Hebrew educational enterprises in the city. From Bălți in Bessarabia he brought the poet Ya'akov Fichman to Dunayivtsi, who taught Hebrew to the youth for two years. From Courland

[Page 152]

he invited the learned and polished and somewhat depressed Dr. Knopping, who served as a teacher in a "Improved Cheder" that was founded at the time. Yosef Blank was one of the most active in the management of this "Improved Cheder," intended for the children of the affluent, and a "Talmud Torah" for the children of the poor.

He would donate his limited time on Saturday afternoons to teach Mishna to artisans and simple people. A kind of Jewish version of the Russian popular movement "Going to the People."

The problem: "Hebrew or Russian," which stirred up emotions in those days, or even "Hebrew or Yiddish," didn't worry him.- What is this "Hebrew or Yiddish?" He loved them both like twins born to the same parents. Well-versed in the ancient sources, a faithful reader of the new Hebrew literature, he was at the same time in love with every artistic work that appeared in Yiddish.

The first sounds of the folk songs of Warshawsky, heard in the city, came from the house of Yosef Blank. He sang them together with his sons, accompanied by a violin that his eldest son played.

All the books of the "Tushiya," "Ahiasaf," and "Moriah" publishers in Hebrew lived peacefully in one basket with the writings of Shalom Aleichem, Mendele, and Peretz in Yiddish. In his house were found the magazines "Ha-Shilo'ah," "Ha-Tzofeh," and "Ha-Tsfira," together with the newspapers "Haynt" and "Moment" from Warsaw and the "Gut Morgen" of Lewinsky which appeared in Odesa, where he also published from the fruit of his pen for many years.

He established associations, organized clubs especially for the youth, and instilled in all strata of the people enthusiasm, national pride, and faithfulness to the Zionist struggle.

The saying that "there is a good man who demands and there is no good man who fulfills" did not apply to him. He infected his sons and daughters with his enthusiasm and his deep belief in the revival of the nation, and he did his best to educate them as Jews and free and proud people at the same time. When he decided in 1913 to send his two young daughters to Israel to work as pioneers and to continue their studies at the same time, his sister came at him indignantly: why is he sending children at a tender age to such a distant place. - "Children, you say? I sent people" - he replied.

His extensive Zionist activities often caused him friction with the Tsarist authorities. The Zionist movement was declared, as we know, to be an illegal political organization and Zionist work was conducted under the guise of the legal Odesa "Hovevei Zion" committee. And here it happened, that Yosef Blank, together with all the members of the committee of the Zionist Federation in Podolia, "were caught" in the house of the lawyer Schleifer in Kamyanets Podilskyy and prosecuted for belonging to an illegal organization. It was in the days of the blackest reaction after the short "spring" of 1905 and all the members of the committee were expected to be sentenced to imprisonment from six months to three years. But a miracle happened: the investigating judge was a liberal person and a personal friend of the lawyer Schleifer and the trial ended well.

Yosef Blank visited Israel for the first time in 1914 and settled there in 1925. In 1926 he went to Chernivtsi to visit his sons and died suddenly in Vatra Dornei in Bukovina.

N. Avi-Chaim

* * *

I heard a lot about the Zionist activities of Yosef Blank already in my youth. His reputation preceded him in the towns of Podolia and Bessarabia. He was known as an outstanding propagandist and his influence on the Zionist youth was strong. I was a young girl when I left my town of Briceni in 1904 and went to study in Belz, the district city of Bessarabia. I came to the house of Itta and Yisrael Steinberg (brother of the writer Yehuda Steinberg). Their home was a meeting place for the Zionist youth. I, a passionate Zionist from my youth, started with a group of friends in community action. We organized a Zionist association and its meetings were mostly held at the Steinberg's house. There, too, many mentioned the name of Yosef Blank.

On one of the evenings while I was sitting in my room, a man about 45 years old appeared, tall, handsome, with a black beard that added to his face, and introduced himself: Yosef Blank. He said that he wanted to talk with me a bit and that's how our acquaintance began.

The conversations between us were ongoing. Every time he visited Belz for his business, he would come to me. He also visited our association. Under his influence, we began to engage in cultural work and held lectures on the essence of political Zionism and on the practical work in the Land of Israel. After the lectures, we sang the songs of the Land of Israel in a group. The connection with the country grew stronger. Yosef Blank also insisted on the need for practical work: collecting funds for Keren Kayemet, which was not an easy task in those days because of the vigorous opposition to Zionism in various public circles. In our conversations, Yosef Blank always guided me, advised and inspired, speaking as friends with surprising simplicity.

I learned a lot from these conversations and so they are etched in my memory. I was certainly not the only one among the Zionist youth that Yosef Blank would meet with and inspire. This individual approach was an interesting innovation in those times and there was a great blessing in it.

In 1905 I returned to my parents' house and the days - the eve of the revolution and the pogroms.

The Jewish youth in Russia, and of course also in our town, were under the influence of Marxist socialism. There were heated arguments between them and our Zionist association. Both sides would invite respected speakers. Socialist Zionist speakers from all its streams would come to our association, but mainly - from "Po'alei Tsiyon" from the Land of Israel. We had arguments with outside forces, but things were not right at home either. The rift between the "Tsiyonei Tsiyon" and the territorialists grew deeper.

Yosef Blank would also visit me at home, and in the association he would demand to study Hebrew history thoroughly: without a thorough knowledge of the people's history, it is impossible to understand our connection with the Land of Israel. The days of the Seventh Congress were approaching, the first after Herzl's death, a Congress in which the decision should be made: Zion or Uganda. Spirits were agitated. Yosef Blank's hectic work began. He would come to us often, gather the members of the association, and prove that only the Land of Israel would solve the homeland question for the people of Israel.

He was a good orator, his lecture was clear, he spoke with true youthful fervor and also influenced the territorialists in our association. Despite being under the influence of Po'alei Tsiyon, we chose him as a delegate to the Congress. I remember that once I had to consult him on an urgent matter in connection with the congressional elections. I went to his hotel. They brought me into his room and here he is standing in a tallit and tefillin -

[Page 154]

and praying. With a wave of his hand, he invited me to sit down and he continued his prayer. When he finished, he came over to discuss with me the matter I had brought to him.

In 1907-1908 I studied in Odesa and already worked among Po'alei Tsiyon. And here comes Yosef Blank to Odesa because of Zionist matters. We met and from our conversations I realized that his view on Zionism in general had not changed. Nevertheless, he encouraged me in my work. All roads lead to Zion, he said. The friendship between us had not been damaged.

We met several times in Israel and I had the impression that he was also active in the Zionist party there. But it was clear to me that the man was sick. In 1926 he went to Chernivtsi to visit his family and died there.

Esther Hen

Avraham Lerner

A marvelous figure, humility with precious virtues of the spirit. From the outside - simplicity and innocence mixed with folkiness, and from the inside - qualities and contributions of a distinguished person.

It grew by itself from underneath him, his environment - a typical Jewish community in a Ukrainian town with all the 49 gates of the diasporic existence in it, and his education - the traditional patriarchal upbringing of the family home, rabbi, and righteous teacher in his community. The beginning of his education - the Talmud and its subjects, which the family home acquired for him from the dawn of his childhood and in which he acquired great proficiency, and its end - the original Hebrew philosophy of the Middle Ages and the Enlightenment period and the new Hebrew literature. All this in difficult living conditions, without a teacher and guide, without any outside help and assistance. From the depths of his soul and from the very essence of his being, he aspired, with his great and bold will, to Torah and to knowledge and from it, he also forged his almost unlimited ability to reach the desired perfection in certain areas.

Because the man was whole, whole in his soul and spirit, and he did not know "the rift in the heart" that his contemporaries suffered. These were "carried by the wind." "The air drifted" beyond the Pale of Settlement and he remained "a soft chick" but faithful "under the wings of the Shekhinah."

Indeed, the highlight of his life and work on earth was mainly his educational work in the Zionist area according to the version of Ahad Ha'am because only this elevated man was his teacher to help in the wandering "of the crossroads of his ways" and he stuck to his teachings until the end of his life.

[Page 155]

While still a boy in his father's house, the "town rabbi" filled him up with Gemara, Rashi, and the Toseftas and after that - the fruit of the joys of Hebrew thought and creation. Upon reaching his matriculation, he began to engage in private teaching and trained quite a few students in his city in Hebrew and its literature (the writer of these columns was also honored to be counted among them). Through close contact with the youth, he recognized and appreciated the fresh forces stored in them for the benefit of the Zionist movement and its future and, together with some of his friends, founded the Zionist youth association "Ha-Techiya," which had a prominent record in the history of Zionism in Ukraine.

Due to his delicate health, he was forced to leave teaching and, with his immigration to Israel, he worked for some years as the secretary of the teachers' federation. Despite the difficulties of absorption, he became fond of the country as he was endeared to all his acquaintances and all those he knew for the pleasantness of his speech and the beauty of his manners, however, the great and cruel suffering that came upon the Jewish settlement during the First World War determined his death while he was still middle-aged.

Avraham Rosen

Mordechai (Motl) Roizen

I met him back in my youth. Short, quick in movement and speech, and with dreamy eyes. He was a wholesale grain merchant and on the days of the fairs in our city, you could see him standing since morning by his warehouse, wearing old and dusty clothes and weighing the sacks of grain that the peddlers around the market were buying from the farmers and bringing to him for sale. Usually, he did not have it easy in business. Even in the years of economic good fortune in our city, success did not shine on him and, if he sometimes had a year of good business, then those that came after them ate up all the good until it was not known that they had happened.

Because the man did not know action, not real life with all its flaws and imperfections, with all the deception and the fraud in it. He did not know the crookedness of the complicated and perplexing human desire, which casts jealousy and hatred between humans and leads them to price fixing and exploitation, deceit and theft. He was all spirit, one who embroiders the mask of his life beyond the realm of daily reality and sees his world mainly in the vision of his heart and the sights of his imagination.

He was also a man of the book. When he returned home from the labor market, emotional and thought poor, he stripped away his many troubles and worries, along with his ragged and dusty clothes, and as a Hebrew scholar

[Page 156]

and outstanding student, wore the garments of emotion and contemplation and worked diligently reading and studying books. His library contained the best of Hebrew literature, starting with the masterpieces of Hebrew poetry and philosophy from the Middle Ages and ending with the collections of the Enlightenment period, the periodicals "Ha-Shilo'ah" and "Ha-Dor," the poems of Y. L. Gordon and Bialik, the books of "Ahiasaf," "Tushiya," and more.

And not only he alone enjoyed his library. All of us, the studying youth in the city, were inspired by it and tasted the taste of reading in the selection of Hebrew literature because his home was a meeting place for us and in it, we felt ourselves as part of our own. He would be with us as with his sons and, with his good taste and knowledge, he would guide us along the paths of Hebrew culture and its revival. He would encourage the first steps of "the writers" among us (among them M. Michaeli, S. L. Blank, and the writer of these columns) and would himself, from time to time, publish reports and articles in the Hebrew press.

The Zionist movement, especially the one that came out of the Beit Midrash of Ahad Ha'am, as well as the revival of the Hebrew language and literature, fascinated the man from the beginning of their awakening and over time, they became the fundamental principle in his private life as well, in which he thought and worked day and night and to which he devoted the best of his energy and spirit. I remember, when I was young, that I saw him on one of the Shabbats sitting wrapped in a tallit in the Sadigura Synagogue during the morning prayer and, as the congregation read the "Psukei de-Zimra" with the cantor in a loud voice, he sang pleasantly and enthusiastically "Ha-Matmid" by Bialik by heart. He was entirely glowing and radiant with excitement and the elation of spirit as an enthusiastic Hasid at the time of spiritual elevation.

During the days of the Bolshevist revolution in Russia, he migrated with his family to the United States, where he was engaged in selling Hebrew books. And see, it's a miracle! Even within the 49 gates of the diasporic existence, which he found in his new place of residence, he did not stop planning his dream of the good and the beautiful in renewed Judaism and also dared in his old age to challenge the authorities of the Russian Revolution who brutally oppress the Jews of their country and rule the soul of the Jewish people without mercy. He did this mainly in his series of articles, which he published in "Ha-Do'ar" under the title "Letters from Russia." At the time, the letters made an impression on the Jews of the United States and they opened their eyes to see what was happening behind the Iron Curtain.

Such was the man in his youth and in his old age, a dreamer and a fighter, honest and sincere and loyal to his people and his spirit until the end of his days.

Avraham Rosen

[Page 157]

Zamechov
(Zamikhiv, Ukraine)
48°52' 27°22'

Translated by Marlene Zakai

Under the Polish regime, Zamechov was located in the Podole Province. In 1765, the Jewish Community in the town and surroundings numbered 505 individuals. In 1784 there were 547 and in 1787 there were 518; of them 252 were in Zamechov. When Podolia was annexed to Russia, the town was in Ushitza Province. The number of Jews in 1847 were 958. According to the 1897 census, there were 895 Jews among the 2,217 residents.

[Page 158]Blank[Page 159]

Zamechov

by Yakov Haezri

The town was small and meager. There were approximately 1000 Jews. Among them were Torah scholars, respected and honored by tradespeople and other residents, and from whom they learned a way of life.

There were also Hasidim in the town, followers of the Friedman Rabbinic line (also known as the Ruzhiner Rebbes). These rabbis were from Boyani, Sadagora, Chortkov and Husiatyn. Almost every year the Hasidim would cross the border to Galitzia during the holidays, and they would return refreshed and inspired, with a new nigun (melody without words) and words of Torah from the rabbi. Every Shabbat the Hasidim would gather in one of their homes, for Kiddush and to praise their rabbi. On Hanukah they would celebrate the completion of the reading of the entire Talmud. They would also gather to pray on the Yahrtzeit of the Rizhany (refers to a prominent rabbi from Rizhany). The rest of the town's Jews were connected to one of the rabbis of the nearby town of Krolevetz. Rabbi Yehiel, from Synkiv, would visit the town once a year.

There were no organized institutions in the town. The Jewish residents looked after the poor in different ways (anonymous giving, bikur cholim [visiting the sick], welcoming guests, acts of loving kindness, providing dowries, etc.) To these goals, many contributed without remuneration.

The synagogue was also a Beit Midrash, a house of study. Every evening there was Torah study. The less learned studied "Ein Yaakov" a collection of Aggadic material and commentaries. There was another synagogue, a wooden synagogue that was considered to be the holier one. Education in the town was mostly in Chederim (religious schools) run by those who studied Gemara. From the years 1917-1918 kindergardens and public schools were established, as well as evening studies for adults.

Emigration was mostly to the United States. During this time, only a few went to Eretz Yisrael. There was a Zionist youth group in town. There was also a Bundist club made up of mainly artisans and their apprentices. During the 1917 Revolution, the Zionist movement grew and many of the youth joined Ze'irei Zion (Young Zionists) and similar organizations. During WWI young men were drafted into the army and this resulted in great financial hardship for their families. This was the extent of the suffering, perhaps because they were so far from the battlefields.

[Page 160]

Anti-semitism was not prevalent in the town. There was trade between Jews and non-Jews and it was mostly on good terms. "Shabbos goys" served the community in various ways. During the 1917 Revolution, a few Jews joined the local town council and from among them some were sentenced to death by Petlyura's people. After October 1917, the economic situation of the Jews worsened. Jewish life began to decline due to the difficult economic conditions and young people leaving the town.

During the change in regime resulting from the Revolution, Petlyura's gangs descended on the town, causing extensive pogroms. The goyim of the town and surroundings joined in the looting, destructions and murder. During the Petlyura and Denikin Regime there were more pogroms in the town. Denikin's soldiers burned homes, looted what was left after the Petlyura soldiers finished and they cruelly killed scores more. It is worth noting that during the pogroms there were also some goyim who saved lives. A few Jews managed to flee to a neighboring town, the new Ushitza. The synagogues were burned by the rioters and after that religious Jews prayed in private homes.

When the Soviets entered the town there was rejoicing at being saved from the pogroms, but the economic condition worsened and there were further signs of decline of the small community. The few that remained suffered from hunger, and if not for the help of their fellow Jews that managed to escape to the United States, or Israel, they would have all died of starvation.

Before the Germans entered, the town organized self-defense with a few weapons which they were forced to give up when the Germans occupied. By this time there were no young people and no one to continue the Hebrew Culture. During the Holocaust, the Jews were taken outside of town where they were forced to dig their own mass grave, after which they were shot and killed.

[Page 161]

Zhvanets
(Zhvanets, Ukraine)
48°33' 26°30'

Translated by Monica Devens

A town on the bank of the Dniester river, at a distance of about 16 versts from the regional city of Kamyanets Podilskyy. Its existence is known from the 15th century. In 1653, the Heidmak regiments laid siege to the Polish army of King Casimir in Zhvanets, which ended in the conclusion of a peace treaty between Bohdan Khmelnytsky and Casimir.

On June 22, 1769, Zhvanets was again forced to suffer in a cruel battle between the Russian army and the main concentration of the Polish rebels, who numbered 2,500 men and who barricaded themselves in Zhvanets and in the nearby town of Okopy. The battle ended in a major defeat for the rebels.

The Jewish population in Zhvanets counted 1,134 people in 1765 with 4,335 in the surrounding area. Due to the political events, and especially the military, their number decreased and in 1775 the town counted only 395 souls, with 126 in the surrounding area. In 1784, however, the Jewish community grew to 617 souls. However, it never reached the numbers of 19-20 years earlier.

The topographical situation of the town on the banks of the great river Dniester contributed to its recovery over time. Because of the Dniester, towns had trade relations with other towns, mainly in the sector of wood for building and for furniture.

There were in the town a pharmacy, a synagogue, 4 Beit Midrash, 2 schools for boys, a school for girls, and one mixed school. In 1847, during the reign of the Tsars, the town had a Jewish population of 1,619 souls and, according to the census of 1897, out of the general population of 5,005 residents, 3,353 were Jews, that is 67%.

[Page 162]Blank[]Page163]

Defense in Zhvanets

by A. Stit

Translated by Monica Devens

The town of Zhvanets lay on the banks of the Dniester and in the days that will be discussed below, its borders were triangular - on the one hand it bordered on the region of Bessarabia, with the Dniester river cutting between them and where the Romanians ruled and annexed it to their borders, and the other border was Galicia under the rule of the Poles where the Zbruch River separated them.

It was in 1904 or 1905. The renown of the self-defense in the town of Zhvanets, Podolia region, reached me and I was still a child in the second or third grade of the Hebrew grade school in the town where I was born;

From views of the city

as children, we were eager to know what the grown-ups hid from us, the things that were talked about in whispers and secret exchanges. These were the days of the Russian Revolution and after it. There was an active branch of the "Russian People's Association" in the town - a movement whose leaders and movers came from the right-wing and the extreme reactionaries in the Russian public sector; they were always involved in inciting riots among the Jews and in organizing them, and the clergy helped them through their Sunday sermons in the church. The ignorant crowd saw in them messengers of the Messiah and the Tsar. The organization was famous throughout Russia and especially in the area of the Jewish Pale of Settlement. They excited the masses with the well-known slogan, "strike the Jews and save Russia." Most of the rulers of Russia were appointed by the Tsar from this group. The local branch of the association established a consumer cooperative in the town and the surrounding countryside in order to create for itself a public base for its activities and in order to deprive the Jews of trade. They established the branch of the market precisely in the Jewish trade center and they would persuade the Christians to avoid buying from the Jews and, in this fashion, to cut off their livelihood. They flavored the lobbying with propaganda and incitement against the Jews as enemies of Russia and the Tsar

[Page 164]

and the causes of their disaster. It was an act of destruction and expropriation under the guise of cooperation and party propaganda hostile to the Jews. The cooperative did not exist long; after the danger of disturbances passed, it was closed, whether because it could not compete with the Jewish trade or whether because it did not achieve its other goal - to cause riots against the Jews. At the head of the organization of the disturbances was a popular teacher in the Christians' elementary school and around him was concentrated the Christian population of the town, the farmers, or the middle class, and the Ukrainian intelligentsia. These days were gloomy for the Jewish population, the days of October-November after the revolution. The cold that started to show its signs and the black clouds that hung over the town's sky added to the insecurity and fear of what was to come.

For the first time, we heard about the self-defense that began to be organized, about training in small arms and meetings in the forests of the town, and that the Jewish population is armed with round iron bars, a weapon of defense for anyone who does not know how to use firearms.

The frantic preparations to meet the rioters in an active manner and not to be a sheep to the slaughter became noticeable. In the town it was known that the day of the disturbance was approaching. The farmers who came to the town began to openly threaten that when the day came, they would riot against the Jews. I remember, I saw one of the farmers being led home and he was all wounded and bleeding as he waved his fists while threatening and shouting. It was two

The Defense Committee of 1918

or three days before the appointed day, later I heard stories at home that in the plaza of the city market, this farmer and others started threatening and shouting, then some people from the town approached and started beating them, and they grabbed one of them by the back of his neck and threw him with great force face down into a pile of gravel and his face was completely covered with blood and wounds. At the time of this act, all the villagers panicked and within an hour the town was emptied of villagers. The Jews of the town warned and threatened the residents of the nearby village that as soon as disturbances started - they would set the village on fire from all four sides. The very fact that the Jews were ready to fight back stifled their unrest. A rumor spread among the villagers that the Jews were preparing mechanized weapons (then

[Page 165]

there were still no machine guns) that they would activate on the day of the disturbances. The bullets of this machine would not harm Jewish pedestrians, but only Christians.

It can be assumed that in those cases when Jewish organization advanced - the defense people had the upper hand, prevented riots, and managed to stand up for themselves and save their property. It was clear that the villagers incited by the black federations to riot did not do so out of patriotic feelings or loyalty to the Tsar and his regime, but out of hatred of Jews.

The year 1918. The state of the town was in every way bad in terms of security. The authorities would change frequently, once it was the Germans, who retreated from Kyiv, once it was the Poles who advanced and retreated. And then the Ukrainians and the Bolsheviks who came in and out in turn and at the twilight of alternating governments - irregular military units or just bandits operated. The Jews were always between a rock and a hard place and it was necessary to create a self-defense force to protect the Jewish population caught up in fear and helplessness. In those days, another trouble appeared. At the initiative of the Ukrainian government, an uprising broke out in the villages of the neighboring Khotyn district in Bessarabia. The uprising by Ukrainians was forcefully suppressed by the Romanians with artillery fire on the rebelling villages. For many days, pillars of smoke and fire from the rebelling villages could be seen in the town. The rural population fled out of terror of the occupation and the fires, together with their families and the little possessions they could save, crossed the Dniester, and found refuge as refugees in our town of Zhvanets until the fury passed.

Once again we were forced to organize self-defense due to the disturbances that broke out in Ukraine, the great massacre in the city of Proskorov (= Khmelnytskyi), the riots and the massacre in the town of Pilshtyn. The staged provocation by the Ukrainian authorities served as a reason for the riots, who orchestrated a coup in favor of the Bolsheviks and only after that, arranged a massacre that cost about 400 Jewish lives.

All this was known to us young people. However, the homeowners' circles were hesitant to accept the idea of self-defense and there were those who opposed it and fought against this idea and reasoned with them: "it might provoke

Youth Group (A)

[Page 166]

the anger of the Christian population and the authorities." The young people had nothing to start with - no weapons and no money to buy them. It was also necessary to obtain some kind of legal approval from the authorities to establish defense. On the basis of a regulation of the Ukrainian government on the existence of Jewish self-government, as the secretary of the local Jewish community, I appealed to the governor of the district to approve self-defense for us. The answer was not long in coming - its gist was that he had no weapons and no ammunition. In the confusion devoid of power that characterized this government - this answer satisfied us. From a formal point of view - they did not refuse to approve the defense and did not even refuse to hand over weapons to us. We could, therefore, shut up the skeptics and the hesitant and say that, while the defense was indeed not approved, it was only for a lack of weaponry. As far as we were concerned, we had the option of solving the question of the weaponry and their purchase by our own means. We started by breaking into the police armory without them noticing and took a few rifles out of a large number that were scattered about in no order and without registration. Second, we purchased weapons and sold some to the self-defense in Kamyanets, so that the Kamyanets defense paid for one rifle the price we paid for two rifles so that we got a rifle for free. That's how we collected a few dozen rifles and armed the members of the defense who were mostly young, those who knew how to use weapons taught the others who were not used to weapons. In those days, cases of theft and robbery increased on the roads and in the town. This action had an immediate result - the thefts and robberies stopped altogether among the Jewish population and concentrated among the Christian population.

The sight of our boys in the dead of night walking with weapons instilled a measure of confidence in the Jewish population, but among the Christians, rumors began to spread that we were holding machine guns and even cannons. Of course, there was no basis for the rumors, but we tried not to deny them.

And here again, like 15 years ago, there were three incidents this time in the town, which proved that the mere existence of the Jewish defense was enough to deter rioters from going wild or to drive them away without the need to use weapons and without the need to bring the defense into any action whatsoever.

The first incident happened in the spring when the Romanian government announced an amnesty for the refugees and allowed them to return to their destroyed and deserted villages. The masses crossed with their vehicles, their livestock, and their families, over the Dniester by Zhvanets in order to return to their places. The beach was full of people, children and infants, and a huge crowd waited for their turn to cross. The bridge across the Dniester had been blown up by the Romanians and the river water rose because of the melting of the Carpathian snows and the crossing proceeded slowly for several days. It was a tumultuous and excited, disgruntled crowd, and even so, resigned itself to its fate and waited impatiently for its turn. However, among the refugees, there were those who were afraid to return and decided to stay in the town. Families of professional robbers who terrorized passers-by and, even during the time of the Tsar and in times of peace, dared to attack convoys that contained mail shipments and money and were guarded by policemen and armed soldiers, but even they knew that there was a defense and that the Jews had weapons, therefore they refrained from any and all intimidation and terror. One of them, who was drunk, grabbed a Jewish coachman and his cart and began to urge him to drive quickly through the town and shoot in the air with his pistol…We didn't know then if it was a mere prank or a planned provocation to scare us. I remember, I went with one of the members of the community then to collect funds for a cultural or economic purpose and I saw the pale and frightened face of the wagoner and the rioter shooting in the air. I recruited some members of the defense

[Page 167]

who started chasing him and even overtook him, took him off the cart, took his gun, and beat him steadfastly until he bled. Finally, they transferred him to the transit camp on the Dnieper to return him to Bessarabia.

This was a gentile, well-built and healthy, but the road leading to the river was about a kilometer and the whole time they did not let up from the blows. Bleeding, humiliated and persecuted, he arrived at the transit camp and began to beg for his life, that they kill him and crucify him so long as they did not hand him over to the Romanians. He started begging the raging crowd to intervene on his behalf and rescue him.

Indeed the crowd started shouting and demanding to fulfill his request. Of course, we did not want to arouse the anger of an agitated crowd and we handed him over to the police.

The second case happened in early autumn. One day around evening time, a small unit of cavalry soldiers with all their weapons appeared and bought themselves a rest at one of the inns. In the unit there were two horsemen from the place, whom everyone knew. The supervisor of the unit called the Jewish head (starosta) and presented him with an ultimatum - bring food to his men, take care of fodder for their animals, and give them 5,000 rubles in cash, and this within 5 minutes and if not - they would destroy the town.

Frightened and trembling with fear and helplessness, the starosta came to me as the secretary of the community. I told him to collect everything and give it to them. And I went to complain at the local police station. The police officer was not there, all the policemen were on vacation and only one policeman was at the station. The policeman answered me that he has neither the power nor the authority to do anything, not even to contact the district authorities. When I asked for a weapon - he replied that he did not have a weapon. It was clear what danger we were in and what might happen. The two cavalry soldiers born in the place - their job is to show the exits of the places and their entrances. And especially to go to the nearby villages to persuade the peasants to come on the appointed day for looting and to participate in the killing. This publicity and the organization of the villagers would usually only take a few days and in the meantime, they rained terror to paralyze all strength and will to resist. The other six, with a group of rioters from the town, their role was to carry out isolated and random raids on residents and houses and to instill fear and terror among the Jews. The gunshots that were heard in the dead of night, with the aim of scaring as well as killing, the knocking on doors and cries for help, the wails that startled the night's rest, and the few murders that were only known the next day - enough to bring the population to despair and lock themselves in their homes, to fear every fallen leaf.

I gathered the defense personnel, put them in the arranged places, group by group, and each of the groups responsible for its area sent out to the streets of the town. It was a guard night for us and that first night - nothing happened. Apparently, the soldiers were tired from the toil of the road and fell asleep immediately. I wandered the streets to visit and monitor those sent out and here the owner of the inn came out and told me that the soldiers of the unit were sleeping and I could disarm them and confiscate the horses because they didn't even set up a guard as they were so sure of their success. Of course, I refused his offer, which did not look right to me, and we planned our actions for the next day and the night after that. We were up all night and with the sunrise we dispersed, each to his home to rest, with instructions on how to act and where to gather in case riots started.

At nine o'clock the next day, one of the townspeople woke me up and told me the story: when the soldiers got up in the morning - their leader called out to the starosta again and said the same words from yesterday: food for the soldiers,

[Page 169]

fodder for the horses and the sum of 5,000 rubles, and this in 5 minutes; and if not - the town would be destroyed. The starosta went out to collect the demanded funds and while he delayed a little in collecting the funds - a policeman approached one of the native soldiers and whispered in his ear - here there is self-defense and it guarded the town all night. Before long, the horsemen did not wait for food, did not wait for fodder, and did not wait for money, but immediately put the saddles on the horses and fled in a panic, and left the town.

The third case happened in the middle of winter that year. With the end of the autumn season and the beginning of the snows and frosts - a somewhat strange creature appeared in the town. By his appearance, he was a short, skinny gentile, wearing a red shirt actually, the color of which indicated the Bolsheviks, and in those days the government was in the hands of the Ukrainians, who were far from being patient with the

Bolshevik regime. We were surprised that the local authorities did not pay attention to his appearance, treated him with tolerance without attention and disturbance.

For several weeks he walked around the town, and we did not know what his actions were and who had sent him. He would appear on the streets and disappear for a while and reappear again.

Once we even learned about a street meeting he had with one of the Hebrew teachers, about political issues, and he immediately started arguing and propagandizing for the Bolshevik regime and, when the Hebrew teacher did not agree with his assumptions and position, he suddenly finished: "Yes, you are one of the people - from the counter-revolutionaries" and left.

That's how we also learned that he considered himself a communist. It was a winter evening.

The town was covered in frost and the snow fell without respite. The cold grew stronger, everything froze from the intensity of the cold. One of the members of the defense appeared at my house and informed me that a Christian wanted to speak with the person in charge of the defense. I went outside, he presented himself as a revolutionary, as a Bolshevik, he heard that self-defense existed. His plan - to carry out an uprising against the Ukrainian regime and he suggests that the defense join him. I gave him an evasive answer, that I should bring the question to the defense committee and it would decide. I added to him - that the self-defense is not a political organization and its only goal is to protect the property and souls of the Jews, regardless of their social class. In the second meeting, I answered him that the committee thinks that it is not within its authority to decide on this important matter without calling a general assembly and asking the opinion of the members of the defense. I presented the question to him - - Why did he choose our town, which is a neglected corner in the government system, and how does he think that with the meager defense forces, it is possible to carry out such a large undertaking. He answered me that in the vicinity of the town there are as many insurgent forces as an entire division, properly armed. We said that we could only act as a force guarding his rear, we would keep the peace in the town, something that should not be taken for granted, then he unexpectedly gave up on the participation of members of the defense in his plan and he was satisfied that the defense would give him its weapons so that he would have a way to arm his bands, he suggested that we visit one of the units of the insurgents located in our town in order to dispel our doubts, and he led us through the dark alleys to one of the two-story buildings that stood at the edge of the town. We went inside. By the light of a small lantern we saw "sheygetzes" walking around dressed in tatters and almost barefoot, unshaven, spiky hair, with a gloomy expression. They didn't have the look of soldiers and military personnel, and we didn't see any weapons, the building didn't have the appearance of a barracks from the inside

[Page 169]

or temporary housing for soldiers. There was disorder in the rooms, they slept on "candles" (sort of beds made of unpolished wooden boards) or walked around doing nothing. We immediately recognized that these were the refugees of Bessarabia. The next day - he disappeared from the town without our seeing him again.

Zionist Club in 1910

[Page 170]

Youth Group (B)

Youth Group (C)

[Page 171]

The "Talmud Torah" in Zhvanets

by Michael Tennen

Translated by Monica Devens

The "Talmud Torah" in Zhvanets was not only an educational institution. It was the institution that, with its founding, changed education in all of Podolia. Following its example, educational institutions were opened in many cities and towns in which they learned according to the "Zhvanets method." None of these were founded with the help of the teachers and practitioners of the Zhvanets Talmud Torah. Its influence was evident even in the "Cheders" like the "Cheder" of Rabbi Hirsch-Wolf in our city.

One bright day, Rabbi Hirsch-Wolf informed us that soon a special teacher of grammar and Jewish history would appear with us. It didn't take long and the promised teacher, Mordechai-Wolf Bernstein, appeared. They replaced the traditional "Cheder" table with benches like the "Talmud Torah."

The age of the students was from 6-15. For eight years, they acquired Torah in this institution in the format of an elementary school and the first grades of high school. The exams were held once every two years, between Purim and Passover. Who among us does not remember the two weeks of the exams? In our eyes, the days of the exams resembled the ten days of repentance. Although there were diligent students who were sure of the results of the exams, there were also those who sinned a lot throughout the year and during the two weeks of the exams, they were tasked to atone for all their transgressions. At night you could see them sitting hunched over their books by the light of a small kerosene lamp and preparing for exams.

And here the "Days of Awe" are approaching. The largest room in the Talmud Torah became an exam hall. Part of it was fenced off for the examiners, teachers and guests. The exams would start on Saturday night and last for about a week. Each student received the grades he deserved, on which his promotion to the higher class depended. The outstanding ones received prizes. The exams were a big event in the whole city, and not only for the students, but also for the parents who were present. The tension of the parents was greater than that of the students. With trembling hearts, they tried to read the fate of their sons or daughters on the faces of the examiners.

The founders of the "Talmud Torah" with Baron Ginzburg in 1906

[Page 172]

The First Lesson in the Russian Language

by Yosef Salzman

Translated by Monica Devens

I left Zhvanets, the town of my childhood and youth, 35 years ago. I still remember all its paths that lead to the Dniester - for swimming in the summer and ice skating in the winter, as if I left it only yesterday. I see the "Talmud Torah," the swings, the tall pillar that each of us tried to climb, the two buildings, the old and the new, and the light-filled classrooms.

The teacher in my class was R. Alter. And who doesn't remember him? The long and white beard, his shining serious eyes. He teaches "Hebrew in Hebrew" - and with success. One bright morning, he informed us that we would start learning Russian. Our teacher was Mr. Pollak. Since we were studying downstairs, we were informed that, when we returned from lunch, we had to go up to the upper room to study Russian there. In the meantime, a guy from Pollak's class came and prepared us how to greet the Russian teacher. He asks us: "How will we receive the teacher?" And we all reply in chorus: "Hello, Teacher, Sir!" The guy erupts in rage: Not like that, not like that! It must be said "Zdavstvuyte Gospodin Uchitel!" We are confused and mumble, but we don't know how to pronounce the difficult Russian words. The guy threatens that, in light of this experience, we will never know Russian. The quick-witted R. Alter replied: "Nu, it's not a great disaster, it won't harm their livelihood." The guy finally calmed down and, with a smile, began to repeat the greeting to the teacher with us.

We went home for lunch and when we returned our faces were washed and our hair was combed, ready

The members of the administration of the "Talmud Torah"

[Page 173]

and prepared to welcome the Russian language. When he saw us, our teacher, R. Alter, sighed deeply: "To become Gentiles, one must be baptized and washed, but to study Chumash and Rashi, it's permitted to have a dirty face…"

At 2:30, we are taken out to the yard. The same guy arranges us in two lines. We are standing and talking - and suddenly a shout in Russian: "Maltshat!" (Shut up!) We didn't know the meaning of the word, but we all kept quiet and again, one after the other, we go over the greeting to the teacher in Russian. Apparently, this time we satisfied his demands. We go up to class. The room is clean and full of light and the benches are clean. We are trembling, hold our breath, and await the teacher.

And here comes the teacher, Pollak. Slim, swarthy, and a clever smile on his lips. He says: "Hello, children!" We all get up in a hurry and at the command of the guy: "Zdavstvuyte Gospodin Uchitel!" That's how we started learning and speaking Russian.

A kindergarten in 1934

[Page 174]

"Talmud-Torah"

[Page 175]

Girls' School

[Page 176]

The Struggle with the Smugglers

by Zev Feller

Translated by Monica Devens

The town lies on the Dniester on the Russian side, on the other side of which is the beginning of Bessarabia. The source of the town's livelihood was, mainly, the timber trade on the Dniester, which was the only sea transport from Galicia-Austria on a fairly long route to Odesa through many intermediate stations. The town is also close to the Austrian border, a walk of only a few kilometers. The border line is quite long and is inhabited by villages, where Jews were forbidden to live. This border developed another livelihood of "stealing the border." Many different people needed this theft and benefited from it, including gentile and Jewish revolutionaries, Jewish refugees from the riots, and deserters from military duty and the like. These two sources of livelihood developed two types of trade and, in any case, two types of traders, the one on the Dniester, official and proper trade, and the one on the border - clandestine trade accompanied by robbery and exploitation and even mortal danger.

With every trouble that befell the Jews in Tsarist Russia, after an attempted revolution, the assassination of rulers, and especially after the riots in general and the Kishinev pogrom in particular, the town of Zhvanets was full of refugees and fugitives who were heading towards the border. Every evening a crowd could be seen - men, women, and children, their possessions with them, loaded on carts. The horses make their way to one village or another, led by a hired "goy" for whom the border paths are clear "precisely" on dark nights and the fate of these refugees is in his hands, for good or bad, life or death, literally. Admittedly, it is not this gentile who determines the fate of the refugees who "steal the border," but rather the trade relations of the "border smugglers" with the gentile himself and with the officials of the Authority,

"Pirchei Tsiyon" in 1909

[Page 177]

which is charged with guarding the border, they are the ones who determine their fate: Is everything in order, is everything paid for? Which means is the road safe on this night of the border theft or not. And more than once, these refugees and defectors were seen who were caught on their way to the border and their end was bitter. And more than once you saw in the early hours of the morning loaded carts bringing back refugees who were killed on their way due to one reason or another. And there were heart-rending sights. But there was no one who could warn about it and no one to warn. Unbridled lawlessness and without any degree of responsibility or justice. Because a "cadre" of border smugglers developed from among the town's Jews who made a fortune, robbed, and plundered, and they were one with the authority on the border and with the gentiles who were doing this. This "cadre" of individuals and entire families took over the town and instilled fear in it.

The Library Committee

But despite all this, Zhvanets was a town of the Enlightenment generation. It had two schools for Hebrew studies and general studies using the "Hebrew in Hebrew" method. It had an organized Zionist circle, which did its work almost openly and without any fear. Boys and girls mastered the Hebrew language and immersed themselves in studying Hebrew literature. Arguments between Zionists and non-Zionists were conducted openly in public meetings. There was organized self-defense in the town in case of riots or attacks and many times these attacks were thwarted, thanks to the defense. Wrong incidents were known and even the officials of the Authority lent their hand to protect the Jews or helped them. The program of the Hebrew school in Zhvanets was brought up as a sample curriculum at the Zionist Congress, which discussed cultural matters. It was a Hebrew town in its full meaning, in which even the non-Zionists, for example, the Bundists, were proud of it.

Nevertheless, these educated leaders, the "intelligentsia" in the foreign language, were attacked by border smugglers. This intelligentsia of the town wanted to establish some order and responsibility in the border trade that developed due to the persecutions of the Tsar, to protect the property and lives of the refugees, and to prevent extortion and robbery. It was necessary to speak openly and publicly. One intelligent gentile helped in this matter. Highly educated and wealthy, who participated in the life of the town, with a sharp and a witty pen, and he published a series of articles in a Russian newspaper severely admonishing the tsar's government over what was happening in the town.

[Page 178]

And then Jews started beating each other. The border smugglers, whose sons and daughters were also educated in the schools and were cultured youth, did not sit idly by and began an attack by informing on the Zionist intelligentsia and their actions. The fight between the two sides increased in the presence of the government authority. Whistleblowers' writings from one and intelligence memos from another. And the result? - The leaders of the intelligentsia were deported to Siberia and in the circle of border smugglers, there was joy and happiness. The "pillars" in the corrupt Russian regime had defeated the "angels."

The Strike of the Roofers

by V. Rozenblat

Translated by Monica Devens

On the banks of the river, the roofers made the wooden shingles in dilapidated shacks on their roofs covered with shavings. They worked in joy and loud singing so that the girls who were walking on the road on their way to the river - would hear the romantic singing. See with your own eyes their jealousy of the joy of life of the roofers. The roofers of Zhvanets, about twenty in number, were like one family; these were fathers with sons, uncles, cousins, etc. They worked a lot, earned a little - but joy did not escape them. For three rubles, they worked a whole week. After much thought, they decided to do something to improve their financial situation.

They called for a big meeting, and Motek Starker was the main speaker, a wise, educated guy, a good orator - he explained: "If you want to achieve something - you have to fight. Organize in a professional association." The roofers did as he said. Each worker paid one ruble, they elected a committee, and they prepared the legal demands against the contractors: twenty kopecks more per 1000 wooden shingles and recognition of the trade union.

It was also decided: if the contractors do not agree to the demands - a strike will be announced.

On one bright Sunday in 1907, the roofers' strike was announced. The contractors did not accede to the demands.

The owners of the warehouses - Israel Cooper, Shimon Berman, Shalom Weingarten, and others were very angry: "Is it possible that brothers and sons will strike against their fathers?" They argued. "My mother kicked me out of the house because I struck against my father."

But all the shouting did not scare us. The workers were full of hope and believed in victory. They set up guards lest strikebreakers come. The workshops were empty. The start of the strike was crowned with success.

But the "proprietors" also organized. Itzik Ben Ha-"Leibeches" and Bobek Starker were their leaders. Bobek was the brother of Motek Starker, the leader of the strike. Bobek was a short guy with a small mustache who always had a sarcastic, naked smile on his face. He and Itzik "Leibeches" managed the negotiations with the workers.

The strike lasted 4 weeks. Seemingly - everything is reasonable: guards, meetings, reports. But nothing moved. Frozen. The proprietors laughed. The strikers began to be indignant, whispers, suspicions. It was then decided to turn to Pini Altman, the son of Shalom Altman, a young man, energetic, a great orator - to take over the management of the strike. Pini agreed. But the fire of the strike died out. The roofers lost faith

[Page 179]

in their leaders. They were suspicious of each other. And when Pini suspected that Motek Starker was passing news to his brother Bobek, the leader of the proprietors - the quarrels between the strikers increased. It is clear that, under these conditions, there was no room to even dream of victory. It was decided to return to work and wait for better times.

This is how the unfortunate strike of the roofers of Zhvanets ended.

"Po'alei Tsiyon" in 1908

A group of Bundists

[Page 180]

My Visit to Zhvanets in 1934

by Karl Blank

Translated by Monica Devens

The summer of 1934. This is no longer the town through which all those who traveled to Bessarabia and Galicia passed. As a result of the First World War, Zhvanets was cut off from Russia and Galicia was annexed to Poland. Romania and Poland did not have friendly relations with Russia. The Dniester was a barrier between two different worlds.

The entire length of the Dniester from Sakowitz to Odesa had only two points where it was possible to cross the river legally. Zhvanets was not included in these two points. The border was strictly guarded and crossing it was particularly difficult. It had one exit for Zhvanets and it was - next to Kamyanets. This road was not completely free either, only the residents of Zhvanets were allowed to enter and exit. Others were dependent on a special movement license from the military police. The only means of connection was the forbidden two-horse chariot of Netta, the water-carrier. Sometimes there would also be builders with a cart carrying passengers. Sometimes there was also a freight car, which went all the way to the Kamyanets train station.

פֿון מאָנדע־ וויו קאַמעניעץ

From views of the city in 1905

When you came from Kamyanets, the first house on your left was the school ("Shkula") which became a Jewish collective farm (kolkhoz). It was the center of a new class among the Jews, a class of land workers. Here you saw Jews, "owners," walking barefoot in the fields, as if they had been born farmers. It was a very poor collective farm, which lacked the machines and horses needed to develop the farm. This collective farm employed more Jews than any other branch of the economy in the town. When you left the collective farm and went to "Baranivka," you saw only destroyed houses. There were no more shops. Even in the market, you saw the big difference between "then" and "now." Most of the "shops" were closed. Others were occupied by the cooperatives and the craftsmen. There was only a cooperative "shop" in that place. There were no "fairs" because the farmers were not allowed to sell their produce in the market. Rarely did you see a farmer woman on the threshold of the Boyan "enclave" selling fruits and vegetables.

[Page 181]

The composition of the majority of the Jewish population were old men and children. The youth migrated to Kyiv, Kharkiv, and other cities. There was a kindergarten in the town where the children received their food because the parents were busy with their work at the collective farm.

During the summer months, the Jewish school was closed. In some houses, you could find textbooks in Yiddish and children aged 12-14 could join you in a debate about political economy and the state of the worker in America.

The affairs of the town were managed by the local Jewish "Soviet," headed by a Jew from Dunayivtsi. In terms of religion, the town was completely dead. The great synagogue was destroyed. Only in the Sadigura "enclave" would Jews gather to pray. On the collective farm they also worked on Shabbat.

Sometimes a film would come to the town and the "Soviet" served as a central meeting place for the town's residents. In the summer, the boys and girls would return to their town from the big cities to vacation and enjoy the fresh air and sun. There were almost no differences in the contents of the house. The same poor furniture, the same dishes. Gas lamps gave their light. Only the government buildings had electricity. Soldiers lived in many of the houses and the relations between the citizens and between them were fair.

From the outside, the houses looked as if they had become hunchbacked over many years. Their joy and pride disappeared, as if they were lamenting the young sons and daughters who had left them. In the streets, you could see pigs raised by Jews for sale. The peace of the night was disturbed only by the voices of the crows and the frogs. The air was dry and cold. The stars shone and as if they asked not to disturb Zhvanets's rest.

"Talmud Torah" for girls in 1906

[Page 182]

A student's report card from the "Tushiya" School in Zhvanets

[Page 183]

Personalities

Shalom Altman

by Israel Goldman

Translated by Monica Devens

He was born on December 16, 1864 in the village of Rukshyn in Bessarabia. His father was a devout, God-fearing Jew and an ardent follower of the Admor of Sadigura. The child, Shalom, received a traditional education and studied Torah from prominent teachers in the nearby city of Khotyn, 5 parasangs from the village. The father's wish was, of course, for him to follow in his path, but he entered the "garden" of education, "took a look and was hurt"… At a young age, he married a woman in the nearby town of Zhvanets, sat for two years, as was the custom of those days, at his father-in-law's table, studying and reading a lot. After that, he opened a manufacturing shop in the same town, where his wife, as an expert in the matter from her youth, was the merchant, and he continued to look through books of knowledge…

His affinity for "Hibbat Zion" probably came from the literature and newspapers of those days. He became an enthusiastic Zionist. His love for the Land of Israel and his dedication to revival projects became miraculous in the passing of time, even in the eyes of his acquaintances and relatives. Everyone's opinion was that he was "insane" for Zion. When he was 25 years old, he immigrated to Israel, worked as a laborer in Rishon Lezion and Rehovot, which was one of the founders, and became very friendly with Moshe Smilansky, with whom he shared a room. His financial situation was not stable at all, nevertheless he decided to go to Russia in order to get his family and return to Israel. Due to the decree of the "yellow certificate," he was forced to return alone after his participation in the "Hovevei Zion" conference in Odesa that year. He worked in Israel until the year of 1886 and then returned again to his town of Zhvanets. He did not return discouraged, but with a doubled and redoubled love for the Land of Israel and all that is in it. From then on, he sacrificed himself entirely for it.

* * *

First of all, he tackled establishing a school in the town. The Hasidim in the place did not rest and were not quiet, they convened meetings, and consulted to interrupt his idea, they rained curses and boycotts on him, they sent special messengers to Admors in Galicia "to overturn the evil of the decree." But Shalom Altman, both energetic and stubborn, was not deterred by anything and not least by the actions of the Hasidim. In the year 1887, he founded the school that he named "Talmud Torah" and he alone was the educator, the manager, and took care of its existence and success all the time. The institution developed day by day and it gained a reputation in the entire region. Many parents from other towns also sent their children to study and be educated at the school in Zhvanets. This school was used throughout the area as a kind of Zionist "workshop." And indeed, many Zionists and politicos came out of it, who later distinguished themselves in the areas of Zionism and universality all over Russia and abroad.

At the beginning of the First World War, all Jewish residents were expelled from the border towns and among them

[Page 184]

also the Jews of Zhvanets, which was one of the richest towns and which was depleted and completely destroyed. On his return from exile, Shalom Altman settled in Kamyanets Podilskyy, a distance of 17 parasangs from Zhvanets. He returned from his exile shattered and broken by the disaster that happened to him there when his only and beloved son, Pinchas Altman z"l, a passionate Zionist and possessed of enormous talents, died. This son studied at the American College in Beirut and, because of his father's exile, was forced to stop his studies and get a job as the secretary of the "Herzliya" Hebrew Gymnasium in Tel Aviv. During the war, he was expelled from the country as a Russian citizen, caught a cold, contracted tuberculosis, and died of it in Astrakhan in 1917 at the age of 29, may his soul be bound up in the bond of everlasting life.

But the great Zionist work during the days of the revolution in Russia in general, and in Kamyanets in particular, awakened in him the "veteran Zionist," dedicated and loyal, and he overcame his pain and sorrow and entered the work with his enthusiasm as then and always. He was the authorized person and the treasurer on behalf of the Joint for those affected by riots in Ukraine, he was a member of the city council, and a member and treasurer of the democratic community in the city, and a delegate in the council of the communities in Ukraine that took place in Kyiv, and twice a week he would visit his town of Zhvanets and help the politicos there with their work.

* * *

In 1920, he immigrated to Israel and settled in Jerusalem. He was the secretary of the "Talpiot" neighborhood and later the director of the school for the blind. For a short time, he also worked in Tel Aviv as a clerk in an ice factory, but he was overcome by homesickness for Jerusalem and he returned there. Every Friday evening, it was customary for him to welcome the Shabbat Queen by the Western Wall.

The founders of Kiryat Anavim - people of Zhvanets and Kamyanets - his students at school and his helpers in Zionism before - remembered the kindness of his youth, built him a special house in Kiryat Anavim and, after a few years, he moved there with all his worries about them. After a while, his second wife, Dr. Wortsman's sister, died and he remained sullen and bitter, despite the fact that all the members of the group and their families treated him with respect and love and treated him as devoted and loyal sons to a dear and loving father.

Even here, in Kiryat Anavim, he did not sit idle. He worked for several hours every day by the trees and flowers around his beautiful house with vigor and exemplary dedication. He also served as a librarian in the group's library named after him, which includes several thousand volumes: "Sifriyat Shalom" in recognition of his actions in the past.

S. Altman made sure that, in the first Zionist Congress, Dr. Yehezkel Wortsman, who was then a student in Bern and later came to the town to deliver a report on the Congress, would participate as a delegate born in the town. Immediately, two Zionist organizations were founded in Zhvanets - "Bnei Tsiyon" and "Bnot Tsiyon" - and another second school for girls, and he conducted them.

He was not satisfied with these results, and always demanded and required from himself and from others more and more actions. He was considered a "perpetual critic" and in this also he influenced others until the Zhvanets Zionists were famous all over the area as "staunch critics" of Zionist affairs.

He was a member of the regional Zionist Committee from the day it was founded in Podolia in 1907 and, in 1911, sat with all the members of the committee on the bench of the defendants in the district court in Kamyanets for the committee's actions as an illegal organization. And the members of that committee, his partners in "crime," will be remembered here, and they are: the lawyer David Schleifer, Shlomo Blank, Menashe Altman, Israel Drachler, Zvi Iserson, and the writer of these columns.

[Page 185]

* * *

In 1909, S. Altman and the writer of these columns were chosen as delegates to the Ninth Zionist Congress in Hamburg. He is from Zhvanets and I am from Kamyanets. We traveled together and I remember a typical episode. On the day of the trip, early in the morning, I came to him, as it is said, to travel to the train on time. But Shalom Altman is not in a hurry. He has to make every event a "Zionist commodity," and in particular a Zionist event such as the trip of delegates to a Zionist congress. Therefore, he gathered all the students in the courtyard of the school and, in the presence of many parents, he said goodbye to them with an enthusiastic speech. The children answered with "Ha-Tikvah" and accompanied him with applause.

All the residents of the town, big and small, respected and loved him, including the Hasidim in the town who, over time, accepted his actions and admired him very much. But a small group of the "border smugglers," the people of the underworld, despised him because of this "that his hand is in everything and he is alert to everything." Therefore, they reported him to the authority and, as a result of this, he was exiled in 1913 to the Narym District for five years. Even there, in his place of exile, he did not sit idly by and gained the love of all the residents with his good deeds and, in the year 1917, he was elected to the Zionist Conference in Petrograd as a delegate from the city of Astrakhan.

Rabbi Alter

by H. Sharig

Translated by Monica Devens

Many years have passed since I was fated to be under the supervision of this dear and great man, to live in his area, to live and to work near him. He was full of goodwill and tolerance for the knowledge and views of those around him, grace and kindness for his acquaintances, his relatives, and his students.

After the First World War and the destruction of the town, I worked with him for a short period of time teaching at the "Talmud Torah" school in Zhvanets. The town's residents began to return to the place and rebuild its ruins, and the few students who returned crowded into the renovated and repaired building.

Rabbi Alter was an ultra-Orthodox Jew and taught Tanakh and Talmud at the school, exposing generations of students to Torah and wisdom. And he knew how to be long-suffering and patient with his colleagues at work, who were mostly "liberal" and even opposed to his religious views.

His students adored and respected him and treated him with love and respect. He was known for a special affection and an attitude of respect and courtesy from his colleagues at work.

[Page 186]

Yehoshua (Schika) Malchi

by D. M.

Translated by Monica Devens

Among the facilitators of the founding of the Kiryat Anavim collective farm and the shapers of its image and the fighters and zealots for its values. The stages of his life pass before my mind's eye. As a child - the one of his brothers who remained alive and therefore constant anxiety on the part of his parents for his health. The material situation is good. He grew up - alert, sociable, intelligent, lively. The Zionist idea was quickly absorbed in his hometown of Zhvanets and he stuck to it. Decides that he should acquire an education at the first Hebrew gymnasium, "Herzliya," in Tel Aviv and the parents make this sacrifice for their only son. World War I comes. He is expelled from the country with others and returns to his parents' home in the diaspora, burning with the zeal of Zionism. The idea of "serving the nation for at least two years" was born in his heart before M. Ussishkin. He participates in the "Tse'irei Tsiyon" conference in Moscow. The time has come, the tools should be prepared, the youth should be organized to join hands with other parties with ability and cleverness; to give a speech, to inspire, to expand its activities in Kamyanets Podilskyy and its surroundings, to acquire the language and prepare to emigrate.

The parents' house is finished, the comfort, the concern for health - revolutionism and in completeness.

At home, they are not satisfied with his way of life, but he does not pay attention. Returns home late at night, becomes a "pioneer," goes down with a youth group from Kamyanets and Zhvanets to the Crimea. There they work, plan, and go right up to the rocky ground of the Judean Mountains; doing clearing work, building stairs, living in shacks, and lo - and behold: water sparingly and roses climbing on the shacks and there is also shade. Going out to afforestation on behalf of Keren Kayemet and he travels and plants, running every time to see if the seedlings have taken hold - and there is no limit to joy.

The reality - work and minimalism in living conditions to extremes. The clothing is patched, no exaggeration of the extras, and one can be satisfied with a large spoon and without knives and teaspoons. He is zealous for minimalism, identifies in his heart with the building of the country, and accepts everything without grumbling. Writes articles to substantiate the idea. The mood is uplifted and alertness is maximized. Sees himself at the center of life - and creates. The dirtiest and hardest work - is the most engaging and persuasive. The past - gone and forgotten. You have to follow the groove, to be among those who fulfill their dreams in heart and soul. After work - a Hebrew lesson for a new friend and then to the library, to which he devotes a lot of time and guards it as the apple of his eye, sits in meetings until dawn, and does not know exhaustion. And so - until it was concluded.

He died on March 21, 1962 at the age of 68.

[Page 187]

Hadassah (Etya) Lerner

by Y. A. Bar-Levi

Translated by Monica Devens

In the summer of 1907, a large fire broke out in Zhvanets, in which most of the town's houses caught fire and hundreds of families were left homeless.

On behalf of the Zionist Federation in Kamyanets Podilskyy, we were then sent to the scene of the disaster to organize first aid for the victims of the fire.

The first people, with whom I came together in the matter of the aid organization, were the old Zionist politicos, R. Shalom Altman and R. Yechiel Lerner. After a short consultation, it was decided that among my tasks was to organize a soup kitchen in the place, where bread, tea, and sugar would be distributed free to those in need.

When I asked them to put at my disposal and my aid someone among the youth in the town, they introduced me to a young girl about 15-16 years old who participated alertly in our conversations and with great understanding. This young lady, with a slender body, a delicate face, and deep, alert eyes, was the eldest daughter of Yechiel Lerner, Hadassah, or as they called her in the town - Etya.

When we started work, I could closely observe the character and mental qualities of this daughter of Zhvanets. The main virtues, which stood out in her character, were patience and tolerance and the ability to listen to the words of those who turn to her. These latter were people who were desperate and at a loss for advice as a result of the disaster that had affected them and who needed not only material help, but also spiritual advice and relief. And here, despite her young age, Hadassah knew how to encourage these unfortunates and to give them hope in their hearts, that things would be sorted out in their favor. The people related to her with respect and admiration.

Hadassah Lerner was born in Zhvanets and was raised there in the home of her educated and passionate Zionist father who excelled in his honesty and strong character. She grew up, therefore, in an atmosphere of Zionism and love of the work. The spirit of Hebrew culture that prevailed in the town and the guidance of a family friend, R. Shalom Altman, also had a considerable influence on the shaping of her personality and character.

In addition to her general and Hebrew education, Hadassah also excelled in her mental intelligence, which was inherent in her from birth and which was very noticeable in her interactions with mankind. She was gifted with cleverness, a sharp analytical mind, and a subtle sense of humor. She knew how to consider other people's words, but she always knew, too, how to express herself. Her argument on community or party matters was fair and matter-of-fact, which earned her respect from friends and opponents alike. Even on her own opinion she knew how to stand firm, but blessed with expressions sometimes seasoned with humor.

Zhvanets stood on the Russian-Austrian border and was known as a place of smuggling and border theft.

[Page 188]

People who wanted to leave Russia because of the Tsarist regime or for other reasons and to immigrate to distant countries passed through this town..

Some of its Jewish residents engaged in the "work" of smuggling in cooperation with the "goyim" from the nearby villages. In general, these smugglers did not hesitate to rob the immigrants of their money and even their belongings. The heads of the town, Shalom Altman and Yechiel Lerner, began to fight against these "black" elements in order to stop their harmful activity. But even these did not sit idly by and they reported to the authorities about the two aforementioned politicos that they are revolutionaries, running Zionist propaganda, and collecting money for illegal funds. S. Altman and Y. Lerner were arrested administratively and exiled to Ural in Siberia. This expulsion depressed the town and especially Hadassah Lerner.

Despite her tender age and weak body, she took upon herself the difficult task of freeing the two exiles. For a long time, she knocked on the doors of Zionist politicos and the government offices in Kamyanets and Kyiv and even reached the ministries in St. Petersburg at the Rabbi's urging, and her limitless firmness, which she invested in this action, surprised many.

Indeed, when she reached a dead end, she did not give up and asked for the help of the chief rabbi in Moscow, Jacob Mazeh. Thanks to the rabbi's connections with the people of the central government, the exiles were returned to their town after being in exile for about three years.

Hadassah Lerner's noble qualities qualified her for the role of an educator and. until the expulsion of the Jewish population from the town in 1915 by the military authorities, she was employed as a practical kindergarten teacher at the local kindergarten. After the deportation, she organized, together with her friend, Bat-Sheva Chen, the first Hebrew Kindergarten in Kamyanets Podilskyy.

During the First World War and the Russian Revolution, she was active in the "Tse'irei Tsiyon" Party as a member of the city committee. On her way to Israel in the fall of 1920, she was delayed in Vienna and finished her studies there under the supervision of Prof. Z. P. Hayut, and in 1922, she immigrated to Israel. Because of a serious illness, she was forced to return to Vienna about 5 years later to ask the advice of her doctors, where she also died during surgery.

[Page 189]

Israel Drachler

by X

Translated by Monica Devens

I. Drachler was known as a community politico in the field of culture and an important member of the Zionist labor movement. He was a teacher and writer, as his literary works attest: stories, poems, plays, and opinion articles, which were published in various newspapers and collections.

Drachler was also blessed with a talent for cultural and community work. During the days of his activity, he occupied a prominent place in Jewish communal life in Europe and America.

In the years 1919-1920, he was the chairman of the committee for the Jewish archive in Kamyanets Podilskyy, which collected material on the pogroms in the Podolia region. He was also a member of the council attached to the Jewish Ministry in Ukraine, which fought against the pogrom spirit in the Petliura army. About this activity he published important articles in the newspaper, "Der Tag" and other newspapers.

He started teaching when he was 16 years old. At the same time, he visited the towns of Podolia and helped to found modern Hebrew and Yiddish schools there, and at first he also taught there. A considerable number of his students are now teachers or cultural politicos in America, Canada, and Israel.

In 1924 Drachler came to America with his family and was accepted as a teacher in the Jewish schools in New York. In 1928, he worked as a teacher at the Shalom Aleichem schools in Detroit. After a few years, he became seriously ill and had to stop his teaching job, which he loved so much. Despite his poor health, he was active in Jewish communal life in America and also participated in the work of the Jewish secretariat of the "Community Council" from its inception. He was also the first to help found the Zionist Youth Federation, "Ha-Bonim," in Detroit and, thanks to his advice and dedicated help, he brought the idea of the Ha-Bonim camp, "Kinneret," to fruition.

[Page 190]Blank[Page191]

Minkovitz
(Myn'kivtsi, Ukraine)
48°51' 27°06'
by Moshe Berman
Translated by Marlene Zakai

The town of Minkovitz was located between the mountains and the forests near the district town of Ushitza. The main road that ran through Minkovitz led to Ushitza's town center. The Jewish residents were merchants and craftsmen. The Jewish population grew to 5000. There were 2 rabbis, 5 synagogues, a credit union, a fire station, and a Bikur Holim Society.

[Page 192]Blank[Page193]

The town of Minkovitz (in the Ushitza district) was located about 12 kilometers from the town of Ushitza, between the mountains and the mouth of Ushitza River. Jews lived in the town center, where there were about 2000 apartments, each housing 5–6 residents. All together there were about 5000 Jews. According to tradition, the town was founded by a Jew by the name of Brenen who was accompanied by Hefritz from Galicia. There were rows of houses and a main street with a cattle and sow market in the center. The big, annual fair took place during the Christian holy days. During this time many came to the town to buy and sell goods.

The Jews were merchants, grocers, and craftsmen. The principal commerce was buying and selling field crops. There were also wood traders, tailors, shoemakers, carpenters, tinsmiths and furriers.

Every Sunday and Wednesday, there was a town fair. Villagers from the surrounding areas would come to town to buy goods and sell their harvest.

There was no post office in town so mail would be brought from Novo–Ushitza.

There were two rabbis in the town, and 5 synagogues. The wooden synagogue was the biggest. It was built around the time of the founding of the town. Especially noteworthy was the ark curtain decorated with 12 signs of the Zodiac. The ark was beautifully decorated. The craftsmen prayed n this synagogue. There was a special place for names to be inscribed.

The second synagogue was white and was built by my grandfather Berman. Lubavitchers were engaged in communal work and ran most of the town's affairs for many years.

The third was known as the "red" synagogue. The fourth was the Rabbi Levis Kloiz (a Yiddish word for small synagogue). The fifth was Rabbi Heimel's Beit Midrash (house of study).

Near the bath house was the "Kodesh," a hostel for poor and homeless people. There were public institutions in the town, for example, a fire station, a Bikur Holim (care for the sick) Society, a weigh house, a society to welcome guests, and burial society. There was a credit union to help residents of the town with loans on comfortable terms.

There were 2 medics and a doctor that cared for sick residents. Among the townspeople there were Maskilim (those who adhered to the Enlightenment movement) and Hasidim, Hovevei Zion and Zionists. An event that created upheaval in the city was when the Zionists wanted to arrange a memorial service for Herzl at the Beit Midrash, and the pious Jews objected. After this there were many arguments in the town. In some of the chederim (schools) the teachers punished the children who were studying Torah by hitting them. Some of the children received a secular education in the nearby town of

[Page 194]

Novo Ushitza. With the end of World War I, when regiments of soldiers began to return from the front, pogroms were expected. In preparation, the young people organized to defend the town.

Some young people prepared for Aliyah and eventually went and settled in the Palestine. The rest of the Jewish Community was completed destroyed in the Holocaust. We remember them forever, in a special Kupat Holim Building (Israel's Medical Insurance) that was built with funds from Minkovitz' Jews living in America.

Memories of My Town

by Haim Drukman

Translated by Marlene Zakai

I will not attempt to write my memories of Jews in the Ukraine during the period of 1917–1920. The Jews lived under malicious and wicked reign that changed hands frequently. There was looting, rapes and murder. Even for the small town of Minkovitz I cannot write about it. The best way is to just say "Amen." Instead I will describe a personal story that I will never forget.

It happened in 1919 on the eve of Shavuot as the sun was coming up. I had just started to fall asleep because at that time, as a 17 year old, I was doing guard duty, wearing clothes that hadn't been changed in weeks. Tired from lack of sleep, hungry and afraid, I closed my eyes and suddenly something awakened me. Panicked and fearful, I jumped. When I opened my eyes, before me stood "Geidemak." He had a wild look, had an acne scarred face, reddened eyes, was fat, healthy, decorated in the uniform of the Petlyura. He wore wide trousers with red stripes, an embroidered shirt, his hair was cut in the fashion known as "herring." He carried arms of all kinds. In short, a true "Geidemak."

"Get up, despicable Jew," he said to me. I got up and went, because I didn't have a choice. I walked in front, and he was behind me with a rifle in my back.

My mother ran after him, howling and screaming. "Gevalt, save his life, they are going to shoot him!" I don't know where my mother had the strength to run to the Jewish elder/official and ask for help, as if he could help. Wasn't his life as worthless as all of ours? My little sisters, scared to death, kissed the hands of the murderer and begged, "Leave our brother, he is now also our father." (My father was by then in America.) "Leave me alone, pitiful worms, before I shoot you like puppies" said the Cossack.

My aunt was in late stage pregnancy. She begged, stroked and kissed the murderer's boots. All this was for naught. He sat on his horse, with me to his right just a few steps from him, with his rifle at my head. In this way, we arrived at the road from Minkovitz to Novo Ushitza. "Why are you taking me, honored master?" "Because you are a Jew, and all the Jews are Bolsheviks and we need to shoot all of them like puppies," he answered. "Where are you taking me?" I asked. "To the headquarters," he replied. "Where is the headquarters?" I asked. He answered, " in the forest, Jew."

[Page 195]

In those days, Jews were expendable. A murderer did not have to account for a murder of Jew. The forest meant certain death. He was on the horse, and I was to his right. Thus we moved along to the new bridge, where we could see the forest up ahead. I spoke to him, I begged, but I did not shed a tear. I will never forget my words or my begging. Suddenly he told me, " Go, Jew, tomorrow I will come to get you." I thanked him and began to take a few steps away from him. He commanded me to return. The game of cat and mouse continued, "Go! Return!" It was not enough to kill but they also had to torture us. He was on his horse, I by his side. We arrived at the Jewish cemetery with the forest getting closer and closer. Again I beg, and again I ask for mercy and again he says, for the fifth or sixth time, " Go! But I am coming back for you!" Again I thank him and I walk away very slowly. I do not run. My instinct told me to be very careful, not to run. Any minute I expected a bullet in my back, but something unbelievable happened. My mother's howling, my sisters' tears, my Aunt Sarah's fainting seemed to have done their work. The murderer allowed me to return to my loved ones.

Mass grave of the victims of Petlyura

Jews of Minkovitz and the Royal Court

Translated by Marlene Zakai

Echoes of the 1905 revolution did not reach Minkovitz until 1907. Among the youth it was popular to find illegal literature. Speakers from the big cities appeared in town. They led workers demonstrations made up of about 70 people each from all of the professions. They would gather secretly in the surrounding towns, in the ravines and in the hallways of the old synagogue.

[Page 196]

This synagogue was the ideal place for these sorts of gatherings because there was a popular tale among both Jews and non-Jews, that the dead gathered there for prayers at night. Therefore, people avoided going there at night. The agitators and the revolutionaries demanded labor strikes in order to gain a 12 hour work day, which included 4 hours of study. The goal of the study was to create equality between the working youth and the proletariat, and between the sons and daughters of those in charge.

The laborers organized under the heading of the Bund but it was not clear if they wrote it with a "Tet" which meant "revolt or revolution" or if they wrote it with a "Dalet" which meant "connection with others."

The demonstration organizer of the surrounding towns was a young man from Minkovitz whose name was Neska. When this became known to the Czar, arrests and imprisonments began, which were carried out by the local police. They managed to free the prisoners by offering bribes and the "prisoners" escaped to America. A few did not really understand what this game was about. Other young men tried to extract large sums of money from their mothers, or to save their coins from their lunches to spend at the Red Synagogue to hear a modern "magid" who gave Zionist sermons peppered with Biblical references that they understood, instead of the sermons of the old "magiddim" that didn't appeal to them. How excited and filled with holy awe they were when they contributed their coins to the Keren Kayemet box! And here is another picture: A young boy with tfillin wrapped under his arm, running to the Beit Midrash on the 20th of Tammuz (a day observed by Jews- the day that the Romans breached the walls of Jerusalem), the day that Dr. Herzl died. I was so jealous of those young men who put on tfillin that was part of the redemption of Eretz Yisrael, to eliminate the diaspora and to look forward to a generation that was completely worthy. I envied them as they ran to pray for the memory of a man who would liberate his people and build the glory of Israel. If this was connected to politics, we didn't really know, not us or our parents.

When the district ruler appeared and brought Jews to vote in the Starosta elections for chief administrator, even then we did not connect this to politics. It was a game and an event in the boring life of the town. On that day they would sit with the administrator himself and then they voted for whoever promised more wine for Kiddush.

The Jews of the town were very interested in life in the royal court; weddings, births, funeral, sickness and healing. For each of these events a decree would appear that cancelled taxes or fines. There were many fines: lack of permit to sell herring, or to teach children, for dumping and splashing water in the street, for playing cards, etc.

Births, weddings and deaths in the town were reported to the registrar, the Rav Mitm. He was a merchant that spent most of his time on business trips to fairs and markets. One of his family members would be delegated to take down the registration of the births and there were many mistakes. Instead of Chaya, they wrote Haim, instead of "shlemah" (complete) they wrote "Shlomo." And when a girl became 21 sometimes a family would receive a draft notice for the army, and when a boy died and the registrar forgot to record it, it was not unusual for a family to receive a draft notice for the deceased youth!

Many fled the country to evade military service. The parents of the draft dodger were fined 300 rubels. Of course they didn't pay, because who among the Jews of Minkovitz had that sum of money?

[Page 197]

Those who had resources transferred their estates to another name. There were others who tried to get the debt removed from the area registers. They would annoy the authorities non-stop. The debt could only be forgiven by the Royal Court. Perhaps this helps you understand the entanglement and interest of the Jews in the Royal Court.

At the grave of the holy victims of the pogroms

Minkovitz in My Youth

by Aaron Elman

Translated by Marlene Zakai

Minkovitz excelled in its wise and learned, especially among the youth. No small deal- those Minkovitz youth! Anyone interested in study did not work, did not engage in commerce. They expected a good shidduch (arranged marriage) with a respectable dowry. In order to accomplish this, one needed to be very learned, and in order to be learned, a young man would study and then engage in endless Talmudic and religious debates. To this goal the library in Minkovitz had many Yiddish, Hebrew and even Russian books.

[Page 198]

Even when out walking with girls on one of the famous bridges of Minkovitz, then they did not refrain from debates on books and authors.

In the town there were six oil manufacturing facilities, as well as tanneries. There was also dried fruit manufacturing, especially plums. These manufactured products were sent to inner Russia. Jews also dealt in the harvest, mainly lumber. Only one or two of Jews dealt in lumber but there were many other Jews whose businesses were connected. One was a broker or middle man, another dealt in real estate. However, lumber was a main topic of conversation in Minkovitz.

There were disagreements among the Jews in town. I remember one big argument that started between the Zinkov Hasidim and the Husatin Hasidim when the Husatin Hasidim decided to build themselves a separate yeshiva…

A Story of a House[a]

by Meshulam Tuchner

Translated by Monica Devens

A town called Myn'kivtsi, embedded in the steppes of Ukraine, adjacent to its river, isolated in its valley, and on the horizon - obscuring forests. Around it an immovable peace, and inside it - everything is frozen in its wake. The synagogues are alternately emptying and filling. Sometimes the cantor speaks and the audience repeats after him, sometimes the opposite. At dusk there is Minchah prayer, and then - Arvit prayer. The street is crowded on market days and shut down on other days. Into the night, shaking sounds are also sprinkled from time to time. The girls are noisy, the boys argue. Night. Day and again night, and one day the calm becomes weak and goes away.

R. Mendel Falik, one of the town's elders, receives a message from the authority. Hands are shaking. The paper is coarse, the letters - foreign letters, and the glasses are not helpful either. R. Mendel slowly comes out of his house, sits down as he usually does at a time of anticipation on the large stone leaning against the back of the house and looks around him. Indeed the house is large, in the heart of the town and standing in its center, with columns on its front and multi-story, wide windows in its walls. To his right is the synagogue, to his left is the Beit Midrash, and between them is his Excellency. R. Mendel sits, his cane between his legs, dispirited, denying his future.

Who is R. Mendel Falik waiting for? His eldest son, Yudel, uprooted himself from the town and has been far away from it for a long time. The father's ways and the son's ways separated. Other life paths and a different landscape. Yudel married a woman from a pedigreed family. His home was in the city of Berdychiv, he became integrated there and didn't return. While the second son, Yehoshua, humble and weak-bodied, although his home is here, but his livelihood is in the forests. Leaving and coming, returning and moving away. Sometimes arriving early and sometimes coming late. Will he visit the members of his household today? Will he come early and decipher the secret code?

[Page 199]

A heart attracts a heart. And a relative comes from afar. The son gets off the cart. The father hurries to get up, but he breathes heavily. Extends the written message and says:

Take, Yehoshua, this writing and say what its nature is.

The son is surprised at the father's expression, pauses slightly and fixes his eyes on the message. His face shows more and more amazement, perhaps ridicule, perhaps fear:

- Strange…strange, father. This letter is not intended for you or me, but for Yudel, and not even for him, but for Avrahamele, may he rest in peace, come listen to what is written here: - "Since Avrahamke, son of Yudel Falik, has reached the age of twenty-one, he must appear before the military committee on this and this day."

- Didn't Avrahamele die in childhood?

- It means, apparently, they forgot to send a message about it.

- God be with you, R. Mendel trembled, I delivered the message with my own hand. Yudel sent it to me from Berdychiv.

There are no words. R. Mendel slowly falls on the stone again. The day packs up and goes, swallowed up in the gloom. The town raises its lights, a pale yellow grid. Light and dark are used in a mixture. Rabbi Mendel's head tosses from side to side, sleep and no sleep, past and present, life and death. Avrahamele stands in front of him in all his figure, in full likeness of his pale, childish face. The days are far away, seemingly embroidered from the twilight of dreams and the coldness of

A group of local Jews by the old synagogue

[Page 200]

death. Indeed, the road is long, tiring and weary to the ancient cemetery. The ground opens wide, and a handful of dirt is thrown on a young, immature body.

* * *

Morning comes. R. Yehoshua goes to the clerk's office. It's cold in high-ceilinged rooms. On the table are volumes of books from leather, books of the living and books of the dead. The clerk bends over them, comes out and browses, says and reads:

- Indeed, yes… that's how it is… - tilting his head, a sly smile on his face… Avrahamele was indeed born, lived and died on January 3, 1889, but Avrahamke did not die, he was not deleted from the registry of the living.

- How? Aren't Avrahamke and Avrahamele one and the same? R. Yehoshua is astonished.

- Why do I need to know your names? Avrahamele is listed as dead and Avrahamke is listed as not dead.

- But Avrahamke and Avrahamele are two names that are one - R. Yehoshua modulates his voice.

- If so, why, oh why, is it sometimes written Avrahamele and sometimes Avrahamke, sometimes Yudel and sometimes Yudke?

R. Yehoshua whispers and hints:

- Perhaps it is a mistake, an unintentional mistake?

- Perhaps because of the clerk:

- It is well known that the Jews evade the army, therefore they mix and confuse the names, Avrahamke with Avrahamele, on purpose!

The son returned to his father with a simple statement in his mouth:

- We will live and see, God will help.

The days slip away and again a message: if he does not show up at the next date, he will be punished, a fine will also be imposed on him. R. Mendel immediately: He will not pay the fine! And again orders and accusations and so forth. Yudel himself is far away from here, makes light of matters, gives advice in his letters, and Yehoshua still does nothing.

And the town is in turmoil: who doesn't remember Avrahamele, a soft, pale-faced boy, not of this world, who passed away and was buried, and who doesn't understand that Avrahamke is Avrahamele, but what else? They wrote him down once like this and once like that, and what of it? Who would pay attention to such little things?

However, the matter gets more and more complicated. Ruling clerks come, inspect the house, surround it from all sides and write in notebooks. A rumor goes: a fine was imposed and not paid. The house will be sold. There is, apparently, someone eyeing the house, perhaps he covets the house itself, perhaps the post office, the horse post located in its yard. The speculations intensified, the fears increased: the ancestral inheritance will be confiscated, the inheritance of generations will be for nothing.

R. Yehoshua turns again to the authorities and again the doors are locked in his face.

* * *

It's dusk. A cool sun is setting. The frogs from the ravine are croaking. Dark is approaching. And suddenly - a magnificent carriage is in the town, the thundering of proud horses, a sharp ring, and a sudden stop. A foreigner gets down, tall and moustached. He approaches the house, wonders at it, glances around, gets back on the cart and disappears into the thick of the darkness.

[Page 201]

There is no longer any light, stars are falling, the boys in the Beit Midrash are noisy. R. Mendel sits on the stone, hunched over, collapses: who would have guessed what was expected? The authorities announced an auction of the house. They say that same gentile will win it. There is a lively fury in the town: what does this gentile have in our midst? What does he have and who does he have in the center of the town? He will turn to the right - the synagogue, to the left - the Beit Midrash, and even the heavens are already dedicated to God!

The house is sold. No Jew was found who asked to buy it, it fell into the hands of gentiles, the same gentile - Ivan Markevich - won it. Yehoshua returned and asked to pay the fine, but he was not accepted. Avrahamke was prosecuted, he is required to appear, alive and not dead.

A restrained mourning in the town, it seems that even the days have turned gray, the lines of the forests have darkened. R. Mendel sits stuck to the stone, wondering about his world and wondering about the house. A strong building and ancestral monument. It was as glorious today as it was then. But when and who built? Maybe old men will remember it and young men will not know. A mistake is in the hands of mankind, he didn't establish and he didn't strengthen it. His relative, R. Alter Shilman, designed the pattern, with the breadth of his knowledge and the strength of his intelligence, he laid its tiles on a foundation and set up thresholds. A man of miracles was R. Alter Shilman, legends encompassed him. He was infinitely rich and had no sons. No one knew where his wealth came from and no one knew where his little children had disappeared to. The "Weicher" (the storm) took them - the tradition says. It is indeed a mystery. R. Mendel, too, did not know its meaning. He also did not know when R. Alter Shilman asked to adopt his son, Yudel. R. Mendel stood before him, shaken to the point of unconsciousness. He wanted to protest, he wanted to hold his son - and he swallowed his words. A living limb was torn off and there were no objectors. R. Alter Shilman was an ancient figure, his countenance powerful. His word was law, his words were a command, say and do. Yudel grew up with the comfort of kings, he grew up and became distanced from him. And when R. Alter Shilman passed away and bequeathed his house to him, Yudel did not pay attention to his inheritance and did not return to his town.

R. Mendel Falik spread his wings over the house, placed Yehoshua and his household in it, and guarded the inheritance with all his heart and all his might.

* * *

R. Mendel awakens, transient visions, and changing experiences. The heart beats and the mind is stormy: what have years of life been spent on, on nothing but preserving the inheritance? And now will foreigners live in the house? And a cry was uprooted from his heart:

- Alter, Alter, where is your salvation?

R. Yehoshua stands and looks at his father's face in bewilderment. Old age is growing, yellowing pages and flowering letters:

- What's going on, Abba?

The old man stands up, blazing fury, strangled words:

- Yehoshua, Yehoshua, why are you silent?

The son bends and answers:

- You know, Abba, I am not a man of war, not a man of battle, my time is devoted to livelihood. With what can I save, and if the inheritance is not for Yudel, where will Yudel be?

- Forget about Yudel, you will inherit the house!

[Page 202]

- And suddenly R. Mendel got up, grasped his son tightly, pushing and pulling him at the same time.

- Where to, Abba?

- To your father-in-law, to my father-in-law, to Hirsch Kleiderman. If he does not stand up with you in your trouble, if he does not rescue you - and the house is lost, it will be lost to you, it will be lost to the members of your household, and it will be lost to the entire town.

The son was surprised and surrendered. R. Mendel pushes and walks slowly. They come together and walk. R. Hirsch Kleiderman stands on the threshold of his house, filling the entire opening up to the door frame. Height and size, a white beard and a wise forehead. He reaches his hand out to his in-laws and pulls them in, man touching man, each man knowing the other's secrets:

- Get up and do it! - shouts Mendel Falik - it is essential for your children.

And Yudel will inherit?

- Forget about Yudel, the house is Yehoshua's. If you save the sheep from the mouth of the wolf, he will inherit!

Around the heavy-legged table, staring at each other, the soul locked in its hiding places, lurking with pounding heart. R. Hirsch Kleiderman remains, standing fully and resolves:

- We will do and we will understand, my father-in-law!

* * *

R. Hirsch Kleiderman travels to the regional city, to Kamyanets Podilskyy he directs his way. To Satnovsky, "the advocate," his destination. Firm in his mind and resolute in his decision, he comes inside the house. He will not be afraid, he will not retreat. Halls and carpets greet him, statues and pictures. And in the corner a glowing candle. A nation, a nation and its faith, a man and his belief. Seemingly a Christian by birth and by heart resides here - and not. Satnovsky is a Jew from birth and nothing else. The sea is vast, open to all sides. But only those who take off their clothes can swim in it…

In essence, his heroism is the "advocate," Satnovsky: his face is full, old age has only thrown a little at him. He glances at the person entering and marvels - a man of intelligence, comes close and listens closely. Heart to heart he will speak even if there is an abyss between them. The beam penetrates the thick shadows and the light scatters. He takes his hand and says:

- I know, "Gospodin" Kleiderman, what a town is and what an inheritance house is, I know that Avrahamke and Avrahamele are one and the same, all this is known and known to me, R. Hirsch Kleiderman. Let us therefore fight, let us fight, my brother, let us save the stolen property.

R. Hirsch stood in all his wisdom, a yarmulke on his head and a beard of faith across his chest, shaken and upset: to praise or to cry?

* * *

And in the meantime, the same gentile appears again, the same Markevich, wearing a top hat, wearing shiny leather boots, opens the door of the house forcefully and the privacy of the rooms is desecrated. R. Mendel breaks down and says with a pleading voice:

- What is there between you, Mr. Markevich, and my house, why are you harassing us? I am old, let me close my eyes between the walls of my home… I…

The gentile is dumbfounded, rolls his eyes with a generous laugh and says:

[Page 203]

- Forgive me, Mr. Mendel, this house is my house, with the best of my money I paid for it, and why so many words. Mr. Falik has sons, surely they will take care of him, surely they will buy him another house and everything will fall into place in peace.

R. Mendel recoils, the laughter is the evil of the heart. R. Mendel knows - his house is gone.

* * *

That day was a winter day. The town is wrapped in white robes. The sun makes its way behind gloomy, angry clouds. Ice crystals hang from the ends of roofs with polished tips. That day they appeared. They came to inherit the house. The people of the town gathered near the portico. Standing in place like people coming for a funeral. Snakes' anger in their hearts and restrained rage in their hands, one boils with anger and slams fearlessly:

- Mr. Markevich will listen, the right thing to do is. There is no God in the world, aren't we humans!

The gentile responds with a laugh:

- And that I am guilty, young Gospodin? If I hadn't bought it, someone else would have bought it.

- This is not true, no one would buy, but you!

Markevich slips away and ignores. Clouds hanging overhead, there is no limit to their size, they passed into the distance, their terror diminished. Markevich was afraid of the moment, watched him with pent up tension, but he did not move from his corner. R. Mendel Falik leaves his house, closes the door slowly as if parting with a hidden oath, comes out from the portico, and walks away and with him the Shekinah of the house.

* * *

The days were wild. Shocked, the town sank into unrelenting tension. From afar, the faces of the town followed the new neighbors. They peered into the veiled windows, raised their eyes to the columns of smoke that extended from the red chimneys, inclined an ear to the boys' chanting, marveled with pent up rage at the grown girls who, despite the intense cold, sat on the windowsills and polished the shining windowpanes.

The sky was the same sky, the glare the same glare, the stream froze like every year, but the storm of blood did not subside. R. Yehoshua, when he got into the town, wandered around it without rest. He looks as if astounded towards his house and fixes his eyes on the ground. Markevich removed the stone from the back of the house. It was no longer needed.

* * *

One did not let go. The "advocate" Satnovsky worked secretly and openly. The ant was crawling in its burrows and no one knew what it was doing. One day the citizen Markevich was called to appear before a committee of inquiry to re-examine the issue of the house. When Satnovsky saw the faces of the members of the committee, he whispered something in R. Hirsch Kleiderman's ear. After they drank the tea prepared in a Jewish house, which had cleared its lounge in their honor, and after they finished smoking their cigarettes, they approached the actual discussion. Immediately, however, when citizen Markevich claimed with hidden glee and demonstrable equanimity: "I didn't know anything, I bought the house at a public and legal auction," Satnovsky once again whispered in Kleiderman's ear: "For every ruble we gave, he gave ten."

[Page 204]

After a short negotiation, the committee decides: "Citizen Ivan Markevich's purchase is kosher." But sweetly, the chairman adds: "It is possible that there is a reason to claim adequate compensation from the government." Markevich calmly gets up. Satnovsky stares at him with gloomy eyes and whispers: "We'll see. It's not over yet."

* * *

Months pass. R. Mendel in his last days stands at the door of his new apartment and glances with dull eyes towards his house. Apparently the face of the house has changed. It was repainted, but its glory still stands. There was a hard tone in his heart, the tone of vanity, vanity, everything is vanity. The townspeople bow their heads and say not a word.

R. Mendel Falik passed away; dead, and his eyes are directed towards his home. The congregation marches and sings chapters of Psalms, passes near the house and pauses. Markevich stands in the shadow of the pillars of the house, exposed and hiding, even his daughters are peeping through the curtains. The two camps face each other and R. Mendel Falik's coffin is between them.

Lethargy spreads throughout the town. Now it's clear: as long as the house does not return to its owner - joy will not abide in it.

* * *

And all of a sudden fate strikes with its force. Markevich is dead, dead and he is still in full force. It was evening. The rumor spread like wildfire, accompanied also by a lively incantation - the revenge of R. Mendel. R. Yehoshua sits in the heavens. Markevich offered him a compromise, and he, too, was cut off. There is mourning in his house also. There are two who do not rest and do not remain silent: Hirsch Kleiderman and Satnovsky. Satnovsky knocks on "Madame" Markevich's door and is rejected with a snort and a fit of rage. But the hidden destiny does not let go. Again its thunder roars with a warning of revenge. The youngest daughter is also dead, actually dead today and her song is in her mouth, they dressed her in the clothes of her youth and carried her in an open coffin. The Jews of the town watched her from between the cracks, watched and whispered trembling:

- She will run away from here, the widow. R. Mendel takes care of her there…

But she did not run away. She closed the shutters of the house and, behind the portico of pillars, she closed and hung a heavy lock on the front door from the inside - To enter, they would enter from the yard.

* * *

And the days are not normal. It seems as if they are holding their breath. The decision is imminent. Satnovsky comes and goes, brightening faces and giving hope. The committee gathers again, this time things are discussed to the end. Satnovsky is fiery. Avrahamke is Avrahamele. The truth bursts forth with force. The committee recognizes the right of Yehoshua Falik's ownership of the house. The house will be returned to its owner and Avrahamele will rest in peace.

Like an ignited spark, the flame spreads. The town is crying out from all sides, big and small, old and young. Everyone is flocking to the house. Surrounding it from all sides. Besieging its windows and kicking the door. There is no sound from inside. The sea winds are stormy; the waves are rising, who will stop them?

The young men arose enthusiastically and tore the door off its two locks. A cry of terror and a threat roll like thunder. From deep within the house, Markevich's widow bursts out, blood curses in her mouth. The Jewish crowd knows its sin and retreats silently. Not an hour passed and R. Yehoshua Falik was imprisoned.

[Page 205]

Satnovsky had not yet finished his work. The widow Markevich wants blood, demands revenge. R. Yehoshua Falik was sentenced to one month in prison according to the law of breaking locks. Regret in "grabbing" is weighed against all the suffering. R. Yehoshua sat and the town sat with him.

But everything has an end. Day and night and day again. R. Yehoshua comes out of darkness into great light. The house is returned to him and the town brings him up to the threshold of the house. The stone is also returned to its place.

[Page 206]Blank

Original Footnote:

1. From the memories of my family concerning an event that happened to it in Myn'kivtsi in the preceding century.

[Page 207]

Smotrych
(Smotrych, Ukraine)
48°57' 26°33'

Translated by Monica Devens

A town on the Smotrych river in the Kamyanets Podilskyy district, at a distance of 30 versts from it. One of the oldest urban settlements in this area. In the middle of the 13th century it was destroyed by the troops of Batu Khan.

During the reign of the Lithuanians one of the princes fortified the town and established his seat there. Because of the quarrel between the princes, the town passed into the hands of the Poles. In 1448, it was included in the Podolia Voivodeship and received the Magdeburg Constitution from the Polish government.

In 1712, there were found in the Jewish community there, together with the surrounding settlements, 375 people.

In 1808, the town came under Russian rule and was recognized as a second-class city; in 1837, it was returned to the status of a town.

In 1847, the town counted 1,274 Jews and, over the next 50 years, according to the population survey of 1897, the number went up to 1,725 in a general population of 4,399.

[Page 208]Blank[Page 209]

Smotrych

by Moshe Hochman, Mordechai Schneiderman

Translated by Monica Devens

Our town was named after the Smotrych river that runs through it. It was a small and quiet town, with a Jewish community of about 400 families, among hostile rural and urban settlements, most of whom were farmers, sugar factory workers, and potters.

From views of the city: the Smotrych River

The Jewish population existed here for generations, they were innocent, honest, and quiet Jews like all the Jews of the surrounding towns. They barely made a living, through heavy toil and hard work; they engaged in trade (including the export of agricultural produce beyond the Austrian border, which was about 30 km from the town), in crafts, and in clerical work.

The town had never been blessed with great wealthy people. However, the difficult life did not prevent the Jewish community from an excellent spiritual life.

Who among the inhabitants of the town does not remember the great synagogue? Many legends were woven about its construction and upkeep. Its walls were beautifully painted and the Ark of the Covenant excelled as a masterpiece. Indeed, for sanctity reasons, the walls were never cleaned. The Central Committee for Folklore in Petrograd, headed by Dr.

[Page 210]

S. An-Sky, studied the evidence of the synagogue and found it of great interest. Unfortunately, this synagogue was destroyed by order of the authorities.

There were 8 more synagogues in the town, belonging to various Hasidim and to craftsmen and around them, the spiritual life of the place was conducted. There were "Cheders" of different types in the town as well as a "Yeshiva" where even older Jews studied Torah.

It is necessary to mention the great light of Hasidism which illuminated quite a bit the gray material life of our town. There were also disputes and fights between the different Hasidic sects and all for the sake of heaven.

Even before the First World War, as a result of various national movements in Russia and in the whole world, Zionist associations began to be organized in our area, too, which attracted the hearts of the Jewish youth and gave them a refreshing spirit of revival. At the same time, a Hebrew school was founded, imbued with a distinct national spirit and with excellent teachers who inspired hope and aspiration for a new life. A Zionist organization was founded with factions of "Tse'irei Tsiyon," "Mizrachi," and "Po'alei Tsiyon." Workers' organizations, the "Bund" and "Mahane Yisrael" of the religious, were also formed. Similarly, institutions for mutual help were also founded: "Ha-Chevra le-Ashrai Hadadi," "Gemilut Hesed," "Hachnasat Orhim," "Matan Be-Seter," "Linat Ha-Tzedek," "Chevra Kadisha," and more.

The results of the First World War and the great Russian Revolution influenced the Jewish youth to strive for education, for self-defense, and for standing up for the dignity of the nation and the individual. During the disturbances in Proskorov (= Khmelnytskyi) and Pilashtyn, Smotrych youth also came to the aid of the injured with medical supplies and food.

We established a large library which contained many books in Hebrew, Yiddish, and Russian,

A group of pioneers

[Page 211]

and many people received education and knowledge through it. The library served not only the townspeople, but also the people of the surrounding area.

A group of "He-Halutz" was organized, talented and cohesive, which worked on the land of Graf Pototsky in Smotrych. The members of the group would go to various hard jobs: cutting trees, cultivating beet and sugar fields, paving roads, repairing dams in flour mills, and more, and served as a personal example for Jewish workers. In this, they laid the foundation for a shared life in preparation for immigrating to Israel. And it is true that the whole group immigrated to Israel and after it - more young people, too.

Despite the vicissitudes of the fate of Russian Jewry, after the revolution, vibrant life still flowed in the town. There was also an emigration movement to overseas countries. Some of the residents moved to the Russian steppes, to the big cities, overseas, and to the Land of Israel; nevertheless, there remained another nucleus around which life was woven, as it did in the old days, until the terrible days of the Holocaust came and the hand of the damned Nazis cut off every trace of our town.

[Page 212]Blank[Page213]

Frampol
(Kosohirka, Ukraine)

49°06' 26°45'

Translated by Monica Devens

A town in the district of Kamyanets Podilskyy, the region of Podolia. In 1847, the Jewish community counted 570 people and in 1897 - 1,240 residents in total, of whom the Jews were - 1,216.

[Page 214]BlankPage215]

Frampol

by Zev Mayberg

Translated by Monica Devens

The period in which the town called "Frampol" came to be lies in the hidden place of history. About 200 years or more or even earlier, there lived and worked a small Jewish community in the same place where the village of Savyntsi now exists, at a distance of about two kilometers from Frampol (=Kosohirka) presently. Remains of tombstones of the residents of that community still existed in my youth, in the ancient Jewish cemetery of that village. Some of the elders of the city in the days of my youth would still go to the ancestral grave of one of the last ones named "R. Abele" who was buried there. He was a holy Jew from the descendants of the first Hasidim.

Apparently the first settlement of Frampol (=Kosohirka) centered around the wall called "Aavstria," which was built during the "Fanshtashina" (=Panchizhni, i.e., "Fortification") period. This place was the market center of the town. This wall was built in a square shape.

Its southern side was a residence in the form of a palace and the other three sides contained about twenty stores for food, flour, textiles, and other household needs for the surrounding area, which numbered about twenty villages with the aforementioned Savyntsi, which was the largest and closest village.

Frampol (=Kosohirka), along with the nearby villages, formed an economic unit whose population made their livelihood off each other. The shop owners and artisans supplied the needs of the farmers with clothing, footwear, and other necessities. The farmers, besides being workers on their farms and on the farms of the Polish landowners, would rent themselves and their carts out to transport goods between the two largest commercial centers in our region: Kamyanets Podilskyy and Proskorov (= Khmelnytskyi).

Our town was exactly on the main road between those two cities and its main street from the western part of the "Aavstria" served as a long line of inns for the merchants and wagoneers going back and forth between the two big cities which were centers of trade, industry (in the magnitude of that time), district government offices, etc.

And as the center of the town with the "Aavstria" at its head prospered and became successful, people with initiatives appeared from the first residents and built shops close to "Aavstria" as well as a residence with shops in front and taverns for the farmers who came for the market day twice a week. (On Sunday and on Wednesday).

The Frampol market made a name for itself in the district area and drew to it for its market day, too, farmers

[Page 217]

from the villages that were outside its natural domain. By this, some of the merchants and craftsmen of the other towns in our district were also attracted.

Its very location on the main road between Kamyanets Podilskyy and Proskorov (= Khmelnytskyi), being the center of all these villages, was an important factor in its growth and in its economic prosperity and, at the same time, also culturally.

But while they were paving, in about 1850, the road between the two big cities mentioned above, when engineers presented the owners of the inn (who profited more than anyone due to the position of the town) a demand for a bribe of about one hundred rubles, these refused to respond to their demand and for that reason, the engineers diverted the road a distance of about ten kilometers from the town. Because of this deviation, the town froze in place and its prosperity and growth stopped. And not only that, but since the large transport on "the dirt track" stopped - the large inns remained empty and without livelihood. The main street, which in previous days was bustling with people, became like a city of evil spirits.

And although the livelihood from the farmers of the area and the market days was still available as before, since weeks and months passed without seeing any new faces in the town and the people of the town did not come into commercial, social or cultural contact with the distant world, the news from the wider world arrived in our town very late. The winds of the Enlightenment, which began to blow in our Jewish world in the second half of the last century, did not reach us until after the great storm that was unleashed in the world by the Dreyfus Affair and the first Zionist Congress that followed it.

In about 1898, some young people arose from the students of the enclave and the Beit Midrash, who already smelled the scent of the new era from afar, and their degree of idealism was really much greater

Yiddisher school

[Page 217]

than their knowledge and education, and they decided to open a Talmud Torah for the children of the poor whose parents were unable to pay tuition fees to the city's teachers and, because of that, were expected to grow up in ignorance and boorishness. They decided that they would teach in the Talmud Torah, together with the Pentateuch, Rashi, Tanach, and Talmud, Hebrew grammar as well and - the Russian language. Then a great war arose against them on the part of pious homeowners who announced: Are they going to establish a Talmud Torah? No, because they want to establish "Talmud writing"! And the war took place all over the town: in the market, in the synagogues, and on the other hand, in the bath house and up to the rabbi of the city, R. Simcha Kahana.

The opponents of this idea went to the rabbi and complained about the "heretical scandal" in the form of the "Talmud writing" that was about to be created. And he, the rabbi, did not listen to their complaints and ruled in favor of the proposed idea. (I will continue to talk about the rabbi, R. Simcha, in the course of this article).

I remember that war very well because my brother, Shmuel, my nephew, Eliezer, and I, the little one, were among the first students of that institution. Our parents, Yosel Feysis and Volvel Feysis, were both Torah-observant Jews and their sons, even without studying in the teachers' rooms, were not expected to grow up without Torah and without good manners. We were sent to study at the same main institution - because of the prospect of receiving a general education, even to a small extent, and secondly, out of gratitude to the idealistic young people who were willing to give of their time and money, not in order to receive a prize, but in order to teach Torah to the children of the poor. Our parents entered into the thick of things with all the power of their reasoning and their glibness for the establishment of the institution and fought with the opponents until they won on the whole front.

As far as I know, only one of those initiators of the Talmud Torah is still alive, after so much time, and he is Mendel Kramer, who went to America, graduated as a dentist, and retired from this profession only two or three years ago.

Those young men were all single in their twenties and after some of them got married and left our town, the supervision of the institution and its development fell to Yitzhak Rabin and his brother-in-law, Yitzhak Eliash. These two Yitzhaks were the backbone of our city because of their belonging to the spiritual aristocracy in it. The first was the son of Meir Rabin. The erudition of the latter was no less than that of the great rabbis in Israel, but he did not use his knowledge to earn a living and instead engaged in trading grain and flour. His son, Yitzhak Rabin, did not fall behind his father in his learning, he even mastered the secrets of the new Hebrew literature and Russian literature, and so did his brother-in-law, Yitzhak Eliash. Both were grandsons of "Reyzel, the Matriarch" of our town. Reyzel, after whom her son-in-law, Meir Rabin, was called: "Meir Reyzeles" it was after she became a widow, practiced hospitality in her home that was unparalleled in our area. All the poor who came to our city knew her address and of her adherence to the teachings of Abraham our father, and her good name preceded her in all the surrounding cities.

They, these grandchildren of Reyzel, dreamed of a modern "Improved Cheder" for the town and pinned their hopes on the first students and "graduates" of the Talmud Torah. The graduates themselves also dreamed of that time when they could in some way repay their debt to their benefactors and their town, but in between came the First World War with its vicissitudes and turned all those dreams into nothing.

[Page 218]

The Zionist resistance movement in town

I want to mention the good of other types of our town's Jews. The first in value and importance is certainly the rabbi, R. Simcha Kahana mentioned above. He was from a famous family of rabbis whose genealogy reached as far as Don Abarbanel. Apart from his great knowledge of Shas and Poskim, he was a man of common sense and the reputation of his wisdom went far and wide. He would participate in the arbitration of various disputes between the merchants of the area up to a distance of dozens of Russian miles. "The Frampoler Rabbi" was a household name in the entire Podolia region.

My father, peace be upon him, belonged to the Zinkiv Hasidim who prayed in the large enclave and R. Simcha used to pray in the "Beit Midrash," a place where he served as a community emissary during the terrible days. And even though we shed quite a few tears at the Arvit Shemoneh Esrei prayers of Rosh Hashanah and Yom Kippur in our enclave, where the prayers ended earlier than those of the Beit Midrash, we still entered the Beit Midrash immediately after our prayers concluded to hear the rabbi's "Le-David Mizmor." In my mind's eye, I see the old rabbi standing erect in front of the Torah scrolls and pouring his heart out in front of his Maker, praying for himself and for his congregation, the congregation of the Children of Israel…

At the beginning of the first war, when R. Simcha reached old age, he resigned from the rabbinate in favor of his son, R. Nahum, who was the son-in-law of one of the rabbi of Chortkiv's gabbais. R. Nahum was then a young man approximately, with beautiful attributes, and sampled a little of the Galician education in Chortkiv. On him, as on his father, was the pride of the city. He served as a rabbi and teacher in the town until the middle of World War II. When Hitler (may his name be obliterated)'s troops entered the town and demanded of R. Nahum that he hand over ten Jews from the town as guarantors, he replied that he could not present anyone other than himself. Of course they did not delay to take him and executed him in the center of the city. They executed him infamously, but his memory will remain blessed and glorious in the hearts of all the citizens of the city until the end of all generations.

[Page 219]

And a few words about another two or three Jews, members of "Amcha," simple because of their innocence and righteousness. The first is "Moshe Volis," the bookbinder in our city. When they gave him a book for binding, they never knew when they would get the book back. Simply, there are so many prayers in the prayer book and so many psalms to say every day, and you also have to go to the mikveh every day, and you also have to collect alms for the poor, and to prevent that anyone might "suspect of kosher things," he stole for himself one grush each time from what he had collected. On Friday nights, in his two-room house, apart from the Shabbat candles, about twenty large lanterns were lit and the light there was of great fame, "almost seven times the light of the sun"…

There was one couple in our city that God did not bless with sons of their own, Yoel Yehuda Leyves and his wife, Devorah. Although they were childless, they "raised" sons and daughters from the poor of our city and helped them with their dowry and wedding expenses, and by doing so, they were blessed with many grandchildren.

I will mention just one more name from the residents of our city that I was not privileged to get to know. He died a few years before I was born, but his name was remembered with great fame by the elders. His name was Itzi Tolner, a tenant farmer. Were Y. L. Peretz among the people of Ukraine, I would say that Itzi Tolner served him as a prototype for his story, "If Not Higher." Exactly the same righteousness that Y. L. Peretz sets an example in his account of the tzaddik of Nemirov was said by the elders of our city of this "down-to-earth" person, Itzi Tolner.

A group of "Po'alei Tsiyon"

[Page 220]

Personalities

by Moshe Mayberg

Translated by Marlene Zakai

Dr. Yaakov Hoffman

I am reminded of that wonderful character, that great, revered, and lovable man, whose name was Dr. Yaakov Hoffman z"l, who came to us from afar, from Yelisavetgrod (=Kirovohrad), that is to say, he did not come to us directly from there, but stayed with us by chance. He came with the Red Army retreating from the front in the first war. The army was stationed at the time in the town of Yarmolyntsi and from there, we persuaded him to stay with us in Frampol (=Kosohirka) since we didn't have a doctor.

His first work among us was to organize the community on democratic foundations. Under no circumstances did he agree to serve as a private doctor, he wanted to be an employee of the community and to receive his salary from it. He would visit the sick without pay and, of course, that the payments to the community would be progressive.

The wealthy people, who had to pay more, raised a cry, they don't need a doctor and didn't want to pay the community the amount it charged them. But the typhus epidemic that was raging at that time did not spare the houses of the rich either, so they came running to the doctor: Doctor, help! He then reminded them: since you don't need a doctor, why did you come to me?

I remember a case where he demanded 500 rubles from one of these wealthy people for a visit, it was a very large sum at the time. He received the money, but on the spot, he destroyed it and then went to visit the patient.

Dr. Hoffman brought a lot of life to the town. He spent most of the money he earned from the large rural surroundings on the school he founded in the town. He brought from Yarmolyntsi the young teacher, S. Shafan, known here in Israel, and kept him at his own expense in housing and food.

Dr. Hoffman and his wife saved the town more than once from riots. I remember one case where the then infamous Ukrainian army had to retreat at night and Dr. Hoffman understood what might happen at such a time. He gathered some more or less decent officers and arranged parties for them and held them all night, until they heard shouts from all sides: "Help!" He got on horses together with the officers and together they drove the soldiers out to the very last one.

[Page 221]

Kupyn
(Kupyn, Ukraine)
49°06' 26°35'

Translated by Monica Devens

During the rule of the Poles in Podolia in the 18th century, the town belonged to the Kamyanets Powiat of the Podolia Voivodeship. In 1765, there were 405 Jews there who paid the poll tax. After the division of Poland and the transfer of rule to Russia, the town was included in the Kamyanets district, Podolia region, and in 1847, there were 923 Jews living there. According to the census of 1897, there were 1,351 Jews in the town.

[Page 222]Blank[Page223]

Kupyn[a]

by Avraham Rosen

Translated by Monica Devens

This was a small town, surrounded by mountains and forests in the Kamyanets Podilskyy district. In its center, there was a large and spacious market and around it several streets and alleys, mostly inhabited, mainly those close to the market, by Jews and in the minority, further away from it, by gentiles. At the edge of the market stood the great synagogue with the Beit Midrash and the "Zionist enclave" next to it and, on either side of it, stood one-story residences with large and small shops in front of them selling groceries, haberdashery, manufacturing, building materials, and more. All of the weekdays the market was almost empty and desolate of people, and only on the days of the "fairs" was it filled with a lot of farmers who came from the surrounding area and brought the crops of their land for sale. Thanks to the proximity of the Austrian-Galician border (about 25 km), the local Jewish merchants used to export various commodities abroad, especially poultry and eggs.

Besides shopkeepers and merchants, the town also had various craftsmen and artisans, such as: tailors, furriers, shoemakers, carpenters, blacksmiths, and more. Some of the town's residents served as clerks in the Jewish factory for the sugar industry, which was nearby.

The Jewish community there numbered about 2,000 people. Apart from synagogues, a Chevra Kadisha, a bathhouse, and a volunteer firemen's company, it had almost no other public institutions. The sanitary situation in the town was very neglected and, due to the lack of roads and sidewalks, its streets were literally drowning in mud and mire during rainy days. There was no doctor or hospital in the town and the residents made do with their local (Jewish) medical assistant or ordered a doctor from the nearby town of Gorodok (=Horodok). There was no post office there either and a special messenger would travel every day to Gorodok (=Horodok), put the letters and packages that were given to him in the post office there, and bring the mail from there to the town. With the exception of "sacred vessels," such as: rabbi, ritual slaughterers, cantors, and shamashs, the Jewish community in Kupyn had no paid public servants and, when necessary, its affairs were conducted by synagogue gabbais or volunteer homeowners. The registration of births and deaths was also done by the "rabbi on behalf of" the aforementioned city of Gorodok (=Horodok).

Indeed, in its economic and social situation, Kupyn was no different from the rest of the small and remote towns

[Page 224]

in Podolia. However, in its activity in the field of national revival, and especially in the branch of Hebrew education, it surpassed many of them and was even considered among the most advanced in these areas. Thanks to some of the local Zionist intelligentsia, and in particular to the well-known Zionist businessman in the area, Aharon Vajnbaum, the Zionist idea penetrated almost every Jewish home in the town and Zionism was in control of all public business and directed it in the channels it desired. Under the initiative of the local Zionist association, a Hebrew school ("Talmud Torah") was established, which accommodated almost all the town's children from all walks of life: poor and rich, ultra-Orthodox and free. The "Cheders" were completely closed and without any objection from the ultra-Orthodox "homeowners," who also, as mentioned, sent their sons and daughters to the "Zionist" school. The number of students in this institution, which was run by the parents' committee headed by the aforementioned Aharon Vajnbaum, reached approximately 120-150 and its program of studies included, in addition to Hebrew studies (Tanach, Talmud, Hebrew, Israeli literature and history), also general studies. In the last ten-twelve years of the existence of this mixed school, the method of study was adapted to that of the all-national "culture" in Russia, and

"Hebrew in Hebrew," which was a kind of innovation unknown in the surrounding towns, took its place. Every year there were public exams for the students and this made a lot of publicity for Hebrew in the town.

The institution's budget came from the tuition fees collected mainly from the children of the wealthy. During the First World War, there were several interruptions of their regular studies due to the capture of our sons by the Russian army that passed through the town on its way to the Austrian border. Indeed, these disturbances did not undermine the institution, which continued its existence until the Soviets took over the area.

In collaboration with the school teachers, most of whom came from different cultural centers, rather diverse national cultural work was conducted by the local youth. For lack of a public library and reading room,

The teaching staff of the "Talmud Torah"

[Page 225]

a kind of Shabbat club was established, where teenagers of different ages would gather for conversations and readings. From time to time, debates on various literary topics were also held there. There was also an association of "Hebrew speakers" for a while, whose members would meet together in one of their homes every Friday night to talk in Hebrew about different things. Over time, several theatrical talents were also discovered there and a group of amateurs was formed that managed to put on an almost constant stage for performances in Yiddish and Hebrew. Plays by Sholem Asch Peretz Hirschbein, Yaakov Gordin and more were presented. One of the members of this group of amateurs, Shifra Ashman-Rifnitzer, who later immigrated to Israel, was one of the first actors in the Israeli theater, "Ohel."

However, with the coming of the Nazi Holocaust on Ukrainian Jewry, the small Kupyn community was wiped off the face of the earth along with the rest and became as if it had never existed. But its memory will never end among her surviving sons, who were brought up in it in a distinct Zionist national spirit and came to Israel to work it and to fertilize it as the ancestral homeland of the entire nation.

Original footnote:

    a.   With the kind permission of "Yad va-Shem," the memorial authority of the Holocaust and heroism.

My Town

by Hayyim Sharig

Translated by Monica Devens

Kupyn in the Kamyanets district, Podolia region, in the vicinity of Grayding (=Horodok), on the fertile land of Ukraine, was located among the gentiles - people who worked the land, who made their living from agriculture. In the center of the rural settlement, in an area of forests and streams, the Jews of the town crowded together, surrounded by settlements of Ukrainians who hated Jews. The surrounding nature was all green, forest fields and a waterfall, which in the summer attracted the townspeople to bathe. The town was small and poor and its inhabitants were few - only about 300 families who mostly made a meager living, but excelled in good spirit and aspiration for a more interesting life. The town was far from the railroad and there was desolation and a lack of economic development. Suffering and sorrow were the lot of its inhabitants, especially in winter, a time based in mud and rain.

Despite these difficulties - cultural life stirred in it.

Although there was in the immediate vicinity a sugar factory owned by the Zaytsev family - Jews from Kyiv - only the gentiles benefited from it, by supplying it with sugar beets. The Jews of the town had no enjoyment.

The Jewish residents of the town were mostly engaged in petty trade, shopkeeping, and crafts: tailoring, shoemaking, furriery, etc. In these crafts, they served the people of the area and also provided for the needs of the Jewish community.

The residents of the town were mostly observant and were faithful to the tradition and customs of their ancestors. As Torah scholars and Hasidim, they were connected to one rabbi or another. The children were educated in "Cheders" in poor sanitary conditions.

Kupyn was one of the main towns in Ukraine that founded a Hebrew school - an "Improved Cheder,"

[Page 226]

which, in the course of time, became a "culture" school where they studied according to the method of Hebrew in Hebrew and general studies, too, were taught in Hebrew.

I must mention here commendably the teacher, Zalman Malamud, a dynamic personality with initiative and activism in the field of Hebrew teaching. He arrived in our town from Khotyn in Bessarabia. He was invited to run the local Hebrew school and to be a teacher in it and he served as an example to many in his dedication and love for the Hebrew language.

Among the Jews of the town there were also differences of opinion and differences of views - between Hasidim and Mitnagdim, Zionists and Bundists, and the like. I remember, when the Zionists wanted to hold a memorial for Herzl in the first anniversary of his death, a fight broke out in the Beit Midrash, which caused a great commotion, and the opponents of Zionism did not allow the memorial to be held, to the displeasure of the Zionists. However, if the majority of the town's residents were inclined to Zionism, then the margins of the tailors and cobblers belonged to the "Bund."

The poor economic situation and the lack of an outlet for the local young energies increased the desire to leave the town for the rest of the world and to immigrate - to America and Argentina. There were also attempts to immigrate to Israel, there were cases where old people immigrated to Israel to live out the rest of their days there. After the revolution - when Jewish life was undermined and the hopes planted in the revolution were disappointed - many of the townspeople went abroad and to the Land of Israel.

In the town there was a sort of Jewish self-rule - subordinate to the local authority. The Starosta (Mukhtar) was elected by the residents of the town as a qualified representative vis-a-vis the authorities and responsible for the regime, in his hands were the collection of taxes (savchenoi savur), issuing certificates of non-criminal record, and border crossing. I remember that Shmuel Schreiberman (my grandfather) continued in this position in the town as Mukhtar (as Starosta) for about 25 years and was occasionally elected in secret ballot with white and black balls. The elections were organized in the Beit Midrash.

The "Talmud Torah" in 1909

[Page 227]

The "Talmud Torah" in 1913

[Page 228]

Many of the townspeople were Hovevei Zion and later also political Zionists. Their souls were also given to the Hebrew language, and any Hebrew newspaper or monthly that appeared in Russia or in the Land of Israel - would also reach the town. Over time, an association of Hebrew speakers was also founded.

During the 1905 revolution, when the peasants revolted against their oppressors and enslavers who owned estates, they expelled the representatives of the government from the villages, refused to pay taxes, and burned the barns and the estate buildings and the grain silos - the Cossack regiments arrived on the scene in a punitive expedition to suppress the rebellion. The Jewish residents of the town were the most affected by this, even though they did not take part in all the uprisings. The Cossacks, who dispersed the demonstrations of the farmers, ran amok in the town, rioted, and looted the property of the Jews. Then one of the town's members was killed - without any reason or cause on his part and the townspeople went through a period of terror and fear until the Cossack regiment left the town. Faced with these acts of the Cossacks, the government stood by completely passively and did not intervene, as if it did not see what was happening. The town's politicos tried to appeal and protest to the district government and the bailiff, but to no avail.

During the World War in 1914 - when our town, which was close to the border, served as a transit station for the Russian army that crossed the border into Galicia and the Carpathians, life was in danger and tension, although economically the Jews benefited from the trade with the soldiers - until the military defeat and the withdrawal of the army. The security of life was undermined and everyone was depressed.

The soldiers who returned from the front in a panicked retreat, without order and discipline, passed through the town and harmed everyone they met on their way. Then began the revolution of Kerensky and a desire for freedom, for a new life, and everything was done at that time at the will and outbursts of the soldiers; in the face of these dangers, the self-defense of the local youth was organized together with Jewish soldiers who returned from the campaign and got delayed in the town. They joined the defense and also served as instructors and suppliers of small arms and the necessary ammunition. The defense group numbered about 40-50 people.

In the first clash with the soldiers who poured in from the front and wanted to enter the town for plunder and the defense tried to prevent them from doing so, several of the defenders were killed. Considering the large number of the attackers' forces, the defense decided to retreat and leave the town at night.

The next day, the soldiers penetrated the place with probing and caution, with the help of the local gentiles who served them as guides, and when they saw that the Jews had left their homes, they began to rob the property in cooperation with the surrounding gentile neighbors, but they did not harm anyone. Some of the Jews reached nearby Grayding (=Horodok) and some hid with their neighbors - their gentile friends. I think it was the first pogrom in Russia after the revolution. After three days - the Jews returned to their homes and renewed life both on their own and with the help of the Joint, which had begun then its aid operation in Ukraine.

Alongside the economic institutions in the town, a discount supermarket was founded for self-help, for the needs of the economy and basic consumption, which sold the goods to its members at cheaper prices; in particular, the craftsmen and workers organized themselves in a consumer association.

A mutual aid fund was founded. Everyone put in a membership fee and the Joint also contributed money for this purpose.

[Page 229]

The craftsmen in the town organized themselves in times of hardship and scarcity for mutual help. An association for Hebrew (culture) existed there, which had conversations and lectures in Hebrew, evening classes and shows by amateurs in Hebrew (such as "He Went Out and Returned"). The member, A. Rosen (Rosenzweig), who worked as a teacher at the Hebrew school and devoted a lot of his time to the strengthening of the activity and the spreading of Hebrew, helped a lot in this action. There was a Zionist association there which mainly dealt with the recovery of the Zionist shekel in an operation for the Keren Kayemet, etc. The living spirit and the main worker in this operation was Aharon Vajnbaum, who saw it as a pleasant duty to devote himself to Zionist action with all his heart, managed publicity among the members of the association, spread the Zionist idea, and solicited donations for its funds. He was also sent to the Zionist Congress as the association representative.

Until the revolution, Zionist activity was illegal. During the revolution, the "Tse'irei Tsiyon" federation was founded in the town, which was connected to the national federation of "Tse'irei Tsiyon," whose center was in Moscow, later in Kyiv. From there, circulars and instructions for organizing and immigrating to Israel were received.

Under the initiative of the "Tse'irei Tsiyon," the pioneer group was also founded and the first pioneers immigrated to Israel (the Grossman brothers). During the war, with the invasion of Hitler (may his name be obliterated), the town was wiped out and no trace of it remains.

[Page 230]

Personalities

Translated by Monica Devens

The Vajnbaum Family

In every town in the Pale of Settlement in Russia, there was some one, and only one, family whose members were above and higher than the rest of the people. They dealt with public needs in faith and alone carried the spiritual struggle and burden of the community. In Zhvanets, it was Shalom Altman, in Khotyn - Hana Rayz, in Dunayivtsi, which was a little bigger and more developed, there was actually more than one family. In my memory, the personality of Motel Rosen stands out the most. In Kupyn, it was the Vajnbaum family.

Aharon Vajnbaum

The father, Shmuel Hirsch Beres, was the patriarch of the family, a man with a magnificent form and a noble soul, he was of the type of Nachman Krochmal. He was an expert in the Talmud and the Poskim, the first and the last, on the one hand, and in religious and philosophical research, on the other. He was frequently called to all kinds of arbitrations among the merchants of the area, to compromise and to reconcile the generations in negotiation disputes among themselves and also between Jews and Russian or Polish landowners. He gained their trust by being wise, sharp, and known for his honest intellect and his dedication to the verse: justice, justice pursue. His two sons, Nachum and Aharon, were "made in their father's image." The two of them had the "average" face of their father, each of them inherited some of his advantages. The elder, Nachum, inherited his inclination for theoretical and constitutional investigation. He was a "lawyer" for the town, writing the "prushenyes" (requests) to the government on behalf of the residents of the city, gentiles and Jews, and also "explained" the civil law to them. He was a "Tolstoyist" and a "Gordonist" before the latter appeared in the skies of our culture and movement, believing in and preaching self-reliance and realizing it. He fixed his family's shoes himself, did all kinds of carpentry and building work in his house, and also used to spice up his exhortations with proverbs and articles from the giants of Hasidism and of the scholars of today and of the past. He immigrated to Israel in the days following the communist revolution in the early 1950s and he lived into his 80s. He used to walk around the streets of Tel-Aviv and the Jaffa border with his saw and his axe on his shoulder to fix what needed fixing in the houses of the poor neighborhoods for a minimal fee. Aharon, the younger brother, inherited from his father his love for social and cultural life. His devotion to Zionism, to Hebrew literature and culture, cost him many sacrifices in family matters and in his private businesses that were neglected by him. He was the chairman of all the public organizations and associations founded in the town: of the Zionist Association, of the "Hebrew Speakers" Association, of the lovers of dramatic art in the town, etc., etc. Nothing concerning Jewish cultural life in the town was alien to his spirit. And despite being devoted with all his heart and soul to the treasures of the nation and its culture and his coat pockets were always full of newspapers, pamphlets,

[Page 231]

shekels, stamps, and books of all kinds and on all his favorite subjects, he would also entertain his listeners with his stories and popular jokes and with his great knowledge of Jewish folklore, it was like an gushing well.

One episode by way of these two brothers: when the proposal for the territory of Uganda was raised at the Sixth Zionist Congress and the differences of opinion and the dispute between "Tsiyonei Tsiyon" and "Tsiyonei Uganda" reached its height, a quarrel was discovered between Nachum and Aharon, against the background of the difference of opinion that existed between them regarding their Zionism. The former was inclined towards Herzl and Nordau in accepting the territory from Britain and the second one was among "those saying no." The quarrel intensified to the point that they could not continue with their joint business and they separated.

During the days of the Bolshevik revolution, Aharon went through all seven layers of hell, both as a representative of Zionism and Hebraism and as a "capitalist," so to speak.

In one of his last letters to me in 1926, he poured out his bitterness about the cup of sorrow that had happened to him and expressed his dismay at his fate that his brother, Nachum, the "Ugandist," was granted the privilege of being among the happy ones who lived out the rest of their days in Israel and reaped in joy what others had sown in tears and he, the Zionist, was forced to die in the "Land of Desolation."

Zev Mayberg

Meir Ha-Ezrahi (Munia Zak)

At the age of six he was orphaned from his mother and went to live at his aunt's house of the Brodsky family in Kamyanets Podilskyy. Here he grew up in a Zionist atmosphere and received a general education at a technical high school. At the end of his studies he entered the college, "Psycho-Neurological Institute," in Petrograd, but due to the political upheavals of the years of the revolution, he did not continue his studies and devoted himself with all his fervor and energy to public-Zionist work.

A propagandist according to his character and talents. He also stood out as a good organizer. Honest and upright. Free of personal positioning. Liked by all who knew him for his ability to walk with humanity. From the day he became aware of Zionism, he was among the general current in the movement, but he also knew how to value the labor movement in Zionism and treated it and its members with loyalty and appreciation.

He visited the European diaspora a lot and garnered supporters to the Zionist idea and to the Keren Kayemet for Israel. When the position of the director of the organization department in the main office of the Keren Kayemet became vacant, Meir Ha-Ezrahi managed the department until his last day.

Y. A. Bar-Levi

[Page 232]BlankPage233]

Kytaihorod
(Kytaihorod, Ukraine)

48°39' 26°48'

Translated by Monica Devens

A town in the Ushytsya district, Podolia region, sitting on the Ternava River, which flows into the Dniester River.

During the rule of the Poles in Podolia, in 1765 the town counted - 489 Jews who paid the poll tax. During the days of the Russian government, there were 642 Jews in 1847, in 1897 1,745 Jews out of the total number of residents of 2,794.

[Page 234]BlankPage235]

The Rabbi Refused to Say "Tzidduk ha-Din"[a]

by M. Kapeliuk

1

Quiet-peacefulness rested in the small Podolian town in Ukraine. From its three sides, it is surrounded by fertile valleys, streams and rivulets full of water and fish, and above these valleys - a kind of dark green wreath, large and thick with forests and young trees, beyond which - large and small Ukrainian villages, scattered among large and wide areas of black and fertile soil.

For many years the town existed, with the passage of time the tradition about its founding was lost. As a reminder of distant days, the old cemetery at the edge of the town was used where, from most of its sunken gravestones swallowed by the ground, after a lot of study, it was possible to read with great difficulty the years T'… TQ'… LP"Q, on some gravestones that had been gray-blackened out by years of age. The same cemetery, surrounded by the remains of the wooden fence that is sinking and sagging, was visible in front of the old synagogue, which, according to tradition, was built after an incident by one of the ancestors of the Polish nobleman, the owner of the estates and properties in the town. Near the town stretched the large Ukrainian village.

In spring days, when the mud and slush began to dry, and soft and slippery paths would cross them, the town boys would go for a walk to the village, sit in the shade of the poplars, pick without looking the white and fragrant cherry blossoms. At the beginning of summer - the unripe fruit.

The Jews of the town had a good neighborly life with the gentiles of the village. Every Jew - whether a merchant or a shopkeeper or a craftsman - had his loyal "customers," and for every gentile - a Jew who was loyal and trusted him. And not only in negotiations was the neighborliness and closeness expressed, but also on days of rest and joy, when a Jew would marry off his sons, the gentile friend would pluck from the produce of his land, from the fruits of the garden and the field, on top of that: a rooster

[Page 236]

with an upright comb, and with him one of his "wives," a white-feathered hen (it was customary among the gentiles to be careful not to bring a black hen to the Jews); and the Jew would bring a colorful "Malorussi" cloth as a gift for a Ukrainian bride and a bottle of "96" schnapps, sealed with a sealing material and a royal inscription stamped on its cork.

Among the gentiles of the village, the "Soviet Meiyurke" was accepted ("The Saint Meir," that is Rabbi Meir the miracle worker) and many conversations and legends were told about him as a Jewish miracle worker on Ukrainian soil. When it happened that one of the villagers became seriously ill, he would come to the cantor of the town and donate to the fund of Meir the Miracle Worker, so that he would be a good interceder and would remove his illness from him. Among the old women of the town, Yavdoha the "Zanakharka" ("soothsayer") was famous, an old gentile, whose thick oak stick with fibers did not move from her bony hands. She was invited to the patient after neither the doctors nor the "rebbes" were helpful, and she was bent half over and her weak eyes with their thick eyebrows gave her a frightening appearance, would be stirring herbs and various markers in water and whispering. Believers in her magic said: "If Yavdoha doesn't cure, the potter will not be useful either."

And this is how they lived near each other; the Jewish town and the Ukrainian village. Each of them knew and recognized his own and the other's weaknesses and strengths, and it seemed that they accepted them without objection. And when 1905 came, a year when an order was given from above to provoke the Jews a little and one of the educated men from the regional city took pains to come there and began to demand and "explain" what the nature of a Jew is - the people of the village took him aside and whispered in his ear: "This is not the place." This one understood and listened to the hint - and not a few days passed and he left in the same manner that he had come. And when one day the people of a distant village, who had come to the town's weekly fair in order to harm the people of the town, the people of the village came to the aid of the Jews and beat and wounded the attackers and expelled them in disgrace from the boundaries of the town. For years, the shame of the defeat that they had received at the hands of the Jews and their allies, the people of the village next to the town, was etched in the memories of those attackers.

2

During the First World War, the town was not damaged. From the distant battlefields, the silence of the night was accompanied by the weak sounds of cannon shots. From the time the rumors arrived about the mass deportation of the Jews from places near the German border, the Jews of the town began to sigh in horror and great fear. Then the town was divided into two camps: the one, the big one, was on the side of "Uncle Velvel" (Wilhelm, Emperor of Germany) and of Franz Joseph of Austria ("Uncle Ephraim Yosef") and the second camp, the unfortunate one, was of those loyal to "Aunt Reyzel" (Russia). And the war was happening between the two camps, and heavy skirmishes would take place occasionally: between Mincha and Maariv, at midday on summer days, on Shabbat or during the long winter nights when they would gather at the rabbi's house or at a rich man's house for a cup of cholent while making small talk about politics. And they would bring there the only issue of the "Kievskaya Misl," of which the town's apothecary was a subscriber, and read in this newspaper, which was held as a newspaper that "it was possible to squeeze many true things out of it 'if you only knew how to read it.'"

They would read "between the lines" (no one paid attention to the actual lines) and would reveal news and secrets about the situation on the war front and what was expected for the near future. And each of the two camps proved with reasonable explanation

[Page 237]

and evidence from what it read between the lines what it wanted and its guesses. And so they would argue and clash, until one day the change occurred that the town did not feel it coming about at all.

3

On one of the last winter days, the fat "Uriadnik" suddenly disappeared, whose jaws hung down from too much fat, and after him the "Strazhniks" (the policemen), armed with swords, went away and were gone. Rumors spread in the town that "Tsar Nikolaike" had been overthrown and that there would be a republic and the Jews would be given "ravnopravaya" (equal rights).

A few days later, the outer space of the town was filled with the song of the "Marseillaise," which was sung by the boys and girls of the town. For weeks and months, this first freedom song, along with the other songs of the revolution, did not stop, from the mouths of the young men and women who would sing them with great enthusiasm. And on the first of May, all the youth, the boys and girls, gathered and went to the regional city to celebrate this day and they returned from there cheerful and full of awakening and hope.

4

Some months passed.

During the winter days, when the snow was piled up next to the walls of the houses and the window panes were covered with tall frozen palm trees - there was an echo in the town that "something was changing" because the "Bolsheviks" (a word that seemed so strange at the time) were about to seize the reins of government. Piles of conjecture and expressions were spread about them. A rumor spread that they were going to uproot evil from its roots and create complete equality between the small and the great, and there were some who exalted them to the heart of heaven, and others made fun of them and said that they would not be able to change the way of nature and that "they were about to smash their heads against the hard rock of human nature." The town did not have the privilege of learning the nature of these because one clear morning at the end of winter, when the town had been for several weeks without any government whatsoever, the townspeople saw the streets full of steel-helmeted Germans and Austrians wrapped in gray hats with strange brims and red-faced Hungarians who were constantly uttering vigorous curses. The old "Strazhniks," whose name for some reason was replaced with "militiamen," returned to the town.

The days did not last long and the soldiers from Ashkenaz and KY"RH (a popular Jewish nickname for Austria) (KYR"H=Kisar yarum hodo=may the glory of the Kaiser be raised) started flocking to their home: the crowns of Kaiser Wilhelm and the King of Austria fell one after the other. And on one bright day, the Ukrainian town was emptied of its soldiers and also of its policemen who disappeared together with them.

5

When the rumors started coming of riots, killings, and pogroms by the Cossacks and the Heidemaks of the "Batku" Petliura and his otamans, a kind of gloomy cloud descended on the town. Things developed gradually: at the beginning, they told about the murder of the "Arndaris" (a nickname for the Jews of the village) (=tenants), about a Jew who was found dead on his way to the fair, and after that - about the "pogrom." Terrible and horrible was this short two-syllable word, which was often heard before Passover. With the beginning of the melting of the snows, and when the first signs of spring were already felt in the air, and somewhere in some hidden corner of the heart, the flutterings of joy woke up

[Page 238]

to greet the spring that was about to come - the news about the pogrom in Proskorov (=Khmelnytskyi), where more than three thousand people were killed, as they said, fell like a thunderbolt. Among the horror stories of the massacre, the names were integrated: Petliura, Semesenko, Tyutyunik, and were an integral part of these events, and the face paled at the sound of these names.

And since Proskurov (=Khmelnytskyi) is not very far from the town, after a few days the details of the massacre that took place on Shabbat afternoon, when the Jews of the town went out for a leisurely stroll, became known. With the delivery of the details of the events, they realized that the first reports were not an exaggeration, as they had believed. On the contrary: the reality was much more terrible than the imagination, apparently, of the narrators.

6

Every week, another list was added to the killings and massacres in the Jewish communities in Ukraine. The people of the house would already notice when the man returned from the morning or evening prayer with an expression of concern and sorrow hidden in his eyes and on his gloomy forehead. And when he was asked - and the answer was first short: the name of a well-known Jewish town and the number of those murdered and tortured, and then details of superhuman suffering and torture. And the woman would sigh and cry, and the little children, at the sight of the faces of the recounting father and the crying mother, would press into her dress as if begging for protection. From the mouths of father and mother a murmur of prayer was heard: "If only we have been saved at least thanks to these babies who did not sin"...

The mists of fear and worry for the future spread in the space of the town and its inhabitants walked like shadows. The relations with the people of the neighboring village did not change, moreover there were also promises from the "feni" that "this time, too, they would not allow riots to be brought into their quiet place," but peace and security were far from their hearts. And it happened on Tuesday, the day of the regular weekly fair, when the thugs of the "sheygetz" were greedy for their money and something "got stuck" in their hand casually (which on days when they were better they would have considered snatching it from the hands of the injured shopkeeper) - this time it was as if it had been agreed to turn a blind eye and not to pay too much attention to such pranks in order to not give room for conflict, which could damage the traditional friendship between the town and the village.

7

For two to three weeks the "big ones" entered (a nickname for the Bolsheviks among the Jews of the towns). The town knew and they themselves knew that they did not enter for long. Difficult days of war faced the revolutionary government from Kolchak and Yudenich and the rest of the white generals, and from the Czechoslovak units, and last but not least: Petliura and all the otamans and gang leaders and over them the armies of the Polish "szlachtas." All these did not allow the Bolsheviks to hold large parts of Ukraine. The thought that long-haired Petliurovets, their hair hiding a long red cloth above their hats, would soon come, would freeze blood in arteries and knees would tremble and fail.

On the eve of Shavuot, when the weekly fair took place in the town, a commotion suddenly arose. The army, which received an order to hurry up and retreat, moved through the market and grabbed the farmers' carts to transport the army and its equipment. The peasants beat their horses and made their way through narrow alleys in order to escape the seizure of their vehicles and long journeys with the retreating soldiers. The pursuit of angry soldiers,

[Page 239]

beatings the dodgers and rebels with rifle butts, cursing those who are caught - filled the space of the market. The shopkeepers hastened to close their shops and locked their shutters as well and in a few moments all living things disappeared from the market. How strange and amazing it was to see the market empty and desolate since moments before it was speckled and bustling, full and crowded with carts of buyers and sellers, taking and giving, and Jewish women walking around with their full and overflowing baskets, and children trailing behind them and holding on to their aprons. Emptiness and desolation all around them, and only the dogs who are used to always walking cautiously on the sides of the street, fearing that a farmer's club or a stone of one of the passers-by would emerge, walked with complete security in the heart of the market, free; and sought out and smelled with their noses the straw and reeds scattered among the remains of fruits and vegetables, which the villagers left when they fled. The large challahs that were braided in a special braid in honor of the holiday of Shavuot, which lay next to the heated oven ready to be baked, looked like orphans and seemed as if someone had put them down by mistake. In the boiling of the dishes on the stove, something like a loud and sullen commotion that portends evil was heard ... And when the boiling water of one of the pots was overflowing, the mistress of the house, who was walking gloomily and helpless, did not pay attention to it. As if what is done in the kitchen in honor of a holiday does not concern her.

In many houses, they would pack the belongings and household items. However, while packing the pillows and covering the most necessary objects, the big question mark appeared and stood in front of the packers: "Where to?" … To escape to one of the towns - is it not clear that they all have the same fate and there is only a matter of sooner or later … There is another place of refuge and it is: the city of the region, which the Ukrainian directorate (government) chose as the capital city. There, in the capital, people said, for sure disaster will be avoided. But how to get there and the road is obstructed by the Heidemak gangs and just murderers who called themselves: "insurgents," and not just one Jew who set out on this road was killed by cruel torture… the "no escape" and the terrible despair hung in the space of the town and was apparent everywhere.

8

The "sleepless night" was that same night of the Feast of the First Fruits. Not only for the elders of the city and the God-fearing who spent this night for years as usual in reading Tikkun Shavuot, but for all the people of the town from small to big. Even the little children were not allowed to take off their clothes. In the morning, several shots were heard from one of the valleys surrounding the town. The shots were accompanied by a drunken and wild Heidemak song. More than the gunshots, the voices of the song that glorified the blood of the townspeople who were debating in their closed and sealed houses paralyzed. Those entering was a unit numbering several dozens and this conquered the town. The "conquest" was accompanied by notices on behalf of the "Ukrainian People's Republic," which were pasted on the streets of the town, the end of which contained a demand for the residents to hand over the weapons in their possession to the commandant (commander). The commandant is young, about twenty-five years old, wearing "galpa" pants and polished and shiny boots fastened to his feet, tall and thin, with a sickly face, which a bad pallor would play with. At the corners of his lips, there was foam of spit that would splash when he spoke. The commandant called the "Starosta" (the town's representative to the government) and ordered him to hand over the weapons, which according to his knowledge (so he claimed) were many in the town. The "Starosta," a Jew about sixty-five years old, who served as the town's official deputy for four decades and was loyal

[Page 240]

always to the government, answered him: "I assure you that no weapon will be seen or found in my town. Upon my word because that is the way it is and not otherwise." This "upon my word," which was said from his mouth only rarely, in times of stress, did not rescue him this time. Swearing and curses accompanied by beatings and shoving was the answer. "Come, old dog, we will search and check and see if your words are to be believed, words of lies and falsehoods!"

First they went to the synagogue, checked the ark, rummaged through the books of the Torah and rolled their scrolls, uprooted planks in different places from the floor and crawled under it. In particular, they bothered with the ankle-deep square in which the cantor stands in front of the ark to perform "From the depths I call you, O God"… Two soldiers stood and uprooted, broke and chopped and dug and groped there very carefully, with their flushed faces sweating and their wild hair, the work of the Heidemaks, stuck to their wet foreheads. After all the searching and rummaging were in vain and all the efforts yielded nothing - a sharp and protracted curse of blasphemy broke out.

9

The next morning, the commandant called the "Starosta" and two other dignitaries of the town to him and informed them briefly: "You must bring in two hundred thousand rubles in fines by three in the afternoon." And when those called to stand came in and asked to cancel this decree against the small and poor town or at the very least to reduce it, he whipped them with his crop once and twice. Offended, pressed, and frightened, they fled from "commandant"'s room.

Like an arrow from a bow, the word of the "contribution" spread in the town and it was the subject of conversation and concern for everyone, though from that decree there was a spark of hope: perhaps their intention was only for property and not for people…

Two Jews came out, one the town's chief and of its dignitaries, and the other a distinguished, respected, and desirable learned person, whose opinion was heard in his group, and they wandered around the town to collect the large amount. At first they appealed to the wealthy. The majority gave in after claims and easy sighs in the same manner as they were put upon them, but there were also those who refused and insisted, some out of the fact that they were trying to save money and some because of inability. And these were negotiating regarding the reduction of the sum that was put upon them, and when they would stand for a long time in their refusal, the learned man would gently persuade the refuser: "Man! There is no trade and negotiation before you, give your soul's ransom, the Petliurovets are before you!" For sure it was in these few words that the refuser would get up and, with a sullen and gloomy face, bring the amount and hand it over to the collectors. And when the time came when they had to bring the "contribution" to the commandant, and the amount was still not complete, those two passed again from house to house and received from each according to his ability and added penny to penny, until after much labor and effort the amount was collected and brought to the commander of the gang. They found him sitting at a party of some of his soldiers, eating and drinking until drunk. The two Jews were not allowed to enter, the deputy commandant went out and received the money, while his mouth spewed curses and insults.

10

The commandant and his deputy occupied one of the beautiful and spacious houses of the town, built shortly before the war. The best restaurant in the town would provide them with hearty meals at the expense of the community and after each meal, the commandant would gallop on his horse through the streets of the town.

The same galloping would be repeated over and over due to an order from the orders that would be renewed every morning. See the commandant's soul longed for a suit of expensive fabric that only before the war was it possible

[Page 241]

to obtain. They tried to offer him another suit, beautiful and good, and he is adamant: "Like this and not another." Every attempt at a different proposal would be answered with blasphemy, insults, and threats. They started rummaging and checking the closets and the bundles of clothes until they found in one of the houses a garment made of a fabric similar to the one the commandant wanted - the town breathed a little sigh of relief.

One evening, an order came to the "Starosta" to appoint a guard from the town's residents. The sudden order was puzzling, but one couldn't refuse. Early in the morning, a few gunshots were heard in the town's area. Many rushed and came down panicked from their beds where they were lying in their clothes and it was learned that, while the guards were walking the streets of the town, they attacked them and shot them. One was killed and others who did not manage to escape were injured, some seriously and some lightly. After that, the gang members raided the houses of the shopkeepers in the market, looting money and jewels and killing one of the married yeshiva students who was famous in the town for his learning and knowledge and liked by all because he was "good-natured," as they termed him, and comfortable with every person, whose entire behavior and manner was in the name of not harming others. The events of that night depressed hearts. Everyone sensed and felt that the end was near and that what was expected to come was getting closer with its terrible steps.

11

The fabric for the commandant's suit was given to one of the best tailors in town. This did not come easily. The tailor pleaded that they spare him and "not hand him over to the murderer" - because what would happen if his work did not please that one, he claimed as if he begged for his life, and I am the father of small children… However, the dignitaries of the congregation sat by him, explained and again proved to him that the lives of tens and hundreds of souls now depended on him, on the tailor. After the many words of persuasion came a long silence. which was considered as consent.

"Sweep the streets, clean well" - this is the new order, which was widespread in the houses of the town. And Jewish men and women came out, boys and girls, with brooms in their hands. They swept and cleaned the lot next to their houses to the halfway point and raised a thick and blinding cloud of dust. And out of the clouds of dust, the hooves of the commandant's horse were heard, galloping through the town. Hearts pounded, the Jews accompanied him with cursing looks, and the Jewish women for whom "Tsena U-rena" and the prayers of Sarah Bat Tovim were routine on their lips, muttered "Would that, Lord of the World, Merciful and Generous Father, his end be like those of Holofernes and the evil Haman" …

Six Heidemaks with stiff faces and bloodthirsty eyes went from house to house to see and check if the last order was fulfilled properly. If one of the places was unacceptable, they would go into that house and beat the owner of the house, his wife and children, murderous blows with their clubs. Screams and horrifying voices interspersed with the wild shouts and crude curses of the villains, would fill the air. Some excessive strangeness casting terror prevailed on the empty streets in the scrupulously swept town, the shouts of the beaten heard here and there and filling the silent space.

And when someone who wasn't usually there was passing through the swept town and saw its inhabitants where every movement of their movements and every step of their steps was full of horror and fear - a sort of fluttering black question mark appeared in his eyes and demanded an answer pleadingly: "What is this cleanliness for?" … .

[Page 242]

12

Twenty thousand "Nikolaevs" (the Russian money named after the last Tsar was worth more than the Ukrainian money) in three hours, don't be late! It was clear to everyone that this new demand was only a pretext and that, in fact, the Petliurovets intended that one of their demands would not be fulfilled … There were those who said that it might not be worth all that big and heavy trouble of collecting the funds. And yet the same two who had collected the first "contribution" went out again and started a new collection.

All that day the Heidemaks feasted and drank, got drunk and reveled. From time to time, the sound of their calls and wild talk and their licentious melodies and songs could be heard.

Individual attacks on passing Jews did not stop during that day. The townspeople started hiding, some in the basement and some in the attic and other hiding places. The houses on the main streets were almost emptied of their inhabitants who went to hide with the women and the children in the poor side alleys, the seat of wretched poor. They said: maybe the hand of the murderers will not reach there. And so men and women filled the little and slouching houses on their thatched roofs, children and babies to the limit. There were also those who went to seek refuge in the village, but the residents of the village refused, fearing that it would be harmful to them. Since not one of the "goyim" had received his punishment for defending a Jew or giving shelter to a Jew in his home. Each of those hiding had a bundle of money that they called a "ransom." Affluent relatives would give sums of money to their poor relatives and friends, which would serve as "ransom" if the murderers came.

A full moon sheds its light on the still town. An old Jew hurriedly crosses the street. A young woman with a baby in her arms, wrapped in a long black winter coat, takes small, quick steps in the direction of one of the abandoned alleys. Looking behind her from time to time with frightened eyes. A black dog with a thin tail walks calmly, rummaging and smelling the respectable and clean ground.

A wail of crying is heard: a soldier stands and aims his rifle… fragmentary words of request and entreaty are heard out of the howl of sobbing… a malicious laugh and a rifle shot… a death sigh and the fall of one wallowing in blood.

A loud cry of a lingering and penetrating "oy va-voy" comes from one of the houses. The father of the family was taken out battered and wounded by a rifle butt. Helplessly he falls. The Heidemaks roll him up and carry him away. Suddenly one of the soldiers calls out: "Guys, how long will you take care of this Yid? There is much work and time, as you know, is limited." And while he speaks, he stabs his bayonet into the victim's chest and a stream of blood erupts… prolonged death gurgling… the family members run away pursued by the killers… screams of terror from the pursued and vigorous and wild curses from the pursuers… frequent gunshots, screams, moaning and falling with arms and legs spread-eagled on the stomach or back.

And so the old butcher and his wife, seventy years old and gout-stricken and walking on crutches, were murdered and killed. The old men had laid down in their beds and were sure that they would not touch them, the old men and the sick standing at the threshold of the grave. The Heidemaks entered there and dragged them out of their beds and slaughtered them both with the long butcher's knife.

They found one, a young yeshiva married man, who was constantly in charge of providing the food and needs of the soldiers among the gang members.

[Page 243]

- Isn't it me, who ran and toiled and brought for you all that your soul craved, take pity on my life. I'm young… I only recently married a wife and a child was born to me…

- For your fee we will make you a beautiful death, said the murderers. And two Heidemaks stood, one facing the captured's back and the other facing his chest, with their rifles ready. The victim would move from one to the other and there were screams and the roars of laughter mixing with the sound of his one pleading cry: "Take pity on my life" - until two shots that erupted at once threw him to the ground and two jets of blood erupted and flowed from his death wounds, creating a wide pool of blood, in which the deceased's body sank.

The seventy-two-year-old cantor was brought out of hiding in the attic of his house, they pulled this old man by his gray sidelocks. One of the murderers tied the cantor's hands. That one began to beg for his life in a half Jewish and half gentile language. They lifted him up and slammed his body into the ground. The wretched man raised a crying voice and recited the "Vidui," they immediately fell on him and tore him and smashed him with their rifle butts and bayonets.

Smashing windows and breaking doors, shouting, crying, a long and interrupted wail, the last moans of the dying, curses, shouts and gunshots filled the space of the town during that night… "Goyim," who are neighbors near and far, enter the empty houses and fill their sacks with everything at hand …

13

The morning found the town strewn with the corpses of victims lying in puddles of their spilled blood that was coagulating with the sun and its heat. Crying and wailing, women wander like crazy, hitting their heads and beating their hearts hard. Here on the corner of the street lies a man with his legs curled up in a last death convulsion and from his hacked head the cells of his white brain are bleaching. Not far from him is his mother-in-law, an old woman, with a blood-soaked turban tied to her head. Her toothless mouth is open with a final expression of death terror and near her right eye a deep gash… Here and there they lay stretched out, some on their stomach and some on their back, their hand folded under their face, dead men, women, old and young.

And in the remote alleys of the town, whose houses were full of people seeking refuge and shelter who thought they were safe from the rioters, the dead were many, lying mostly by families. Here is a man and a woman and their son and daughter lying near each other. Their legs and hands are intertwined and holding on to each other. The heads are mutilated, the swollen faces are soaked in blood that has congealed and dried. There, not far away, as if leaning on the cornice of a lonely and fallen house, lies a nineteen-year-old young man with his eyes open, his chest exposed. Not far from him lies a girl with a deep red-black wound in her side. Her golden, long curls are scattered over her pale face. From a distance, it seems that she is sleeping.

By one fence lies the water drawer and his long black beard is full of blood clots that hang and fall. His face is mashed to the point of not being able to distinguish between his eyes, nose, and lips.

And in the same house, the commandant's place of residence, they found the owner of the house dead near the threshold of the house from the outside, and her son, seventeen years old, lying dead on his bed with his left eye shot out. The boy is lying there, his face soft and innocent as it was, covered and wrapped in a blanket as if sleeping, only the pillow red from his blood.

[Page 244]

Eighty-four victims were felled by the killers during the night. Before they left the town, they wanted to set it on fire, but the Ukrainian peasants stopped them in their place with the justification that the village not be swallowed up by it. The town is plundered and robbed, a snow of feathers outside, tools and clothes that fell from the full sacks of the thieves rolling here and there. The windows are smashed, many doors are broken and uprooted.

Everywhere death, ruin, destruction, and wailing.

After hours of sobbing, horrifying cries, fainting, and madness of some mothers and fathers, a murmur began to pass through the rabbi's mouth: "Enough, the martyrs to the grave of Israel." They went and hired a few carts from the gentiles of the village, and these came with their furry and tall hats pulled down to a little below their eyes … These would only look to the side …

Some pairs of the "Chevra Kadisha" held the hands of the slain who were gathered together in one place in the market, lifted them and placed them carefully on the cart. The wave of the dead grew that much. Hands and feet and slumped and destroyed heads slipped away, one on top of the other … All the people of the town who were left alive, from small to great, were gathered by the carts loaded with the corpses of their fathers, their mothers, and their slaughtered children, and the wailing and the sobbing grew and the place became one of anxiety and horror. And when the cantor mentioned the name of one of the dead in the "El Male Rachamim," the wailing of the relatives of the mentioned deceased grew amidst all the crying voices and the bitter eulogy.

The rabbi of the town, a young man with a gentle face, whose black beard added special beauty to his profile, conducted the rite of burial of the martyrs in the cemetery He read the prayer and the chapters of Psalms. With great effort, he continued to say the verses that needed to be said.

And when he came to saying the "Tzidduk ha-Din," suddenly there was a long silence. Everyone is waiting for him to say the verse: "God gave and God took away, blessed be the name of God," but the rabbi still stands in his place and does not utter a word.

He coughed as if preparing to say what was required to be said, but look the audience heard explicit words coming out of the rabbi's mouth: "I can't say the Tzidduk ha-Din, I won't say the Tzidduk ha-Din," and while saying this, he pointed to the dozens of fresh mounds, under which the victims of the massacre were concealed.

Original footnote:

1. This list was published 35 years ago in the "Ha'aretz" newspaper (issues 8-9.1928) under the title "Town" and signed by K. Menachem. What is told and described here refers to the town of Kytaihorod, which is near Kamyanets Podilskyy, the regional city of Podolia (today the "Khmelnystskyi geographic region"). The pogrom in the town that was carried out by a Ukrainian gang during the rule of Petliura happened in 1919 (June 16, 1919).
    This list was written nine years after the massacre.
    The information is given here as it was published in 1928 with certain omissions and corrections.

[Page 245]

Memorials

Translated by Monica Devens

[Page 246]Blank[Page247]

We Remember

with great pain and sorrow, the souls of our holy and pure brothers and sisters who fell at the hands of filthy murderers for the sanctification of the Name and for the people during the days of the Holocaust in the communities of Israel of

Kamyanets Podilskyy
and the surrounding cities:

Orynyn, Nova-Ushytsya, Stara Ushytsya, Balin, Grayding (=Horodok), Dunayivtsi, Husyatyn. Vinkivtsi, Zhvanets, Velikiy Zhvanchik, Zbruch, Zinkiv, Zamikhiv, Chemerivtsi, Chernivtsi, Yarmolyntsi, Lyantskorun (=Zarechanka), Myn'kivtsi, Solobkovtsy Sataniv, Smotrych, Frampol, Kupyn, Kytaihorod, Shatava.

We will remember the binding of these, our holy ones, with the binding of the other holy ones of Israel and its heroes and may their souls be bound up in the bonds of the eternal life of the nation.

[Page 248]

A memorial plaque for the victims of the Holocaust in Kamyanets Podilskyy and the surrounding cities in the Chamber of the Holocaust at "Yad va-Shem" on Mount Zion in Jerusalem

[Page 249]

Matityahu Segal

by Y. A. Bar-Levi

Matityahu Segal was born in Kamyanets Podilskyy, in the home of his father, cantor Yitzhak Meir Segal, and received a traditional education in the "Cheder" and the "Yeshiva."

When he grew up and it was time to join the army, he left Kamyanets and "stole" the border to eastern Galicia. He stayed there for a number of years and continued his studies in "Yeshivot" and, at the same time, "glimpsed and was struck" and was caught up with the Zionist idea. With the eradication of absolute rule in the February 1917 coup, he returned to his hometown of Kamyanets as a politically mature man and joined the "Tse'irei Tsiyon" party. In the years 1917-1920, during his extensive activity on the Jewish street, he stood out as a popular speaker at public meetings and rallies and won the hearts of his listeners, especially the "fair sex," with words that came from his heart and were spoken with warmth and simplicity.

In the fall of 1920, when the escape from Kamyanets Podilskyy towards the border of Galicia and Bessarabia began, he also left the city and arrived in Khotyn and then Kishinev. There he was approached by the well-known Zionist politico, Dr. Bernstein-Cohen, and Matityahu Segal began to rise step by step in the Zionist and public arena.

In the 20s of this century, a great many Jewish refugees from Ukraine gathered in Bessarabia and concentrated mainly in Kishinev. In that period, the aid institutions of American Jewry operated in Bessarabia. The "Joint" and "HIAS," and Segal was appointed the director of the local branch of the "Joint."

With the reduction of the operation of the "Joint" in Bessarabia, he moved to work as an emissary on behalf of the national committee of

[Page 250]

"Keren Hayesod" in the provincial towns. He served in this position until he immigrated to Israel in 1932. In Israel, he served as the manager of the "Keren Hayesod" office in Tel Aviv.

In Israel, Segal belonged to the General Zionist party and, in the last years of his life, he joined the Progressive Zionists. He was also active in various community institutions and organizations and contributed a lot to them of his energy and time.

He also did quite a bit to renew the activities of the organization of expatriates of Kamyanets Podilskyy and its surroundings in Israel and worked together with the other members of the committee to place a memorial tablet for the Holocaust victims in Kamyanets and its surroundings in the Chamber of the Holocaust on "Mount Zion" in Jerusalem and to publish this memorial book.

May his memory be blessed!

Gabriel Schor (Schwartz)

by A. D. Stit

He was born in 1894 in the town of Zhvanets, Ukraine. He studied at a school where the language of instruction was Hebrew and he was educated in the nationalist spirit and in Judaism. From his environment, he absorbed the love for traditional Hebrew culture and Zionism and these helped him to withstand the currents of the revolutionary ideas of 1905.

At the end of the First World War and the revolutions that flooded Ukraine with Jewish blood, he moved with his family to Kamyanets Podilskyy and continued his Hebrew and Zionist activities. He was among the organizers of a group of young pioneers to immigrate to Israel, with them he crossed the border by a difficult route in life-threatening danger and arrived in Israel in 1920 with the first of the third pioneering Aliyah.

He was one of the founders of the Kiryat Anavim collective farm and the driving force within it. After that he returned for a short time to Russia and, upon his return to Israel, became a construction worker in the name of the conquest of Hebrew labor and its introduction to Jerusalem. He was also among the founders of a Hebrew transportation group in Jerusalem, the first of its kind in the area, and he headed it. From 1934 he worked at the "Zerubavel" Bank as a senior employee and was loved by his friends and bore the brunt of their organization. He was active in the Zionist Federation of the Clerks, in the Cooperative Consumer Council, and a loyal member of the Zionist Federation all his days.

He was a clear social creature and, in every gathering, party or public or family celebration, he was the driving force and excelled in cheerfulness, in communal singing, and in raising spirits.

He was a kind person, ready to support a close or distant friend, and never knew tiredness in any activity that had something for the good of the whole or of the individual.

[Page 251]

Aharon Wasserman

by A. M.

Aharon Wasserman was devoted heart and soul to Zionist work from the day he became a high school student in Kamyanets Podilskyy until his last day.

He was a rank-and-file man and saw himself as one of the unknowns devoting their time and energy to the building of the country.

In 1920 he left Russia with a group of pioneers and wandered for many months in Romania and Turkey. In Israel, he joined the "Koach" group of "Gedud Ha-Avoda," which dealt with community activities in Tel Aviv. Then he started working in the Tel Aviv municipality as a clerk and devoted his free time to public engagement in the organization of the municipality's employees, the "Po'alei Eretz Yisrael" Party, and musical institutions: the Israel Oratorio, the opera under the management of M. Golinkin, and the folk opera.

He was loyal and devoted to his friends, shared activities with them in various areas and, in recent years, took an active part in the establishment of the organization of expatriates of Kamyanets Podilskyy and its surroundings and was one of the members of the committee until the end of his life.

[Page 252]Blank[Page253]

A Memorial Plaque
to the Victims of the Holocaust
in Kamyanets-Podilskyy and its Surroundings

Memorial Days: Elul 3, 4, 5

OKSMAN Shimshon, his wife, Etyl, and his sons, Dovid, Moshe, and Israel, from Kuz'myn.

EINBINDER Eiser, son of Yaakov ("the cook"), from Yarmolyntsi-Kytaihorod.

AURBACH Zisyl, daughter of R. Yehoshua-Eliyahu and Rifka Bernstein, her sons, Moshe, Elazar, and her daughter, Nechama, from Kamyanets-Podilskyy.

EINBINDER Herschel, son of Eiser, from Yarmolyntsi-Kytaihorod.

[Page 254]

EINBINDER Mordechai, son of Eiser, from Yarmolyntsi-Kytaihorod.

BLANK Mordechai, his wife, Fanya, and their son, Nunya. BLANK, Nuta, his wife, Ruchel, and their son, Yuli, from Dunayivtsi.

ELLES Schniur-Zusya, Rabbi, from Zhvanets.

BRAND Yaakov (Yakel) and his wife, Devorah, from Dunayivtsi.

BLANK Yosef and his wife, Chaya (Hayuna) of the Rafalowicz family, from Dunayivtsi.

BRAND Aharon-Meir (Artzi), son of R. Avraham and his wife, Peryl, daughter of Hayyim-Tsvi, from the village of Vil'khivtsi next to Husyatyn.

[Page 255]

BARD Susya of the Lerner family, from Zhvanets.

BRONSHTEYN Hinda, wife of Dov, and their children: Shmuel-Moshe, Chaya-Bluma, Menachem-Nachum, and Miryam, from Kamyanets-Podilskyy.

BROYT Chana and her daughter, Shulamit, from Kamyanets-Podilskyy.

BRONSHTEYN Feige, daughter of Yehoshua-Eliyahu and Rivka, from Kamyanets-Podilskyy.

BRONSHTEYN Dov-Beryl, son of R. Yehoshua-Eliyahu and Rivka, from Kamyanets-Podilskyy.

GUTMAN Sarah of the Lerner family, from Zhvanets.

[Page 256]

GOLDSTEYN Leybish, son of Yisrael, fell in battle against the Petliura forces.

GLUZMAN Avraham and his wife, Tzippora, daughter of Aharon, from Kamyanets-Podilskyy.

GARFINKLE Odeya of the Shlomo and Miryl Richter family, her husband, Aharon, son of Zusya, and their son, Shmuel, from Kamyanets.

GRYNBERG Tzvi (Herschel), son of Avraham and Fruma, from Kamyanets-Podilskyy.

GARFINKLE Menucha of the Shlomo and Miryl Richter family, her husband, Baruch, son of Zusya, and their son, Moshe, from Kamyanets.

HOFFMAN Devorah of the Lerner family, from Zhvanets.

[Page 257]

DR. HALPRIN Mordechai, son of Yaakov - dentist, his daughter, Miryam, his son, Emanuel, were tragically killed in the Holocaust in Kamyanets.

ZICHERMAN Shimon, Shalom, and Moshe, in Zinkiv.

WEISMAN Aharon, son of Levi and Chana'che from Kamyanets, and his wife, Fanya of the Avigdor Krivaviaz family from Dzyhivka - were tragically killed in the Warsaw ghetto.

KATZ Dov, son of Yaakov, from Lyantskorun (=Zarechanka), fell in the battle of Stalingrad.

ZEIGER Roza, from Kamyanets-Podilskyy.

KATZ Leah (Liza), daughter of Yitzchak and Beyla, from Kamyanets.

[Page 258]

KATZ Chana of the Yaakov Katz family and the members of her household, Kamyanets.

MELNITZER Roza, Bella, Shumer Goldoshe, from Kamyanets.

LERNER Yehuda-Leib, from Zhvanets.

MELNITZER Yisrael, from Kamyanets-Podilskyy.

LERNER Michal, son of Yehudah, from Zhvanets.

NIK Chaim, son of Shlomo and Yehudit, from Kamyanets-Podilskyy.

[Page 259]

NIK Miryam (Myronya), wife of Chaim Nik, from Kamyanets.

FISHBACH Yoel, son of Pinchas, his wife, Esther, and their son, Michael.

SEIGALMAN Batsheva, daughter of Tzvi and Peryl Dinitz, her husband, Chaim son of Yechiel Seigalman, their children, Roza and Mordechai, from Dunayivtsi.

FELDMAN Akiva and his family. Peisman Betti and Yaakov Shalita Lipa and his family, from Kamyanets-Podilskyy.

FUCHS Zlotta, her daughter, Feige Rapaport and her husband, from Kamyanets.

PRIZENT Zev and his wife, Rivka, from Dunayivtsi.

[Page 260]

FREYFELD Zalman, son of Yisrael, his wife Rivka, and their sons: Yisrael, Dov, and Yonah, from Kamyanets.

KOTLER Fruma of the Shneiderman family and her sons, Eliezer and Yerachmiel, from Grayding (Horodok).

FREYFELD Yitzhak, son of Yisrael, and his wife Chava, their daughter, Miryam, from Kamyanets.

KAPLAN Elkanah, son of R. Michael, and his wife, Gissya, from Kamyanets-Podilskyy.

FREYFELD Ehreh Ida, her husband Yaakov, their daughter, Blanka, and their son, Aleksander.

KAPLAN Yitzhak, son of Elkanah and Gissya, his wife, Malka-Beyla, and their children: Gissya, Tovah, Elkanah, from Kamyanets-Podilskyy.

[Page 261]

KAPLAN Mordechai, son of Elkanah and Gissya, fell in the battle of Stalingrad.

REIS Chaim, son of Michael from Smotrych, in Kamyanets-Podilskyy.

KAPLAN Michael, son of Elkanah and Gissya, his wife, Reyzel, and their daughters: Pesya and Gissya.

REIS Yitzhak, son of Chaim from Smotrych, in Kamyanets-Podilskyy.

ROZENBLAT Czarna, her husband and three children, SHYTENMAN Gitla, her husband and daughter.

RICHTER Avraham the ritual slaughterer, his wife, Miryam, their daughter, Chaya'ke, in Kamyanets.

[Page 262]

RICHTER Shlomo, son of Feitel and Feige, born on Tu B'Shvat 1866, from Kamyanets-Podilskyy.

SHTERN Leah (Basha), wife of Moshe, their daughter, Czarna, and her husband and two children.

RICHTER Miryl, daughter of Natan and Peryl Kahane, wife of Shlomo Richter, from Kamyanets-Podilskyy.

SHECTMAN Abba, son of Melech, his wife, Chaya, daughter of Yosef, in Kamyanets-Podilskyy.

RICHTER Yaakov, son of Shlomo and Miryl, and his wife, Itta, daughter of Yitzhak Kupershteyn, and their daughter, Gittel, from Kamyanets.

SHNEIDERMAN Itta, in Grayding (Horodok).

[Page 263]

SHREIBER Freyda of the Berk family, from Kamyanets-Podilskyy.

SHREIER Yenta with her family, in Orynyn.

SHREIBER Shmuel, son of Chaim-Yisrael, from Kamyanets-Podilskyy.

SHREIER Yosef, son of R. Mordechai, his wife, Devorah, and her family from Orynyn, in Odessa.

SHREIER Mordechai, son of R. Eliyahu, and his wife, Hinda, daughter of R. Akiva, from Orynyn.

SHERMAN Miryam of the Zichrin family, in Zinkiv.

[Page 264]Blank[Page 265]Blank[Page 266]Blank]

Page numbers refer to original text

Photographs

Translated by Sara Mages

[Pages 253-263]

Page numbers refer to original text

Holocaust Victims in Alphabetical Order

Transliterated by Moshe Steinberg

Edited by Ann Harris

Family name(s)	First name(s)	Maiden name	Sex	Martial status	Father's name	Mother's name	Name of spouse	Place of residence	Additional family members	Remarks	Page
א Alef											
OKSMAN	Shimshon		M	Married			Etyl	Kuz'min			253
OKSMAN	Etyl		F	Married			Shimshon	Kuz'min			253
OKSMAN	Dovid		M		Shimshon	Etyl		Kuz'min			253
OKSMAN	Moshe		M		Shimshon	Etyl		Kuz'min			253
OKSMAN	Israel		M		Shimshon	Etyl		Kuz'min			253
EINBINDER	Eiser		M		Yakov			Yarmolyntsi Kitaygorod		Tova Nik's husband	253
EINBINDER	Hershel		M		Eiser			Yarmolyntsi Kitaygorod			253
AURBACH	Zisyl		F		Yehoshua Eliahu	Rebeca		Kamyanets Podilskyy			253
AURBACH	Moshe		M			Zisyl		Kamyanets Podilskyy			253
AURBACH	Eliezer		M			Zisyl		Kamyanets Podilskyy			253
AURBACH	Nechama		F			Zisyl		Kamyanets Podilskyy			253
EINBINDER	Mordechai		M					Yarmolyntsi Kitaygorod			254
ELLES?	Reb Shniur Zusya		M					Zhvanets			254
ב Bet											

Surname	Given name	Maiden name	Sex	Status	Father	Mother	Spouse	Town			Page
BLANK	Yosef		M	Married			Chaya Chyna	Dunaivtsi			254
BLANK	Chaya Chyna	RAFALOWICZ	F	Married			Yosef	Dunaivtsi			254
BLANK	Mordechai		M	Married			Fanya	Dunaivtsi			254
BLANK	Fanya		F	Married			Mordechai	Dunaivtsi			254
BLANK	Nunya		M		Mordechai	Fanya		Dunaivtsi			254
BLANK	Nuta		M	Married			Ruchel	Dunaivtsi			254
BLANK	Ruchel		F	Married			Nuta	Dunaivtsi			254
BLANK	Yoel		M		Nuta	Ruchel		Dunaivtsi			254
BRAND	Yakov Yekyl		M	Married			Devorah	Dunaivtsi			254
BRAND	Devorah		F	Married			Yakov Yekyl	Dunaivtsi			254
BRAND-ARTZI	Aharon Meir		M	Married	Abraham		Peryl	Ol'khovtsy (Vil'khivtsi)			254
BRAND	Peryl		F	Married	Chaim Tzvi		Aharon Meir	Ol'khovtsy (Vil'khivtsi)			254
BORD?	Susya	LERNER	F					Zhvanets			255
BROYT	Chana		F					Kamyanets Podilskyy			255
BROYT	Shulamit		F			Chana		Kamyanets Podilskyy			255
BRONSHTEYN	Dov Beryl		M	Married	Yehoshua Eliyahu	Rebeca	Hinda	Kamyanets Podilskyy			255
BRONSHTEYN	Hinda		F	Married			Dov Beryl	Kamyanets Podilskyy			255
BRONSHTEYN	Chaya Bluma		F		Dov Beryl	Hinda		Kamyanets Podilskyy			255
BRONSHTEYN	Menachem Mendel		M		Dov Beryl	Hinda		Kamyanets Podilskyy			255
BRONSHTEYN	Myriam		F		Dov Beryl	Hinda		Kamyanets Podilskyy			255
BRONSHTEYN	Feiga		F		Yehoshua Eliahu	Rebeca		Kamyanets Podilskyy			255

ג Gimel

Surname	Given name	Maiden name	Sex	Status	Father	Mother	Spouse	Town			Page
GUTMAN	Sarah	LERNER	F					Zhvanets			255

Surname	Given name	Maiden/Other	Sex	Status	Father	Mother	Spouse	Town		Notes	Page
GOLDSHTEYN	Leybish		M		Yisrael			Kamyanets Podilskyy		Soldier who fell in battle	256
GARFINKLE	Odeya	RICHTER	F	Married	Shloma	Miryl	Aharon	Kamyanets Podilskyy			256
GARFINKLE	Aharon		M	Married	Zusya		Odeya	Kamyanets Podilskyy			256
GARFINKLE	Shmuel		M		Aharon	Odeya		Kamyanets Podilskyy			256
GARFINKLE	Menucha	RICHTER	F	Married	Shloma	Miryl	Baruch	Kamyanets Podilskyy			256
GARFINKLE	Baruch		M	Married	Zusya		Menucha	Kamyanets Podilskyy			256
GARFINKLE	Moshe		M		Baruch	Menucha		Kamyanets Podilskyy			256
GLUZMAN	Abraham		M	Married			Tziporah	Kamyanets Podilskyy			256
GLUZMAN	Tziporah		F	Married	Aharon		Abraham	Kamyanets Podilskyy			256
GRYNBERG	Tzvi Hershel		M		Abraham	Froma		Kamyanets Podilskyy			256

ה   Hey

Surname	Given name	Maiden/Other	Sex	Status	Father	Mother	Spouse	Town		Notes	Page
HOFMAN	Devorah	LERNER	F					Zhvanets			256
HALPRIN	Dr. Mordechai		M		Yakov			Kamyanets Podilskyy		Dentist	257
HALPRIN	Myriam		F		Mordechai			Kamyanets Podilskyy		Died in Kamyanets Podilskyy	257
HALPRIN	Emanuel		M		Mordechai			Kamyanets Podilskyy		Died in Kamyanets Podilskyy	257

ו   Vav

Surname	Given name	Maiden/Other	Sex	Status	Father	Mother	Spouse	Town		Notes	Page
WEISMAN	Aharon		M	Married	Levy	Chancie	Fanya	Kamyanets Podilskyy		Died in Kamyanets Podilskyy	257
WEISMAN	Fanya	KRIVAVIAZ	F	Married	Avigdor		Aharon	Kamyanets Podilskyy		Died in Warsaw Ghetto	257

ז   Zayin

ZEIGER	Roza		F					Kamyanets Podilskyy		Died in Warsaw Ghetto	257
ZICHERMAN	Shimon		M					Zin'kov			257
ZICHERMAN	Shalom		M					Zin'kov			257
ZICHERMAN	Moshe		M					Zin'kov			257

כ Kaf

KATZ	Dov		M					Zarechanka (Lyantskorun')		Soldier who fell in battle in Stalingrad	257
KATZ	Leah Leitze		F		Yitzchak	Beyla		Kamyanets Podilskyy			257
KATZ	Chana	KATZ	F		Yitzchak			Kamyanets Podilskyy	family		258

ל Lamed

LERNER	Yehuda Leib		M					Zhvanets			258
LERNER	Michal		M		Yehuda			Zhvanets			258

מ Mem

MELNITZER	Roza		F					Kamyanets Podilskyy			258
MELNITZER	Bilah		F					Kamyanets Podilskyy			258
MELNITZER	Yisrael		M					Kamyanets Podilskyy			258

נ Nun

NIK	Chaim		M	Married	Shloma	Yehudit	Myriam Myronia	Kamyanets Podilskyy			258
NIK	Myriam Myronia		F	Married			Chaim	Kamyanets Podilskyy			259

ס Samech

SEIGALMAN	Bat Sheva	DINITZ	F	Married	Tzvi	Peryl	Chaim	Kamyanets Podilskyy			259
SEIGALMAN	Chaim		M	Married	Yechiel		Bat Sheva	Kamyanets Podilskyy			259

SEIGALMAN	Roza		F		Chaim	Bat Sheva		Kamyanets Podilskyy		259
SEIGALMAN	Mordechai		M		Chaim	Bat Sheva		Kamyanets Podilskyy		259

פ Peh

FUCHS	Zlotta		F					Kamyanets Podilskyy		259
FISHBACH	Yoel		M	Married	Pinchas		Ester	Kamyanets Podilskyy		259
FISHBACH	Ester		F	Married			Yoel	Kamyanets Podilskyy		259
FISHBACH	Michal		M		Yoel	Ester		Kamyanets Podilskyy		259
FELDMAN	Akiva		M					Kamyanets Podilskyy	family	259
PEISMAN	Batya		F					Kamyanets Podilskyy		259
PRIZENT	Zeev		M	Married			Rebeca	Dunaivtsi		259
PRIZENT	Rebeca		F	Married			Zeev	Dunaivtsi		259
FREYFELD	Zalman		M	Married	Yisrael		Rebeca	Kamyanets Podilskyy		260
FREYFELD	Rebeca		F	Married			Zalman	Kamyanets Podilskyy		260
FREYFELD	Yisrael		M		Zalman	Rebeca		Kamyanets Podilskyy		260
FREYFELD	Dov		M		Zalman	Rebeca		Kamyanets Podilskyy		260
FREYFELD	Yonah		M		Zalman	Rebeca		Kamyanets Podilskyy		260
FREYFELD	Yltzchak		M	Married	Yisrael		Chava	Kamyanets Podilskyy		260
FREYFELD	Chava		F	Married			Yitzchak	Kamyanets Podilskyy		260
FREYFELD	Myriam		F		Yitzchak	Chava		Kamyanets Podilskyy		260
FREYFELD	Ari Eida?	EHRE	F	Married			Yakov	Kamyanets Podilskyy		260

FREYFELD	Yakov		M	Married			Ari Eida?	Kamyanets Podilskyy		260
FREYFELD	Blanka		F		Yakov	Ari Eida?		Kamyanets Podilskyy		260
FREYFELD	Aleksander		M		Yakov	Ari Eida?		Kamyanets Podilskyy		260

ꝗ Kof

KOTLER	Froma	SHNEIDERMAN	F					Gorodok		260
KOTLER	Eliezer		M			Froma		Gorodok		260
KOTLER	Rachmiel		M			Froma		Gorodok		260
KAPLAN	Elkanah		M	Married	Michal		Gissya	Kamyanets Podilskyy		260
KAPLAN	Gissya		F	Married			Elkanah	Kamyanets Podilskyy		260
KAPLAN	Yitzchak		M	Married	Elkanah	Gissya	Malka Beyla	Kamyanets Podilskyy		260
KAPLAN	Malka Beila		F	Married			Yitzchak	Kamyanets Podilskyy		260
KAPLAN	Gissya		F		Yitzchak	Malka Beyla		Kamyanets Podilskyy		260
KAPLAN	Tovah		F		Yitzchak	Malka Beyla		Kamyanets Podilskyy		260
KAPLAN	Elkanah		M		Yitzchak	Malka Beyla		Kamyanets Podilskyy		260
KAPLAN	Mordechai		M		Elkanah	Gissya		Kamyanets Podilskyy	Soldier who fell in battle	261
KAPLAN	Michal		M	Married	Elkanah	Gissya	Reyzel	Kamyanets Podilskyy		261
KAPLAN	Reyzel		F	Married			Michal	Kamyanets Podilskyy		261
KAPLAN	Pesya		F		Michal	Reyzel		Kamyanets Podilskyy		261
KAPLAN	Gissya		F		Michal	Reyzel		Kamyanets Podilskyy		261

ꞧ Resh

RAPAPORT	Feiga	FUCHS	F	Married		Zlotta		Kamyanets Podilskyy			259
RAPAPORT			M	Married			Feiga	Kamyanets Podilskyy			259
REIS	Chaim		M		Michal			Smotrich			261
REIS	Yitzchak		M		Chaim			Smotrich			261
RICHTER	Abraham		M	Married			Myriam	Kamyanets Podilskyy		Shochet — Ritual Slaughter. Picture appears	261
RICHTER	Myriam		F	Married			Abraham	Kamyanets Podilskyy		Picture appears	261
RICHTER	Chayake		F		Abraham	Myriam		Kamyanets Podilskyy		Picture appears	261
RICHTER	Shloma		M	Married	Feityl	Feiga	Myrl	Kamyanets Podilskyy		Born 1866 January 18. Picture appears	262
RICHTER	Mirl	KAHANE	F	Married	Natan	Peryl	Shloma	Kamyanets Podilskyy		Picture appears	262
RICHTER	Yakov		M	Married	Shloma	Myrl	Itta	Kamyanets Podilskyy			262
RICHTER	Itta	KUPERSHTEYN	F	Married	Yitzchak		Yakov	Kamyanets Podilskyy			262
RICHTER	Gittyl		F		Yakov	Itta		Kamyanets Podilskyy			262
ROZENBLAT	Czarna		F	Married				Kamyanets Podilskyy	3 children		261
ROZENBLAT			M	Married			Czarna	Kamyanets Podilskyy	3 children		261

Shin

SHALITA	Yakov		M					Kamyanets Podilskyy	family	?	259
SHUMER	Goldoshe		F					Kamyanets Podilskyy			258
SHYTENMAN	Gitla		F	Married				Kamyanets Podilskyy			261
SHYTENMAN			M	Married			Gitla	Kamyanets Podilskyy			261
SHYTENMAN			F			Gitla		Kamyanets Podilskyy			261

SHTERN	Leah Basha		F	Married			Moshe	Kamyanets Podilskyy			262
	Czarna	SHTERN	F	Married	Moshe	Leah Basha		Kamyanets Podilskyy	2 children		262
			M	Married			Czarna	Kamyanets Podilskyy	2 children		262
SHECTMAN	Aba		M	Married	Melech		Chaya	Kamyanets Podilskyy		Picture appears	262
SHECTMAN	Chaya		F	Married	Yosef		Aba	Kamyanets Podilskyy		Picture appears	262
SHNEIDERMAN	Itta		F					Gorodok			262
SHREIBER	Freida	BERK	F					Kamyanets Podilskyy		Picture appears	263
SHREIBER	Shmuel		M		Chaim Yisrael			Kamyanets Podilskyy		Picture appears	263
SHREIER	Mordechai		M	Married	Eliahu		Hinda	Kamyanets Podilskyy			263
SHREIER	Hinda		F	Married	Akiva		Mordechai	Kamyanets Podilskyy			263
SHREIER	Yenta		F					Orinin	family		263
SHREIER	Yosef		M	Married	Mordechai		Devorah	Kamyanets Podilskyy			263
SHREIER	Devorah		F	Married			Yosef	Orinin	family		263
SHERMAN	Myriam	ZICHRIN	F					Zinkov			263

Name Index

A

A. M., 239
A. R., 5, 148
Abramovich, 18
Aharonson, 56
Alexander I, 99
Alter, 34, 53, 169, 183, 184, 199
Altman, 25, 28, 43, 64, 65, 66, 175, 181, 182, 183, 186, 187, 221, 253
An-Sky, 205
Asch, 45, 216
Ashman, 7, 18, 28, 29, 45, 66, 67, 92, 95, 96, 217
Aurbach, 240, 256
Avi-Chaim, 150
Avnei-Kamenetzky, 4
Axelrod, 51

B

Ba'al-Shem-Tov, 7, 18
Bahat-Buchhalter, 4
Bar Levi, 4, 9, 28
Bar Levi-Weissman, 4
Bard, 241
Bar-Levi, 4, 60, 89, 186, 223, 237
Bar-Shira, 28, 29
Barzin, 72
Bashirovker, 28, 29
Baynvelman, 55, 62
Becker, 35
Beharav, 77
Ben Avraham-Feldblit, 4
Bendersky, 21
Ben-Zion, 4, 143
Berdyczewski, 7
Beres, 221
Berman, 56, 175, 189, 190
Bernstein, 4, 21, 49, 167, 238, 240
Bernstein-Cohen, 21, 238

Betti, 247
Bialik, 74, 120, 122, 140, 154
Biletsky, 17
Blank, 5, 7, 9, 25, 92, 97, 98, 102, 103, 116, 119, 122, 123, 124, 125, 127, 129, 131, 142, 143, 144, 149, 150, 151, 152, 154, 156, 159, 177, 183, 189, 190, 202, 204, 207, 215, 236, 240, 241, 252, 254, 257
Bletter, 118
Blobstein, 24, 29
Bloch, 54
Blovstein, 46, 47
Bograd, 27
Bokser, 127, 128, 129, 130, 131
Borochov, 24, 64, 120
Brand, 241, 257
Brandman, 30, 45, 48, 67
Branzon, 14
Breitman, 54, 56
Brenner, 120
Brieftreger, 120
Bromberg, 30
Bronshteyn, 241, 242, 257
Broyt, 242, 257

C

Cantor, 35, 126
Casimir, 158
Cheifezes, 119
Chen, 187
Chirikov, 45
Chomsky, 33, 34
Cohen, 21, 54, 58, 146
Cooper, 175

D

D. M., 184
Dayan, 58

9 781962 054102